The Story of Cellular Jail

Prison to Pilgrimage

DR RASHIDA IQBAL

To Amma and Abba

Contents

Preface

The Andaman and Nicobar Islands represent a unique miniature of India, reflecting the country's diversity and cultural richness. Throughout their brief recorded history, these Islands have played a significant role in shaping the national freedom struggle. The Islands are physically separated from mainland India, but emotional integration with it can be understood only from a historical perspective. The East India Company began developing the Andaman Islands in the 18th century to provide a safe harbour for its ships.

In 1858, the British established a penal settlement on the Islands, marking a significant moment in their history. The Andaman Islands, historically known as 'Kala Pani' or 'Black Water', have a vague origin for this infamous name. Some experts suggest that the dark colour of the sea contributed to this name. However, the usual belief links 'Kala Pani' to the Sanskrit word 'Kaal', meaning Time or Death. Thus, it symbolises the water of death—a place from which only the fortunate could return. Indian revolutionaries and freedom fighters were condemned to Kala Pani to undergo severe punishment. Yet, their sacrifices immortalised these Islands in the chronicles of India's struggle for independence.

Thousands of people were deported to the Andamans, but many remain unnamed. Only those whose names can be found in the records are mentioned in this book.

Today, the once-dreaded Kala Pani has transformed into a sacred symbol of resilience and sacrifice and is now a pilgrimage site. It takes the readers on a journey into their lives through the perspective of a convict's daughter, who has witnessed the transformation of the Andaman and Cellular Jail into a sacred site very closely.

Rashida Iqbal

One of the corridors of the Cellular Jail-Post conservation

Acknowledgements

Here, I would like to mention that this work was originally undertaken while I was pursuing my PhD at Osmania University, Hyderabad, between 2005 and 2010. Later, I got the idea to publish this work with additions from a reader's point of view. However, it was significantly more delayed than anticipated owing to official commitments. Meanwhile, several parts of the thesis were either displayed on the walls of the Cellular Jail or used for other official purposes. Finally, after my superannuation in April 2024, I decided to work on the thesis again and to get the same published on priority.

From its inception as an idea to its completion in the present form, it owes greatly to several people, most notably my PhD thesis supervisor, Prof G Venkat Rajam. I also wish to express my deep sense of gratitude to my mentor, Dr. Pala Krishna Moorthy, Deputy Director (Retd), Andhra Pradesh State Archives and Research Institute, Hyderabad, who has been of tremendous help and guidance during the course of my research.

I am thankful to all the pioneers and custodians of the history of the Andaman and Nicobar Islands who have not only inspired and encouraged me to take up this work but have also made significant contributions to fostering a sense of pride in the historical legacy of the Islands among the general public and students alike. They include Shri G.S. Pandey, the Late Shri M.A. Mujtaba, the Late Shri Madan Mohan Singh, Shri Robin Roy Chowdhary, Shri Francis Xavier, and Shri Swapnesh Choudhary. Their insights and dedication have played a crucial role in educating and inspiring younger generations about the rich heritage of the Islands. I sincerely thank Shri Mukeshwar Lall, Historian & Filmmaker, for his consistent guidance. His suggestions on various aspects of the subject were very useful for the completion of this book.

I am extremely grateful to my colleagues with whom I have worked in the Cellular Jail for over two decades in various capacities. My thanks are due to Ms Kuldeep Kaur, Ms S Lalita, Ms Salma, and Mr. Damodaran, Librarians of Cellular Jail Library for their support and encouragement. I also thank Mr. Hasan Ali, Assistant Archivist of the Central Records Section, Andaman and Nicobar Administration (now Retd); Mr. Naseem, Incharge, State Library, (Retd) Port Blair; Shri Majeed, Archivist, Regional Archives, Kozhikode, Kerala; Andhra Pradesh State Archives and Research Institute, Hyderabad. I would be failing in my duty if I did not acknowledge my thanks to Dr. P.K. Srivastava, Martyrs Memorial and Freedom Struggle Research Centre, Lucknow, for providing me with valuable documents for my research work. My sincere thanks are also due to all the staff attached to the National Archives of India, New Delhi and National Library, Alipore, Kolkata.

It is important to acknowledge that my book would not have come to completion without the unwavering support of my family, in particular my brother A.U. Khan, Razia Aapa, my younger brother Sudipto and his wife Sumita Roy. This book is dedicated to my Amma and Abba, as no words can truly capture the depth of my respect and admiration for them.

Moreover, I would like to express my heartfelt gratitude to my husband, Iqbal, for his tremendous support throughout the extensive months of research and the completion of this work.

Dr. Rashida Iqbal
1ˢᵗ March 2025

CHAPTER I

Andaman and Nicobar Islands - an Overview

Introduction

The Andaman and Nicobar Islands are a group of Islands in the Bay of Bengal, between six and fourteen degrees north latitude and ninety-two and ninety-four degrees east longitude. This chain of Islands, situated to the east of the Indian mainland, is an archipelago of eight hundred and thirty-six Islands, islets, and rocky outcrops with thirty-one inhabited Islands. These Islands span more than seven hundred and fifty kilometres from north to south, with a land area of more than eight thousand square kilometres. The turbulent Ten Degree Channel separates the Andaman archipelago from the Nicobars.

These Islands lie close to the Southeast Asian countries of Myanmar, Thailand, Malaysia, and Indonesia. The northernmost island is Landfall Island, which is one hundred and ninety kilometres from Cape Negrais in Myanmar. Indira Point, named after the former Prime Minister of India, Smt Indira Gandhi, is the southernmost tip of the Islands, which is only one hundred and fifty kilometres away from Banda Aceh, the northernmost point of Sumatra. Saddle Peak, situated in North Andaman with a height of seven hundred and thirty-two metres, is the highest peak in the Andaman Islands, whereas Mount Thullier, at six hundred and forty-two metres above sea level, is the highest peak in the Nicobar Islands. The only active volcano of India, Barren Island, is also located on these Islands, one hundred and thirty-five kilometres from Port Blair.

The Union Territory of Andaman and Nicobar Islands is headed by a Lieutenant Governor. The Islands are divided into three districts: South

Andaman, North and Middle Andaman, and Nicobar with nine Tehsils. Each district is placed under a Deputy Commissioner. The Andaman and Nicobar Islands have only one Lok Sabha seat. Port Blair, the capital city of the Islands, is located in the southern part of the Andaman Islands. Port Blair is named after Captain Archibald Blair, Marine Surveyor of the 18th century. However, Port Blair has been renamed to Sri Vijaya Puram by the Government of India. It is situated at a distance of approximately one thousand three hundred kilometres from Kolkata, Chennai, and Vizag. It is well connected to the Indian mainland by regular air and sea services.

The Andaman and Nicobar Islands are home to five pristine, Particularly Vulnerable Tribal Groups (PVTGs) viz, Great Andamanese, Jarawas, Sentinelese, Onges and Shompens. All these five PVTGs are at different stages of development. Although the Andamanese and Onges have seen modern developments, they still practice foraging. Jarawa and Shompen are foraging groups and move from place to place according to the season for their survival.

As per the Census of 2011, the population of Andaman and Nicobar Islands is 380,581 out of which 28,530 are scheduled tribes, with a population density of forty-six persons per square kilometre. The literacy rate is quite remarkable at 86.63%.[1] However, the official website of the Andaman and Nicobar Administration shows the total population of the island as 434,192 (EST) in 2019.

The Islands are covered with evergreen tropical rain-fed forests with an exclusive and rich variety of flora and fauna. Several Islands have been declared as National Parks and Wildlife Sanctuaries for better conservation and protection. The 1962-kilometre-long coastline makes the Islands rich in marine biodiversity and an ideal, eco-friendly tourist destination of the twenty-first century, appealing to both domestic and international visitors. The climate of the Islands is tropical and humid and remains generally pleasant. However, the Islands are also experiencing climate change like the rest of the world. Truly, words fall short of capturing the Islands' pristine natural beauty. In the words of F.A.M. Dass, "Their beauty maddens the soul like wine. They invite or await Wordsworth, a Spenser or a Tagore to celebrate them in immortal verse."[2]

The Andaman and Nicobar Islands represent the significant narrative of our quest for independence. The once-feared Kala Pani, now considered a pilgrimage, served as harsh confinement for our freedom fighters and revolutionaries. These individuals, dedicated to the liberation of our homeland, endured absolute isolation and lived under brutal, inhumane conditions in the penal settlement established by the British. The then Prime Minister, the late Mrs. Indira Gandhi, after she visited the Islands in 1968, remarked that "these Islands have in fact been a nursery of some of our great revolutionaries. It is here appropriately that an Indian Government hoisted the national flag before the rest of the country became free."

The establishment of the first settlement by the East India Company on the Andaman Islands in 1789 marked the beginning of the modern history of the Andaman and Nicobar Islands. However, due to the ill health of the settlers, the settlement was eventually abandoned in 1796, leaving the Islands unattended for the next sixty-two years. It was not until 1858 that the British reoccupied the Islands with the intent to establish a penal settlement to suppress the voices raised against their paramount power.

The history of the Islands is broadly divided into five periods – travellers' accounts of the Islands, first settlement during 1789-1796, decades of isolation and incidents of shipwreck, re-occupation of the Islands for the establishment of a penal settlement in 1858 till the Second World War, and the Japanese occupation of the Islands from 1942-1945. Some of the notable events that took place on the Islands include the Battle of Aberdeen, fought between the aborigines and the British, the assassination of Lord Mayo, the then Viceroy of India, and the construction of the Cellular Jail. Besides these, the arrival of heroes of the First War of Independence, the Wahabi Movement, the Kuka

Movement, the Anglo-Manipur War, deportation of political prisoners, Moplah rebels, Manyam heroes, and the Japanese occupation of the island during the Second World War are other important events in the history of the island. The struggle and sacrifices of our freedom fighters, convicts, and settlers, both pre- and post-independence, have shaped the history of the Islands.

Though the Andaman and Nicobar Islands as a whole remind us of the sacrifices made by our fellow countrymen during the Indian freedom movement, a few places in the Islands are more closely connected with the memories of the freedom struggle and hence worth mentioning—Viper Island, for its gallows and Chain Gang Jail, Chatham Island for receiving the first batch of Freedom Fighters of the First War of Independence, and Cellular Jail, now a National Memorial, for the battle fought by firebrand revolutionaries within its solitary cells. The erstwhile Ross Island (now renamed as Netaji Subhas Chandra Bose Dweep), the headquarters of the penal settlement for over eighty years, gives us a snapshot of life enjoyed by colonial rulers through the ruins of structures, which were once the bakery, stores, water treatment plant, church, tennis court, printing press, secretariat, hospital, cemetery, and so on. These landmarks of the history of the Andaman and Nicobar Islands will remain a source of inspiration for the generations to come.

Today, the Islands are known for their unity in diversity, as people from different parts of India have made the Islands their home along with its indigenous tribes, and the harmonious blend of various languages, religions, customs and traditions has enriched the composite culture of the Islands and given it a unique vibrancy as a *Mini India*, a dreamland for every Indian. The tourism department of the Administration invites all tourists and nature lovers with its tagline *"Emerald. Blue. And You."* The future of these Islands lies in its eco-friendly tourism and, above all, its peace-loving people.

Islands in Travelogue

The Andaman and Nicobar Islands remained a mystery for thousands of years due to their geographical distance from the Indian mainland. However, it cannot be denied that the existence of the Andaman and Nicobar Islands in the Bay of Bengal has been known to navigators, cartographers, and travellers since ancient times.

These Islands were noticed by the travellers who passed by the Islands and thus were mentioned in their writings and maps. However, it remained a mystery for the outside world until the sixteenth century, owing to the absence of any reliable accounts of the Islands. While authentic historical records are lacking, the early references to these Islands have come down to us either through oral histories, folk tales or the writings of earlier travellers.

The first ever mention of the Islands is available in the holy Hindu scripture Ramayana. It is believed that the name of the Andaman Islands is derived from the word Handuman or Hanuman. According to a Hindu legend, Lord Rama wanted to utilise these Islands as a bridge to get to Lanka and save his wife Sita from the clutches of Ravana with the help of his disciple Hanuman. While describing this, MV Portman, referring to Wilford, writes, "Hindu legends noticed the remarkable chain of Islands from Cape Negrais to Achin, and ascribe it to Rama who first attempted here to bridge the sea, an enterprise afterwards transferred to Palk Straits and Adam's Bridge." Describing the origin of the word Andaman, MV Portman, while mentioning his visit to Penang in 1885, where he met a well-known Malay scholar W.E. Maxwell, writes, "the Malays had known, and slaved at, the Andamans from time immemorial, that they looked on the Andamanese (who were also known as the Rakshasas) as the Handumans mentioned in the Ramayana, and had consequently called the group, the Islands of the 'Hanumans' (or Handumans as they pronounce the word), hence Andaman Islands as we know them." Portman justifies his statement by narrating a personal incident which occurred during his visit to Penang in 1883 with thirteen Andamanese. He observes, "I was mobbed in the streets by the Malays who called to their friends to come and see the Handumans."[3]

An early mention of these Islands can be found in the literary work *Bodhisathvavadana* by a Kashmiri poet, Kshemendra. He writes that a few Indian traders met with Emperor Ashoka in Patliputra in the third century BC, and they complained to him about the damage caused to them by the hostile natives of the Andamans when their ship passed by these Islands.[4]

Other than the legends mentioned above, our knowledge of the early history of the Islands is primarily derived from references made by occasional voyagers who endeavoured to pass through the Islands.

However, the first reliable reference to the Andaman and Nicobar Islands dates back to the 2nd century AD in the writings and maps made from those writings of the Greek astronomer and mathematician Claudius Ptolemy, who named the archipelago from Cape Negrais to Sumatra as *Buzacata* and described that "it produces quantities of shells, and the inhabitants go naked and are called Agmatae." However, he says that "we cannot determine whether this name was intended to apply to the Andaman Group." Ptolemy did not draw any map, but the earliest maps, drawn by *Agathodaemon*, a mathematician of the fifth (?) century after Christ, are based on Ptolemy's data where the Islands were shown as the *"Island of Cannibals"* called the *"Island of Good Fortune."*[5]

The first authentic historical record of the Islands may be found in the writings of two Arab travellers from the 9th century AD, *Abu Zaid Hasan* and *Sulaiman*. Their accounts of the Islands have been translated and quoted in Pemberton's publication 'A General Collection of the Best and Most Interesting Voyages and Travels in All Parts of the World'. They recorded, "Beyond these two Islands lie the sea of Andamans: the people on this coast eat human flesh quite raw; their complexion is black, their hair frizzled, their countenance and eyes frightful, their feet are very large, and almost a cubit in length, and they go quite naked. They have no sort of barks or other vessels;

if they had, they would seize and devour all the passengers they could lay hands on. When ships have been kept back by contrary winds, they are often in these seas obliged to drop anchor on this barbarous coast for the sake of water when they have expended their stock; and upon these occasions, they commonly lose some of their men." [6]

Marco Polo, the famous Venetian traveller who passed by these Islands in 1290 AD on his way to China, called the Islands *Angamanaian*. While describing the land and people of the Islands, he narrated, "*Angamanaian* is a very long island. The people are without a king and are idolaters and no better than wild beasts. And I assure you, all the men of this island of Angamanain have heads like dogs and teeth and eyes likewise; in fact, in the face, they are just like big mastiff dogs. They have a quantity of spices: but they are a most cruel generation and eat everybody that they can catch, if not of their own race. They live on flesh and rice and milk and have fruits different from any of ours." [7]

Friar Odoric and Niccolò Conti passed by the Andamans in 1322 and 1440 AD, respectively, and, again, described the natives as cannibals. While mentioning the Islands in his writings, Cesare Federici, in 1569, also labelled them as the *Islands of Cannibals*. [8] *A Duquesne*, during his voyage to the East Indies from 1690 to 1691, mentioned that "the inhabitants are the most cruel and savage in the world, they neither trade nor correspond with any other whatsoever, not so much as suffer any to land upon their coast, and if by chance they are so unhappy as to be driven upon, these barbarous savages immediately kill them and dress them for food." [9]

The behaviour of the natives towards visitors can be largely attributed to the exploitation they endured at the hands of the Malays, who frequently visited the Islands to collect bird's nests. During these visits, they would kidnap the natives and transport them to distant lands, where they were sold into slavery. This history of abduction and enslavement has fostered a deep-rooted hostility among the natives, leading them to view all strangers approaching their shores with great suspicion.[10]

The travellers mentioned above provided an incomplete and unfavourable portrayal of the natives of the Andaman Islands. The inhabitants have long been regarded as 'one of the most savage and unapproachable races on Earth'. This perception persisted until Blair, the renowned hydrographer of the 18th century, arrived and offered the first highly favourable depiction of the Islands and their people.

The Nicobar group of Islands has similar stories. The Cholas from Thanjavur, who sailed to Southeast Asia, often stopped by these Islands en route. The Tanjore inscriptions from 1050 AD, which mention Nicobar as Nakkavarum, indicate that with the increase in naval activity in southern India under the Chola kings, Rajendra Chola Deva I conquered many kingdoms in the East. The occupation of Pegu was followed by the annexation of the Nicobar Islands. After failed attempts at colonisation by the Danes, Austrians, French, and Portuguese, it was finally the turn of the British, the most successful of all colonial powers.

NOTES AND REFERENCES

1. *Andaman and Nicobar Islands – At a Glance, Directorate of Economics and Statistics, Andaman and Nicobar Administration, 2019.*

2. *Dass, F.A.M., The Andaman Islands, 1937, Asian Educational Services, New Delhi, Madras, 1988, p. 4.*

3. *Portman, M V, A History of Our Relations with the Andamanese, Vol. I, Government of India, Asian Educational Services, New Delhi, Madras, 1990, pp. 19-20. This book was written at the request of Lt. Colonel R.C. Temple, Chief Commissioner of the Islands.*

4. *Dass, p. 7*

5. *Portman, p. 50*

6. *Ibid, p. 51*

7. *Ibid, p. 52*

8. *Ibid, p. 53*

9. *Cooper, Zarine, Archaeology and History, Early settlements in the Andaman Islands, Oxford University Press, New Delhi, 2002, p. 11. (Cooper quoted A. Duquesne who has given a detailed account of his voyage to the East Indies, titled A New Voyage to the East Indies in the years 1690 and 1691)*

10. *Mouat, F.J., Adventures and Researches among the Andaman Islanders, Mittal Publications, New Delhi, pp. 21-2. (The author Frederick John Mouat was the President of the Andaman Committee constituted to examine the suitability of the Andaman Islands for the establishment of a penal settlement.)*

CHAPTER II

Andaman Penal Settlement

First Settlement and Its Disastrous End

The Andaman and Nicobar Islands, strategically located in the Bay of Bengal, have historically drawn the attention of various imperialist countries, including the British, Dutch, Danes, Portuguese, and French. To safeguard their interests, these countries sought to acquire an excellent harbour in the Bay. It is said that imperialist rivalries were undoubtedly the primary reason for the lack of disclosure regarding the particulars of the official report submitted by Captain Archibald Blair and Colonel Colebrook, as well as the subsequent actions of the Government.[1]

The Andaman Islands were often viewed as an *island of savage people* primarily because the travellers' accounts depicted them as a group of *cannibal Islands*. By this time, the Government was searching for a suitable location for the establishment of a convict settlement associated with a harbour of refuge. In 1777, John Ritchie surveyed the Bay of Bengal and urged Warren Hastings, the first Governor-General of India, to take a greater interest in these Islands. A decade later, Lord Cornwallis took up the project.

Under these circumstances, Lord Cornwallis, the then Governor-General of India, issued directions to Lieutenant (later Captain) Archibald Blair, one of the early distinguished hydrographers of the East India Company, and Colonel Colebrook, the Surveyor General of India in 1788, to survey the Andaman Islands. They were ordered to collect as many details about the Islands as possible. Both officers were men of great ability and had the personal experience of undertaking such challenging missions in the past. Captain Blair set sail from Calcutta with two ships under his command—

the Elizabeth and the Viper on 20th December and reached the Andaman Islands on 29th December 1788. It is quite remarkable that the remains of the wooden wharf built at Chatham, named after an area in Kent, to land stores exist even to this day.

Captain Archibald Blair and Colonel Colebrook meticulously surveyed the Andaman Islands. Captain Blair remained on the Islands for three months and submitted his report in June 1789. He prepared a report supplemented by a chart indicating the important areas and plan of three important harbours deemed safe. The report submitted by Captain Blair and Colonel Colebrook received high praise from the authorities. This was the first reliable account of the Islands and their original inhabitants covering aspects such as water, soil, wind, currents, climate, natural resources, and flora and fauna, which were found favourable by the authorities.[2]

In appreciation of Blair's survey report, Frederick J. Mouat, the President of the Andaman Committee who examined the Islands in December 1857, commented, "The inhabitants were described in such a manner as to leave a much more favourable impression on the mind of the reader, as to their character, manners, and customs, than the narratives of any former writers were calculated to impart. So favourable indeed, was the impression conveyed, that it led the authorities to take measures for the formation of the first settlement on the Andamans."[3] In light of this, the responsibility for establishing a settlement on the Islands was assigned to Captain Blair.

Blair worked diligently to maintain the trust of the Government and proved his skills in founding the settlement. His efforts resulted in the prosperity of the settlement marked by well-managed health and mortality rates. He also succeeded in establishing somewhat amicable relations with the natives. By 1790, Chatham Island was cleared and adorned with vegetable and fruit tree plantations. Additionally, Blair erected a structure on Ross Island, positioned at the harbour entrance, designated as a hospital for the settlers, who numbered one hundred and nineteen. He also allowed the settlers to bring their families to join them in the new settlement.

Commodore Cornwallis, the Commander-in-Chief of His Majesty's Ships in the East Indies, visited North-East Harbour in November 1790 and directed Blair to carry out a survey, which was completed by March 1791. Upon receiving Blair's survey report of the North-East Harbour, Commodore Cornwallis, brother of the then Governor General, recommended moving the settlement from Chatham Island to the new harbour without completing prior arrangements for shifting and founding the settlement in a new site, contrary to their usual practice. However, the decline of the once-flourishing settlement began when the colony was relocated from Port Cornwallis to North-East Harbour on 16th October 1792.

Meanwhile, the settlement at Chatham continued to be healthy. Blair reported in March 1792, "The settlement had been so healthy as to suffer no injury from the absence of the surgeon, who had been to Calcutta on leave, and the natives have been perfectly inoffensive for a long time, and are becoming every day more familiar—they seem now convinced that our intentions towards them are pacific."[4] However, as soon as the decision to move the settlement was communicated to Blair, efforts to strengthen the existing settlement were discontinued. This relocation was prompted by the Government's intention to establish a naval arsenal, following the recommendations of Commodore Cornwallis in view of the ongoing Anglo-French War in Europe.

Captain Alexander Kyd, an Engineer from the Corps of Engineers, was appointed the superintendent of the new settlement. He arrived in the new settlement on 5th March 1793. Captain Blair proceeded towards Nicobar to continue with his mission of surveying. The new settlement was established exactly in accordance with the plan adopted in the first settlement. With the colony, the name 'Port Cornwallis' was also transferred to the new locality. A site on a small island was selected and named Chatham Island, and a harbour was designated as 'Port Cornwallis'. The recently abandoned port was referred to as 'old harbour', a name that remained until 1858 when Dr. Frederick John

Mouat's recommendation was accepted, and it was renamed as 'Port Blair' in honour of Blair, who first surveyed and established the first settlement here.[5]

It is worth mentioning that the settlement in the North-East Harbour was the first maritime operation of the East India Company in the Bay of Bengal. The shifting of the settlement was made during the dry and healthy season, and hence, no health-related problems were noticed in its early days.[6]

Meanwhile, the imperialist rivalry among the European countries led to the war with France in June 1793, and England was also involved in the war. On hearing the news of the war with France, Major Kyd placed the settlement in a state of defence and went to Calcutta to procure more arms and weapons for the fortification of the settlement. This deteriorated the situation as all developmental work in the settlement was discontinued, and instead of using resources for its progress, fortification became the prime concern of the authorities. During the absence of the superintendent of the settlement, Major Michael Symes reached Port Cornwallis on his way to Burma and remained in the settlement for a few days. He reported on the 14th May 1794 to the Council of the Governor-General that "the situation of Port Cornwallis has of late proved very unfavourable to the health of the settlers, but we entertain hopes that the place will become more salubrious in proportion as it is cleared."[7]

The new settlement continued to remain an unhealthy site, with fifty casualties reported during the rains of 1795. This unfortunate situation led to a loss of confidence among the settlers, who expressed a desire to leave the settlement. The combination of a high death rate and escalating expenditure on its maintenance ultimately pushed the settlement to the verge of closure. With the death of Dr. Reddich, the surgeon of the settlement, in January 1796, the Government decided to abolish the settlement.

Under these circumstances, the Governor-General in Council ordered the abolition of the settlement and recorded the minutes dated 8th February 1796: "Considering the great sickness and mortality of the settlement formed at the Andamans, which, it is feared, is likely to continue, and the great expenses and embarrassment to the Government in maintaining it, and in conveying supplies to it at the present period, it appears to the Governor-General in Council, both with a view to humanity and economy, prudent to withdraw it." However, authorities were worried that deserting the settlement in the Andamans might encourage other colonial powers to claim over the Andamans and to avoid such a situation, the board decided to keep a small vessel at Port Cornwallis, which would be relieved every six months. It was ordered to remove all the convicts, numbering two hundred and seventy, to Prince of Wales Island, and settlers, including five hundred and fifty free men, women and children and European artillery and sepoys to Bengal, and thus the settlement was abandoned by May 1796.

Describing the disastrous end of the first settlement in the Andamans, Major Kyd remarked, "... Blair's success in the Southern Harbour had naturally led the Government to conclude that the other harbours would be equally healthy and well-suited for settling in. It was unfortunate that Commodore Cornwallis, who was the brother of the Governor General, should have been so taken with the present Port Cornwallis (though he, of course, regarded it from a strategic point of view only) as his words carried great weight and caused the moving of the settlement to the Northern Harbour on the 12th November 1792."[8]

Colonisation of Nicobar

On the other hand, the situation in the Nicobars was different from that of the Andaman Islands. From the last decade of the 17th century until its occupation by the British in March 1869, the Nicobar group of Islands experienced numerous unsuccessful attempts at colonisation by European countries. The French during the periods of 1701-1742 and 1836-1845 and the Danes from 1756-1783 sent their missionaries to propagate the Christian faith and convert the natives. However, these missions met with disastrous ends on account of the unhealthy climate leading to the deaths of missionaries. In the first half of the 19th century, several incidents involving attacks on the crews of ships anchoring off the shores of the Nicobars were reported. These incidents ultimately contributed to the circumstances that led to the British occupation of the Islands.[9]

Six Decades of Isolation

It appears that, although the Council of Directors in its meeting decided to keep a small vessel at Port Blair to maintain its claim over the Andamans after its abandonment in 1796, this decision was never put into practice. As a result, the Islands entered a period of isolation for the next sixty-two years. From 1796 until the re-occupation of the Islands in 1858, there was a notable lack of attention given to the Andaman Islands.

From the 2nd century until the 18th century, the occasional voyagers and surveyors engaged by the Government published short accounts and reports, which form the basis of our information about the Islands. However, not much information is available from 1796 to 1855, except the narratives of shipwrecked crews of trading vessels, which mentioned the inhabitants as most savage. Several incidents of shipwreck and hostility of the aborigines were reported from the Andaman Islands, which are mentioned in the following paragraphs:

In 1811, six men on a boat were inhumanely murdered by the natives of Little Andaman.

During the first Anglo-Burmese War in 1824, the fleet carrying the army of Sir Archibald Campbell to Rangoon anchored at Port Cornwallis. The aborigines kept themselves away from them.

Dr. J.W. Helfer, an Austrian physician and naturalist who went to the Islands for scientific research, was killed by the aborigines in the year 1840. This was caused as he had little information about them. Helfer wrote in his diary, "We made him understand that we wanted water, and he showed us where it was to be found. My Malay Captain took the savages a bowl of rice. The young man took it and afterwards brought the bowl filled with fresh water. One of my Malay boatmen jostled against them, and unfortunately, the bowl was broken. After that, the savages would not come near the boats anymore but only peeped at us from behind the rocks."[10]

The next incident reported from the Islands was an unusual shipwreck of two British ships carrying the detachments of 50 and 80 Regiments *Runnymede* and *Briton,* which were hit by the cyclone near John Lawrence Island. These ships with six hundred and twenty men on board were wrecked on 12th November 1844. They remained and suffered fifty-four days on the Islands, and many of them died. The rest safely returned to their destination. The last detachment of the wrecked troops sailed for their ultimate destination, Calcutta, in the *Agnes Lee* on 5th January 1845. Before their departure, they named the Island *Briton* and the anchorage *Runnymede Bay.* In later years, two ships *Flying Fish* and *Emily,* under the command of Captain Anderson and Captain Shaw respectively, also met a tragic end in 1849 near the Andaman Islands. The natives looted the ship and killed an officer of *Emily.*[11]

In the following years, more shipwrecks continued: the *Tenasserim* in 1852, *Sesotris* in 1854, and the *Faiz Baksh* on 13th January 1855. The outrages instigated by the indigenous inhabitants of the Islands became a grave concern. The story of the dramatic survival of a 55-day ordeal of the crews of *Runnymede* and *Briton* and subsequent shipwrecks of the *Flying Fish* and *Emily* prompted the British to take serious note of the Islands. Eventually, the Government decided to quash such incidents by re-establishing a convict settlement on the Islands.

The Officiating Secretary, in his letter number 4152 dated 28th November 1855, addressed to the Secretary, Government of Bengal, asked to propose measures for the protection of British subjects in the Andaman Islands. It was suggested, "The only effectual remedy would be the occupation of the Islands in question, but this is manifestly impracticable. However, His Honour in

Council believes that good might be affected by the establishment of a convict settlement on the southwest part of the southern island, which is reputed to be healthy."[12]

Circumstances Leading to Penal Settlement

In December 1855, the Government of Bengal requested Captain Henry Hopkinson, Commissioner of Arracan, to suggest measures for the protection of British subjects in the Andaman Islands. In response, Captain Henry Hopkinson, in his letter No. 18 dated 8th February 1856, suggested various measures to put an end to the incessant murders and ill-treatment of shipwrecked crews. He replied, "…that the only effectual remedy would be the occupation of the Islands, and if this should appear impracticable, then I must still agree that the establishment of a British settlement on one of the Islands, which might extend itself hereafter as circumstances allowed, would be the next best thing."

Hopkinson strongly recommended the occupation of the Nicobars by suggesting that "any project for the re-occupation of the Andaman Islands should comprehend arrangements for exercising surveillance over the neighbouring group of the Nicobars." [13]

While the matter of forming a settlement on the Andaman Islands was under consideration by the Government, the murder of eight Chinese traders by the aborigines of the Islands was reported in March 1856.[14]

In spite of numerous reports of the inhospitable and savage character of the natives, the Governor-General in Council was not in a hurry to form a settlement on the Islands without any prior arrangements. Moreover, by that time, Pegu was occupied by the British, and they were overconfident that no other country could dare to occupy the Islands as the Bay of Bengal was a British sea. It was decided that "…It would be expedient, therefore, in the first instance, that steps should be taken to explore them, and to report upon the sites, which they may offer both for the construction of harbours of refuge on the coast and the establishment of penal or other settlements, not only on the shores but also in the inland parts of the Islands." [15]

While the proposal for the formation of a harbour of refuge associated with the establishment of a penal settlement was under active consideration by the Government, the *Great Mutiny of 1857*, known as the *First War of Indian Independence*, broke out in India, shaking the very foundation of British rule in India.

This was the largest armed resistance against colonial rule throughout the entire 19th century, with individuals from diverse backgrounds actively participating in this struggle. However, this unprecedented armed uprising against the colonial power was suppressed in the most barbaric way. The mass arrest compelled the Government to initiate immediate steps to explore the possibility of the establishment of a penal colony in the Andaman Islands. Accordingly, the Andaman Committee was formed under the Chairmanship of Dr. Fredric John Mouat, Surgeon of the Bengal Army, Dr. G.R. Playfair of the Royal Army and Lieutenant J.A. Heathcote of the Indian Navy on 20th November 1857. The Committee was asked to immediately proceed to the Andaman Islands to study and suggest the site for the establishment of a penal settlement. The mutineers of 1857 were initially intended to be sent there, and the Islands were ultimately designated as a station for receiving all offenders sentenced to transportation from the Indian mainland in the following years.

The mission was time-bound, and therefore, Dr. Mouat was allowed only a short time to make necessary arrangements. Within two days of the formation of the committee, Dr. Mouat and his team left Calcutta for Moulmein on 23rd November 1858 on board the Steam Frigate S.S. Semiramis and arrived on the Islands on 11th December.

The Committee explored and surveyed Port Cornwallis, Stewart's Sound, Barren Island, Chatham Island, Port Campbell, Interview Island, Middle Strait, and Port Mouat in December 1857. The members of the Committee meticulously prepared their notes with exceptional accuracy. Lt. Heathcote took careful note of every hydrographical feature and "made minute enquiries into all that concerned the supply of suitable timber and building materials of every kind." The main aim of Dr. Playfair's observations was to find out "to what extent the Islands themselves could be put under contribution for the supply of provisions to future settlers." The Committee took great care in searching out the perennial source of water on the Islands.[16]

The Committee concluded that Blair's old settlement, then called *Old Harbour*, is the most appropriate site for establishing a penal settlement and justified their observation by stating that "this was the only place, which fulfilled all the conditions considered requisite for a penal settlement. Here was an abundance of wood for building and other purposes; stone in any quantity could be procured; and, what is of infinite importance in these Islands, there were three sources from which, at all seasons, an abundant supply of pure, limpid drinking water could be obtained for the use of settlers and prisoners."[17] In his report, Mouat criticised the then Governor General, who ordered the removal of the first settlement from *Old Harbour* to the *North-East Harbour* on the advice of his brother. Dr. Mouat justified Blair's selection for having preferred *Old Harbour* to all other Islands and recommended the Government of India name the *Old Harbour* as *Port Blair* in his honour.

The Andaman Committee is credited with discovering a port that could not attract Blair's attention during his survey of the Islands in 1788. This new port was subsequently named Port Mouat by order of Earl Canning, in honour of its explorer, who was also the chairman of the Andaman Committee.[18]

The Committee returned and submitted its report in January 1858. At that point in time, the Governor-General was very "uncertain as to the manner in which these mutineers (of 1857) who, however guilty, had not deserved capital punishment, should be disposed of..." But, with the favourable outcome of the Andaman Committee, the tension was released.[19]

However, the origin of an Indian penal settlement was first conceptualised by Sir Stamford Raffles around the 1780s, who first introduced Indian convicts into Sumatra to develop that island. In 1825, upon the handing over of Sumatra to the Dutch, convicts were transferred to the Straits Settlements to supplement the supply of free labour. Later, attempts were made to find another place to which convicts could be deported from India, and in the year 1858, finally, the Andaman came into active consideration.

1857 - Genesis of Kala Pani

The Government accepted the recommendations made by the Committee and immediately ordered Captain H. Man (later General), the Executive Engineer and Superintendent of Convicts at Moulmein, to take over the control of the Islands. It was informed to Captain Man via dispatch no. 87 dated 15th January 1858, that "It has been determined by the Right Honourable the Governor-General in Council to establish a penal settlement on the Andaman Islands, for the reception, in the first instance, of convicts sentenced to imprisonment, and to transportation, for the crimes of mutiny and rebellion and other offences connected therewith, and eventually for the reception of all convicts under sentence of transportation, whom, for any reason, it may not be thought expedient to send to the Straits Settlements or the Tenasserim Provinces."[20]

The orders were implemented, and Captain Man formally took over the possession of the island by hoisting the Union Jack on 22nd January 1858, thus marking the beginning of penal settlement in the Islands. It was made clear to Captain Man that he was being sent to make initial arrangements and a plan for the settlement. He was authorised to nominate an officer as superintendent to execute his plan for the location, employment, and general control of the convicts following the pattern which existed in the Straits Settlements.

The challenging task of establishing the penal settlement was undertaken by Dr. James Pattison Walker, the former Superintendent of Agra Central Jail. He was selected as the first superintendent of the penal settlement as he brought valuable experience from dealing with the 'mutineers' of 1857 and had studied penal institutions in England. His skills were demonstrated during the 1857 Mutiny when he successfully held Agra.

He left Calcutta on 4th March 1858 with two hundred Freedom Fighters of the First War of Independence aboard the Steam Frigate S.S. Semiramis. He was accompanied by an Indian Overseer, Lalla Matton Daus; two native doctors, Nawab Khan and Kureem Buksh; and a guard of fifty naval brigade men under the command of an officer of the Indian Navy. They reached Port Blair on 10th March 1858, marking the beginning of the settlement. Assistant Apothecary Mr. Ringrow arrived on the 20th of March aboard the ship Semiramis from Moulmein. Dr. Gamach, Mr. Richardson, and the Hospital Attendants arrived on the 29th of March from Rangoon.

Upon their arrival, the convicts were tasked with clearing the jungles at Chatham and later at Ross Island (now known as NSCB Dweep). In the following days, Dr. Walker encountered neither environmental health issues nor hostility from the natives. There were no incidents of escapes; however, the situation was soon to change.

Life Amid Hardship in the Settlement

All life and long-term prisoners aged eighteen to forty years who had avoided the death penalty for various reasons in India and Burma were selected for transportation. It was mandatory for all to be medically fit for hard labour before transportation, for which necessary guidelines and rules were established.

Prisoners were deported to the Islands through the Alipore Jail of Bengal, which was the receiving jail for prisoners from North-West Provinces, Punjab, Rajputana, Central India, and Assam. Prisoners from Madras Province went directly to the Andamans to avoid overcrowding at Alipore Jail. Specific space prescribed by the *Native Passengers Ships Act of 1875* was allotted to all prisoners aboard the vessels on their voyage to Port Blair.

These prisoners had to face untold hardships in the open jail of Andaman. The settlement officers inflicted all sorts of inhuman and brutal punishments, including mass execution without any proper trial. The officers chosen for the settlement were experienced in convict management during 1857 and afterwards, and hence, they did not hesitate to treat the prisoners with great severity.

From the first day onwards, Dr. Walker engaged all the prisoners to clear the forest on Chatham Island. Here, he found that the island does not have any perennial source of water. He was of the view that Chatham Island had been chosen as the headquarters of the settlement; however, it is inferior to Ross Island, located at the mouth of the port, which effectively controls the entrance. Ross Island is more favourably situated and has a good supply of excellent drinking water, something that is difficult to obtain on Chatham Island. In case of a requirement, they need to transport drinking water from the other side of the port in casks via boat. In view of this, he sought permission to select Ross Island as the headquarters of the settlement, a decision fully supported by Captain Man. Accordingly, a proposal was submitted to the Government of India to shift the headquarters of the settlement from Chatham to Ross, which was approved in May 1858 via letter No. 743 dated 7th May 1858.[21]

Dr. Walker frequently communicated with the Government of India and kept them informed about the situation in the settlement. His letter addressed to the Secretary to the Government of India is an important source of first-hand information about the initial days of the settlement.

In the initial days of the settlement, ships *Semiramis, Dalhousie, Pluto, Roman Emperor, Edward, Sesotris,* and others continued to arrive at frequent intervals with prisoners on board from Rangoon, Moulmein, Karachi,

Calcutta and so on. The *Roman Emperor*, which sailed from Karachi on 27th February with one hundred and seventy-five prisoners on board, reached Port Blair on 6th April 1858, but only one hundred and seventy-one arrived as four died on the way. The condition of the others was also not satisfactory, as some were sick, and a few others were not in a position to undertake any kind of hard work. Meanwhile, *Dalhousie*, which reached Port Blair on 15th April 1858, supported the settlement by bringing on board other officers besides Mrs. Walker, as mentioned above.

The lives of prisoners in the initial days of the settlement were too miserable. They were transported to the penal settlement without any prior arrangements. Even the basic needs for the establishment of the settlement were received ten days after their arrival. Though Captain Man was ordered to make arrangements before their arrival, he left the Islands for Moulmein after the formal occupation by hoisting the British Flag on 22nd January 1858 and returned to the settlement ten days after the arrival of the first batch on 10th March.

Even during the rainy season, they had no place for a safe shelter other than staying in tents. The condition improved a little by November 1858 when accommodation for one thousand prisoners on Ross Island was provided. [22] The prisoners were accommodated in barracks of a temporary nature with thatched roofs and mat walls, which leaked continuously during the rainy season. Later, from 1877 onwards, barracks with a proper roof were provided for their accommodation. [23]

Discipline on the lines of the Tasmanian settlement (which was inhabited by an indigenous population) was imposed on the Andamans. Dr. Walker was brutal towards the prisoners. "Convicts were handcuffed together in pairs, and these handcuffs were never opened. During working hours, the worst characters were taken to the sea beach, and an iron bar being passed through the fetters of a number of them; they were thus fastened to the earth and made to do what work they could in a sitting posture."[24] This punishment was, however, relaxed on the arrival of Captain Houghton.

The prisoners were put on the hardest labour for about nine hours a day in the tropical climate and dense forest. They were engaged not only in clearing thick tropical jungles but also in digging wells, cutting earth, filling swamps, cooking, and constructing huts. Towards the end of the 19th century, the prisoners were engaged as labourers in works such as forestry, reclamation, cultivation, fishing, making domestic utensils, breeding and tending animals and poultry, fuel, salt, portage by land and sea, shipbuilding, furniture making, metalwork, carpentry, masonry, stonework, etc. [25]

The arrangements for food, clothing, and shelter were not adequate for human beings. They were given a meagre allowance of one anna and nine pice for their food, clothing, and other facilities, which was so insufficient that they could hardly procure a piece of cloth to cover themselves.[26] This allowance was deliberately set at a very low amount in accordance with their malicious intent, as stated in the Jail Manual of 1874, which reads: "Transportation entails hard labour with strict discipline, with only such food as is necessary for health. Any mitigation of the above is an indulgence, which may at any time be withdrawn in whole or in part."

One can imagine the dire condition of the prisoners as described by Robert Napier in the 1863 inspection report. Most of the convicts wore tattered clothing, struggling to manage with their meagre rations. Owing to a lack of adequate medical care and proper nutrition and facing an unhealthy climate, they succumbed to minor diseases such as malaria, dysentery, and pneumonia. Furthermore, they were subjected to gruelling labour in oppressive conditions and were ruthlessly punished for any violations of jail rules and regulations.

The tortures imposed by Walker escalated day by day. With the occupation of Viper Island on 8th October 1858, a new form of punishment known as the *chain gang* was introduced. Prisoners sentenced to this punishment by the Superintendent's Court were bound together and confined at night with a chain that ran through their legs via iron couplings. To enhance the severity of the punishment, a jail and gallows were constructed at Viper Island between

1864 and 1867 by 1870 Additionally, punishments such as flogging with six stripes could be administered to prisoners by a convict officer without any official inquiry.[27]

The selection of Port Blair was also made keeping its excellent location, which is "300 miles from the coast of Burma, 400 miles from any part of the Malay Archipelago, and 700 miles from the coast of India, all this across a stormy and often dangerous sea. Hence, escape is rendered very difficult and perilous." Life on such an isolated island was considered *hell*. The isolation from their homeland and family itself was the greatest torture. While describing this, H.L. Adam observed, "It is, however, only this homesickness which causes the penal settlement of Port Blair to be to the prisoners such a crushing place of bondage..." [28]

Under these circumstances, escapes of convicts were a regular feature in the initial days of the settlement, and harsh measures were initiated against the recaptured convicts. During the first two months, two hundred and twenty-eight convicts escaped from the settlement. Out of them, eighty-eight were recaptured, one pardoned, one was in the hospital untried, and a hundred and forty convicts remain uncaptured. The recaptured eighty-six prisoners were executed by hanging on the 13th May 1858. However, the authorities disapproved of the conduct of Dr. Walker with the remark, "That the return of so many of these runaways, to meet any fate that might await them in the settlement, after realising the hopelessness of living away from the settlement, would, if they had been allowed to live, have acted as a more active, certain, and permanent warning to the other convicts than the execution of the whole of them." [29]

It is unfortunate that, to this day, we do not know the exact date or names of those eighty-six freedom fighters who were hanged on a single day by Superintendent Walker. However, details on the website of Azadi ka Amrit Mahotsav indicate that they were hanged on 18th May 1858. An article titled 'Survivors of our hell' written by Cathy Scott-Clark and Adrian Levy in *The*

Guardian on 23rd June 2001 reveals that eighty-one convicts who returned to the settlement 'pleading for mercy' were hanged by Walker on 13th May 1858. While the exact date may be debatable, the primary aim is to highlight the contributions of these heroes.

In order to reduce the incidence of escapes, Dr. Walker proposed allowing the prisoners to bring their families. He believed that convicts with families in the settlement were reliable in times of need because they had a real interest in the penal colony. It was also necessary to have women in the settlement, and therefore, he strongly urged the Government to make arrangements to provide all facilities for families who wish to emigrate, ensuring their arrival at Port Blair. Meanwhile, Dr. Walker, with much difficulty, convinced twenty-five convicts to invite their families from the mainland to join them in the penal colony and also made a detailed plan to implement the same. He reported via letter on 16th June 1858 in paragraphs 14 and 15 that read, "14) Twenty-five inspected letters from convicts to their wives, requesting them to proceed to Port Blair, are enclosed for approval and transmission to the addressees by post or through the Collectors of the districts in which they may reside. Duplicates of the letters are enclosed with Lalla Mundun Singh's Pervvannah of appointment for delivery to the addressees when he may visit them at their houses to arrange for their transmission to the port of embarkation. 15) The terms I have offered to convicts, whose families may join them, are permission to reclaim and cultivate land free of rent during their and their wife's lifetime; assistance during the first three years (before which the land cannot be expected to yield full crops) to the extent of four rupees per mensem to the convict for the first year, three rupees per mensem for the second year, and two rupees per mensem for the third year. Additionally, two rupees per mensem for each adult female, and one rupee per mensem for each juvenile member of his family for three years, after which, all assistance will be withdrawn." [30] However, the proposal was not sanctioned at that time as the settlement was not 'sufficiently advanced to handle them'.

As per Walker's plan, steps were initiated to relocate the families of twenty-five Bengali convicts to the Andamans, but none of the females agreed to go due to caste concerns. In 1860, thirty-five female convicts were sent from Bengal to Port Blair, leading to several marriages, as these couples were classified as 'self-supporters'. However, issues arose when male term convicts married female life convicts; upon their release, the men often returned home, leaving their wives and children behind. This situation prompted the Government to permit such marriages only if the male convict agreed to stay in the settlement after release. Consequently, about 400 women expressed a desire to marry but had to wait due to this restriction.[30]

Meanwhile, the authorities took severe steps to prevent escapes as per suggestions put forth by Walker. The Company's schooner *Charlotte* was stationed near Chatham Island and *Sesotris* between Ross Island and the mainland.[31]

The settlement officers were not satisfied with the measures taken to prevent escapes and decided to impose severe punishment on prisoners escaping the settlement. Captain Man in his letter dated 15th May 1858 proposed to brand all prisoners transported to Port Blair and recorded, "I would earnestly recommend that all the convicts be marked on some conspicuous place such as the breast or arms. Vessels do, at present, touch these Islands searching for trepang and bird's nests, and these might afford opportunities for the convicts to escape. Once landed on the coast, they would merge with the general population of the country and be secure from detection." Dr. Walker supported Captain Man and suggested that "the branding be on the front of the right forearm, and that the letters P.B./L be marked in the case of life, and P.B./T in the case of term convicts, and that in every case the convicts' register number, which is the key to all information regarding his name, caste, sentence, and personal description, be inserted below the letters…". However, via letter dated 28th August 1858, the Government resolved that the convicts of the penal settlement should not be branded.[32]

These prisoners, mainly the rebels of 1857, not only endured the inhumane treatment administered by the colonial rulers but also suffered at the hands of the indigenous people of the Islands. Since the inception of the settlement, the aborigines launched attacks on the working parties, leading to the deaths of many prisoners while they were engaged in various tasks across convict stations. However, the 'Andamanese tribe' appeared to realise that "the convicts were there under compulsion and their assaults were aimed more at the guards and warders, under whose charge the convicts worked, than against the convicts themselves."[33]

Initially, the settlement officers had a negative attitude towards the aborigines, but they later began to build friendly relations with them. This change occurred because they were afraid of the aborigines and as a result of this, even basic resources, like thatching leaves for huts, were being sourced from the Tenasserim coast, despite the Islands having plenty of the same materials. However, this practice was soon discontinued in May 1858.[34] In later years, convicts were engaged in bringing thatching leaves from dense forests to make huts for themselves.

The miserable condition of the settlement was evident from the fact that during the first three months, there were seven hundred and seventy-three persons in the settlement. Out of them, sixty-four had died in hospital, one hundred and forty escaped, and one committed suicide. Eighty-six were hanged on conviction for escape. Thus, out of seven hundred and seventy-three, only four hundred and eighty-one remained, and out of them, sixty were in hospital. [35] Till 28th September 1858, one hundred and sixty-nine deaths were reported among one thousand and thirty prisoners with a 24 percent death rate.

During the first decade, the death rate was alarmingly high, with the highest being 63%. Nevertheless, during the period of Colonel Henry Man (1868-1870), extensive swamp reclamation and forest clearance were undertaken to make the settlement healthier, resulting in a decrease in sickness and death rates. [36] The death rate percentage during the first decade is given as follows: -

Year	Death rate per cent
1858-59	16.00
1859-60	63.00
1860-61	13.40
1861-62	14.25
1862-63	15.53
1863-64	21.55
1864-65	14.64
1865-66	6.57
1866-67	10.56
1867-68	10.16

The high mortality rate in the settlement was attributed to its location in an isolated tropical region inhabited by hostile aborigines and covered by dense forest. E.H. Man summarised the reasons for the higher death rate as follows:

a)   Transportation of a large number of prisoners who were unfit to endure the climate or perform the required work under exceptional conditions.

b)   Insufficient nitrogenous food.

c)   Lack of a sanatorium for the recovery of invalids.

d)   Continuous employment of convict labour for various tasks throughout the year, regardless of seasonal suitability, leading to a mortality rate during the rains that was nearly three times higher than in the dry months.

e)   Challenges faced by working parties due to persistent attacks from the Aborigines.

According to the available information[37], the general statistics for the settlement during the period of 1874-1905/06 show the number of convicts deported, died, escaped, and executed:

THE GENERAL STATISTICS OF PRISONERS

Particulars of convicts		1874	1881	1891	1901	1905-06
Total received	Male	603	1,102	869	1,232	1,307
	Female	97	100	52	80	34
Life convicts	Male	6,727	7,668	8,033	9,204	9,642
	Female	836	1,122	861	714	673
Term convicts	Male	6	2,657	2840	2,037	4,339
	Female	-	5	4	19	42
Total released	Male	335	64	653	215	300
	Female	4	3	73	32	31
In hospital	Male	11,192	2,531	22,328	22,319	25,991
	Female	842	827	1,094	1,290	1246
Total died	Male	107	534	435	433	529
	Female	9	18	17	17	30
Escaped and not recaptured	Male	24	15	14	5	23
	Female	-	-	-	-	-
Executed	Male	6	13	12	6	5
	Female	-	..	-	-	-
					Medical statistics are from 1900	

Key Landmarks of the Penal Administration

A detailed description of the administration and its policies towards the aborigines is not within the framework of this book. However, key aspects of the administration are described below:

From 1858 to 1864, the settlement was placed under the Government of India and was later placed under the Chief Commissioner of Burma. This decision was again revised in 1868, and on 1st January 1869, the settlement of Port Blair was once again brought directly under the Government of India in the Home Department.

One notable feature of the Indian prison system was the involvement of doctors in governance, who provided essential healthcare services while contributing to the overall management. The first superintendent of the settlement was also a doctor known for his stern approach towards the prisoners. However, over time, many medical staff raised concerns about the harsh treatment of convicts, often clashing with administrative personnel to advocate for more humane treatment.

In 1869, the Nicobar Islands were occupied, and a small settlement was established in Nancowry Harbour. This settlement was withdrawn in 1888, and thereafter, the Nicobar Islands were governed from Port Blair. Following the occupation of the Nicobars in 1869, the post of superintendent was upgraded to *Chief Commissioner of the Andaman and Nicobar Islands*. However, for practical purposes, the title of *Superintendent* was retained, with assistance from various European and Eurasian Officers, including Deputy Superintendent, Assistant Superintendents, and Overseers. Several Indian Warders also contributed to the administration. The Chief Commissioner held both Chief Revenue and financial authority. All land in the settlement was vested in the Crown and was held at a fixed rent under a licence from the Chief Commissioner subject to specific terms and conditions.

For administrative purposes, the settlement was divided into two districts and four subdivisions. The headquarters were located on Ross Island, where all the principal Government offices and other facilities, such as a bazaar, bakery, stores, water treatment plant, church, tennis court, printing press, secretariat, hospital, cemetery, and garrison were situated. The remaining official population was based at the district headquarters on Aberdeen and Viper Islands, as well as other sub-divisional headquarters. The subdivisions remained constant, but their distribution between the districts changed from time to time.[38] (see table below)

DISTRIBUTION OF DISTRICTS, SUBDIVISIONS, AND VILLAGES BY 1906

District Headquarters	Stations under subdivisions	Villages within subdivisions
Eastern District Headquarter- Aberdeen	Ross Subdivision Ross, North Bay, Mount Harriett, North Carbyn's Cove, Madhuban, Middle Point, Rutland Island	South Point, Aberdeen
	Haddo Subdivision Phoenix Bay, Haddo, Tea Garden, Navy Bay, Rangachang, Garacharama, Minnie Bay, Pahargaon	Chatham, Phoenix Bay, Junglighat, Nayagaon, Brichgunj, Bimblitan, Taylerabad, School Line, Garacharama, Protheroepore, Austinabad, Pahargaon, Lamba Line, Dudh Line
Western District Headquarters - Viper Island	Viper subdivision Viper Island, Dundas Point, Port Mouat, Elephant Point, Namunaghar	Mithakhari, Namunaghar, Ograbraj, Chouldari, Port Mouat, Dhani Khari, Homfraygunj, Manglutan, Nawashahr
	Wimberly Ganj Subdivision Shore Point Goplakabang (including Middle Straits), Kalatang, Jatang, Bajajagda, Bindraban	Bambooflat, Stewart Ganj, Wimberley Ganj, Kadakachang, Mathura, Bindraban, Anikhet, Cadell Ganj, Hobdaypur, Tusonabad, Manpur, Temple Ganj, Alipur

The first Superintendent, Dr. J.P. Walker, faced two main problems. First, the hostile attitude of the aborigines and secondly, frequent escapes by prisoners. Though they consistently followed a policy of appeasement towards the Andamanese, severe steps were taken by Walker to punish the recaptured prisoners, which has already been discussed above.

Dr. Walker resigned in March 1859 and was replaced by Captain Haughton on 3rd October 1859, who was a little kind towards prisoners. During his two-and-a-half years of tenure, his treatment of convicts using a more humane method and friendly relations with the Andamanese brought him good results.

Colonel Tytler assumed charge of the settlement in 1862. During his period, the somewhat good relations with the Andamanese were disturbed due to the collision between some men of the Naval Brigade and the Andamanese. However, with the appointment of Reverend H. Corbyn, Chaplain of Port Blair, as in charge of the Andamanese, the relation with the Andamanese was restored and the *Andaman Home* was set up.

In 1863, General Robert Napier visited the settlement and recommended a scheme for reorganisation, which was later implemented. By 1863, there were 3,094 prisoners. The Islands of Chatham and Viper had been cleared and permanently occupied.[39]

Colonel Ford, who took over the charge of the settlement in 1864, had the credit of writing the first ever Annual Report of the settlement in 1864-65. During his tenure, the construction of Viper Jail was taken up. A school for Andamanese boys was also started in 1864 at Ross Island by Reverend H Corbyn.

Colonel Man, who founded the settlement in 1858, joined the administration as superintendent in 1868. He introduced the disciplinary system that prevailed in the Straits penal settlements. These were based on the rules drawn up by Sir Stamford Raffles for the first Indian penal settlement of Bencolene in Sumatra, established in 1823.

After Colonel Man's retirement, General Donald Martin Stewart assumed the charge of the superintendent in the year 1871. This was the time when Mayo, the then Viceroy of India, paid a visit on 8th February 1872 but was assassinated by *Sher Ali* at the base of Mount Harriet. Sher Ali was a prisoner from the North-West Frontier of India undergoing a life sentence and living as a self-supporter in Hope Town convict station.

In 1872, the Administration was raised to the rank of Chief Commissionership. General Stewart was the first Chief Commissioner. Justice Scarlett Campbell visited Port Blair, and the settlement was placed directly under the Home Department. General Norman visited in 1874 and recommended codifying the rules framed by Colonel Man, which later formed the base of the *Andaman Regulation of 1874*. The settlement was placed under the Government of India, which was earlier under the High Court of Calcutta, for all its judicial purposes.

General Barewell took over as the Chief Commissioner of the Andaman and Nicobar Islands in 1875. During his tenure, significant legislative changes occurred, including the amendment of the Andaman and Nicobar Regulation, which was enacted as Regulation III of 1876. This period also saw the publication of the Andaman and Nicobar Handbook, which served as an important resource for administration and governance in the region.

General Barewell was succeeded by Colonel T. Cadell in 1879. His tenure is particularly noted for advancements in various sectors, including agriculture, forestry, road construction, and reclamation work. These improvements contributed to the overall development of the Islands. Additionally, during this time, released prisoners began to settle in the area along with their families, leading to an expansion of settlements both in terms of size and population.

The Lyall-Lethbridge Commission visited the Islands in 1890 to examine the penal system, and their recommendations brought significant changes with the construction of the Cellular Jail.

NOTES AND REFERENCES

1. Mouat, F.J., *Adventures and Researches among the Andaman Islanders*, Mittal Publications, New Delhi, 1995, p. 34.

2. *Ibid*, p. 18.

3. *Ibid*, p. 17.

4. Portman, M. V., *A History of Our Relations with the Andamanese*, Vol. I, GOI, pp. 83-84.

5. Man, Edward Horace, *The Aboriginal Inhabitants of the Andaman Islands*, Mittal Publication, New Delhi, 1883.

6. Portman, pp. 85-9.

7. *Ibid*, pp. 90-91.

8. *Ibid*, pp. 91-2.

9. Ram, S., *Andaman and Nicobar Islands, Past and Present*, Akansha Publishing House, New Delhi, 2001, pp. 11-22

10. Cooper, pp. 12-20

11. Portman, pp. 126-155

12. *Ibid*, pp. 185-9.

13. *Ibid*, pp. 188-196.

14. *Ibid*, p. 197.

15. *Ibid*, p. 205.

16. Mouat, p. 195.

17. *Ibid*, p. 172.

18. *Ibid*, p. 229.

19. *Ibid*, p. 278.

20. Portman, p. 242.

21. *Ibid*, pp. 259-260.

22. *Ibid*, p. 264.

23. *HD-P November* 1878. No. 557.

24. Portman, p. 257.

25. *Imperial Gazetteer of India*, Provincial Series, A&N Islands, 1st Edition - 1909, Reprint - 1985, p. 55.

26. Majumdar, R.C, *Penal Settlement in Andamans*, Gazetteers Unit, Department of Culture, Ministry of Education and Social Welfare, GOI, New Delhi, 1975, p. 121.

27. *Ibid*, p. 126.

28. Adam, H.L., *Crime & Criminology*, Printwell, Jaipur, Reprinted 1997, p. 330.

29. Majumdar, p. 99, footnotes at Sl. No. 4.

30. *Ibid, p. 124.*

31. *Portman*, pp. 268-9.

32. *Ibid*, pp. 262-3.

33. Lowis, R.F. *Census of India, 1911*, Vol. II, the Andaman and Nicobar Islands, Calcutta, Govt. Printing, India, 1912, p. 54.

34. *Ibid*, p. 53.

35. Portman, pp. 260-265.

36. Man, pp. xvi-vii.

37. *Imperial Gazetteer of India*, 1909, p. 65.

38. *Ibid*, p. 55.

39. Lowis, p. 55.

CHAPTER III

Patriots of 1857 and Movements That Followed

The *mutineers* of the 1857 revolt, often referred to as the First War of Independence, were pioneers among the political prisoners in the Andamans. Between 1858 and 1860, 3,000 to 4,000 mutineers from different parts of the country were deported to the settlement through three ports: Calcutta, Karachi, and Madras. The next group of prisoners included Wahabis, Kukas, companions of Vasudev Balwant Phadke, and Manipuri rebels. All these prisoners, except Manipuris, were sentenced under specific provisions of the Indian Penal Code. The Manipuri prisoners, sentenced to transportation after the Anglo-Manipur Conflict of 1891, were confined in the Andaman Islands under *Regulation III of 1818*.[1]

Warriors of 1857

The first batch of freedom fighters from 1857 reached the settlement on 10th March 1858. This marked the beginning of the illustrious history of the island, transforming the once-dreaded 'Kala Pani' into a place of pilgrimage. They landed at Chatham Island, where a memorial stands in their memory today. This memorial was erected in the year 2008-09 to mark the 150 years since the arrival of the first batch of 200 Freedom Fighters of the First War of Independence. Every year, a solemn function is organised on 10th March to pay tribute to the first batch of heroes of the First War of Independence.

The first batch of prisoners was deported without any prior arrangements, resulting in their initial accommodation in open enclosures, mostly tents. During this phase, there were no established rules and regulations, and the functioning of the settlement depended solely on the directives of the superintendent. The inflicted torture was indescribable, as the prisoners were consistently engaged in clearing the forest with fetters on their feet. Aborigines posed a threat, killing and injuring several prisoners while they worked in the jungles. Malaria and other diseases added to their misery. The inhumane living conditions incited the escape of two hundred and fifty-one convicts in March-April 1858. Upon recapture, eighty-six of them were executed in a single day by Walker.[2]

The names of freedom fighters who revolted against British rule in 1857 are lost to history. However, some of them have been recorded in various sources, and their contributions are remembered with respect and admiration. Their courage and sacrifice are an inspiration for generations to come.

This chapter presents the names and contributions of some of the freedom fighters who took part in the First War of Independence in 1857 and several other movements they were involved in. A detailed list is provided in the Appendix, compiled from various records, documents, and letters. However, this list is not exhaustive and requires regular updates as new names are received over time.

The most important work in the field was done during Azadi Ka Amrit Mahotsav—a celebration of the 75th anniversary of India's freedom struggle. The section on 'Unsung Heroes' as part of this initiative is an attempt to recall forgotten heroes, 'many of whom might be renowned yet unknown to the new generation'. Their faded memories of the 1857 revolt, often referred to as the First War of Independence, have been brought to light. Another commendable effort in the field has been made by the Indian Council of Historical Research (ICHR), Ministry of Education, Government of India, which has published volumes of 'Dictionary of Martyrs of India's Freedom Struggle (1857-1947)' in 2019, which are also available online.

It is worth mentioning that the 1857 revolt, often referred to as the First War of Independence, represented the most significant armed challenge to colonial power throughout the nineteenth century. The movement garnered support from diverse sections of society and called for social and economic reforms, as well as an end to the oppressive British policies.

For several months after the uprising began in Meerut on 10th May 1857, British rule collapsed in northern India. Rulers of princely states joined forces with the rebelling soldiers, militant peasants, and national leaders. Among the most prominent figures were Bahadur Shah Zafar, Nana Sahib Peshwa II, Tantia Tope, Rani Lakshmi Bai, Kunwar Singh, Bakht Khan, Rao Sahib, Azimullah Khan, Begum Hazrat Mahal, Khan Bahadur Khan, Bhaskar Rao Bhave, Maniram Dewan, and Rao Tula Ram—a long and distinguished list.

The British took extreme measures to suppress the revolt. Thousands were shot dead, many were tied to cannons and blown apart, and countless others were hanged. When these brutal tactics did not suffice, freedom fighters were exiled for life to Kala Pani, far from their families, where they faced a future filled with torture and suffering. Through these inhumane acts, the British not only crushed the spirit of the patriots but also sent a clear message to the general public about the consequences of opposing their rule.

Among those sentenced to life imprisonment in the Andaman Islands, Musai Singh and Fazal Haq Khairabadi stand out.

Musai Singh, celebrated as a hero of 1857, played a significant role in the Bhadohi Rebellion of June 1857.[3]

Musai Singh - Longest-Held Prisoner of 1857

The Pargana of Bhadohi was ruled by the Maharaja of Benaras when Udwant Singh, head of the Monas Rajput family, declared himself king and appointed Bhola Singh and Ram Raksha Singh as Diwans, raising an army of 2,000 men. The pro-British King of Benaras arranged for their arrest, leading to their execution after a court-martial by W.R. Moore, the Joint Magistrate.

This sparked unrest in Bhadohi, where Musai Singh and Jhuri Singh led around 300 men in an attack on the Pali Indigo factory, resulting in the deaths of Moore and two factory managers. Jhuri Singh and his men were arrested and faced severe penalties, including the execution of eight and life transportation.

Musai Singh, born in 1836 and just twenty-one during the uprising, was sentenced to life transportation for his role in the rebellion on the charges of "being a ringleader in the murder of Mr. Moore and arson, dacoity and rebellion." After 25 years in the Andamans, he received a partial release in March 1884 for saving a woman from an attack by another convict.

Musai Singh, prisoner number 4568, resided with his wife Roop Kunwar and children in the Namaunaghar convict village in the Andamans, where he served as the Village Choudhary. Despite several petitions and receiving recommendations from British officials, it was only through the personal intervention of Viceroy Lord Minto that he could be released from the settlement in May 1907 at the age of seventy-one. Lord Minto believed that releasing him on the 50th anniversary of the 'Mutiny' would be appropriate. Consequently, Musai Singh was conditionally released with permission to reside in Rangoon under police surveillance. An extract of the correspondence on his release is reproduced.[4]

Telegram, dated 1st May 1907, 3-45 p.m.

From—Viceroy,

To—Secretary of State.

Private. Release of Musai Singh from Andamans. Please refer to Home Department despatch, dated 11th April, on the subject. I have just seen the despatch, and consider that his conditional release with permission to reside in Rangoon, under police surveillance, should be sanctioned. He is the last survivor of the Mutiny convicts in the Andamans, where his record has been excellent. I strongly recommend his release, which would be most appropriate on the fiftieth anniversary of the Mutiny. I shall be glad if you will reply by telegraph.

———

The Secretary of State's reply may be awaited. In view of His Excellency the Viceroy's note of the 20th April last it does not appear necessary to make any reference to the Government of Burma at present.

L. J. D'S.,—3-5-07.

A. W. J Talbot,—1-5-07.

———

Telegram from the Secretary of State for India, dated the 14th May 1907.   Pro. no. 55.

Stating that Musai Singh might be conditionally released with permission to reside at Rangoon under police surveillance.

The conditional release of Musai Singh may now be sanctioned with permission to reside at Rangoon under police surveillance, and the Burma Government, the Superintendent, Port Blair, and the memorialist may be informed accordingly. Drafts* put up approval.

*The ordinary form of conditional release has been altered to suit the present case.

His Excellency the Viceroy should see the Secretary of State's reply.

A. W. J. Talbot,—16-5-07.

G. Fell,—16-5-07.

H. A[damson,]—16-5-07.

His Excellency has seen and approves the drafts.

J. R. Dunlop-Smith,—21-5-07,
Private Secretary to His Excellency the Viceroy.

Historians consider Musai Singh as the *hero of 1857* as when the Indians were observing the fifty years of *1857*; he was released from the penal settlement of Andaman after forty-seven years, the longest-ever incarceration. He reached Rangoon in July 1907, where he was directed to present himself before the Superintendent of Police, Eastern Division, on the first day of every month.[5]

✻

A Mutiny Transportee

Mossaya Singh, who was transported to the Andamans in 1859 for having taken part in the mutiny of 1857 has landed at Rangoon and on presenting himself before the Commissioner of Police was ordered to present himself before the Superintendent of Police, Eastern Division, on the 1st of every month. He was forty-eight years in the Andamans.

News about Musai Singh's arrival in Rangoon, published in 'The Tribune' on 5th July 1907, was reproduced in its issue dated 5th July 1972.

Ayodhya Singh, Mannu Singh, Sujan Singh Chauhan, Ganesh Maharaj Gowardhan, Jasmer Singh, Shankar Maharaj and Khedu Laxman were eight associates of Musai Singh who were deported to the Andamans along with him.[6]

Allama Fazal Haq in the Andamans

Fazal Haq Khairabadi, son of Maulana Fazal Imam, was born in the year 1797 at Khairabad, District Sitapur, Uttar Pradesh. Khairabad was considered one of the important centres of Arabic Language and Islamic philosophy. He was a genius from his childhood. He completed his studies in Arabic and Persian in 1809 when he was only 13.[7]

He was appointed as Serishtadar (Administrative officer of the court) at Delhi Residency. Later, he was transferred to Allahabad as an advocate, but he was quite unhappy with his new assignment. In order to join the battle against the British, he resigned from the service and took an active part in the First War of Independence. With his writings, he roused a sense of patriotism among the Indian masses, particularly among Muslims, and inspired them to fight against colonial rule. He was a good friend of the well-known poet Mirza Ghalib and other contemporary eminent writers and intellectuals. He read out a fatwa, jointly signed by prominent persons at the Jama Masjid Delhi and sought their advice to proceed further. The Government was aware of the situation in Delhi, and in view of this, they did not delay the matter and occupied Delhi in September 1857. Cases were filed against prominent leaders, including Fazal Haq.[8]

Soon after the defeat of Bahadur Shah's army and the failure of the First War of Independence, he went to Khairabad, where he was arrested on 30th January 1859. Within three weeks of his arrest, the trial began before a Court of Jury at Lucknow on 21st February 1859. However, after a few days, on 28th February 1859, his case was transferred from Lucknow to the Judicial Commissioner, Awadh Court. Fazal Haq Khairabadi was found guilty of *revolt* against the Government on 4th March 1859 and was sentenced to transportation for life to the Andamans with the confiscation of his property on 20th April 1859. He, along with other freedom fighters of 1857, reached the Andamans on 8th October 1859 aboard the Steam Frigate *Fire Queen* and was registered as prisoner number 3687.

Fazal Haq wrote on pieces of cloth with charcoal sticks and sent them to his son Abdul Haq in mainland India in 1860 through Mufti Inayat Ahmed Kakurri, another scholar rebel of the First War of Independence. These works were rendered in Arabic which are known as Al-*Surat-ul Hindia* and *Al-Fitnat-ul-Hindia,* which describes the events of the First War of Independence and his days in Kala Pani respectively.[9] These works are not only of historical importance but also have great significance in Arabic literature.

Some of the Wahhabi rebels mentioned in their writings that a kind-hearted jail superintendent, who had a passion for astrology and astronomy, attempted to write a book on his interests. He gave a draft of the book to a Maulvi, who was his assistant, for correction. Within a week, Maulvi returned the corrected draft, mentioning that the corrections were made by Allama Fazal Haq Khairabadi. When the superintendent went to thank Allama, he found an old man, barefoot and dusty, carrying a basket. The superintendent was ashamed that they had brought the old man, who was a great scholar and writer, to this position. He later ordered him to sit in the office for official work.

Colonel Haughton, the Superintendent of Port Blair at the time, recommended to the Government the release of Allama Fazal Haq. After much effort, his son, Shams-ul-Haq, succeeded in obtaining the release order from the Viceroy of India. However, fate had other plans; as he arrived in Port Blair on 20th August 1861, he could only join his father's funeral procession.

Exiled Patriots of the United Provinces

Uttar Pradesh, then called the United Provinces of Agra and Oudh, which included Rampur State, Banaras State, and Garhwal Kingdom, has a significant place in the history of India. From here, several rebels of 1857 were sentenced to transportation to the penal settlement, besides the two celebrated patriots mentioned above.

One notable freedom fighter was Maulvi Liaqat Ali, who fought for the defence of Allahabad city. After the defeat in the battle at Cawnpore and Nana's successful escape to the Nepal region, Maulvi continued his resistance activities in northern India. Eventually, he embarked on a southwest journey and established his residence in Lajpur, a village in Surat, as a new centre for anti-British activities. In 1872, Maulvi's elusive journey came to an end when he was apprehended at Bombay Railway Station by British Police Officer Style, who had been pre-informed by Maulvi's own associates. Subsequently, he was brought to Allahabad and faced trial in the Court of District and Session Judge, and he was sentenced to transportation for life on 24th July 1872.

During his stay in the Andamans, he became close to the rebels from the Wahabi Movement and 1857. He died on 17th May 1892 in the penal settlement. Previously, our information about him was based on "Who's Who of Indian Martyrs," which states that he was about to board a ship taking Haj pilgrims when he was captured and sentenced to life transportation to the Andamans.[10] The Wahabi rebel, Jafar Thanesari, mentioned in his book that he offered his last prayer in the Andamans along with Maulvi Liaqat Ali on 9th November 1883.[11]

Many patriots were deported to the Andamans for anti-British activities during 1857. Some of the available information about them is given below:

Mufti Inayat Ahmed Kakurri, an Arabic scholar, was transported to the penal settlement in 1858, a year before the arrival of Fazal Haq Khairabadi. He wrote many books during his imprisonment in Andamans; however, none of the books were based on his life on the Islands. His main interests were theology and astrology. At the request of a British officer, he translated a book, which ultimately resulted in his release from the Settlement.[12]

Hidaitullah, along with his brother Kifaitullah was sentenced to transportation for 14 years in August 1859 with confiscation of his property.[13]

Himanchal Singh and Kura Singh, father and son respectively, residents of Thana Bhavan, District Muzaffarnagar, took part in the defence of Thana Bhavan against the British attacks. Later, they were arrested and transported to the Andamans, where they died.[14]

Loney Singh, a resident of Mitauli, District Sitapur, was sentenced to transportation for life but died on the way while being taken to the Andaman Islands.[15]

Mammu Khan took part in the revolt of 1857 along with Begum Hazrat Mahal and was sentenced to transportation for life.[16]

Mirza Wilayat Hussain Khan, Prime Minister of Banda, was arrested, and Sadar Nizamut Adalat sentenced him to transportation for fourteen years in October 1860.[17] It is said that he died in the Andamans.

Mohammed Ismail Hussain Muneer, son of Syed Ahmed Hussain, was born in 1815 in Agra. He was a well-known poet known as 'Muneer Shikohabadi'. He was appointed as the Munshi of the Nawab of Banda. During his imprisonment in the Andamans, he composed poems and spent most of his time with Fazal Haq Khairabadi. He was released in 1865.[18]

Mohammed Yar Khan was the Naib Nizam of Badaun who was arrested on charges of being a leader. He was sentenced to transportation for five years with confiscation of property.[19]

Niaz Mohammed Khan, a resident of Rampur, was appointed General by Khan Bahadur Khan, the Nawab of Bareilly, with authority over the district of Badaun. He commanded the rebel contingent of Badaun in the action near Shamshabad. He was arrested in Bombay and sentenced to death by the Badaun Court. Later, the sentence was commuted to transportation for life by the High Court of Allahabad.[20]

Jhanda Shah reached the Andamans along with Liaqat Ali in 1858, where he was placed at Hope Town convict station. The settlement officers were of the view that he inspired Sher Ali, the assassin of Lord Mayo. The Home Secretary to the Government, in his inspection report of the settlement in 1885, observed, "he was made a State prisoner after Lord Mayo's murder and is supported entirely by the offerings of convicts, sepoys and others who took him as a deity."[21]

Qutub Shah, son of Baksh-Ullah, was arrested for the murder of Europeans at Bareilly on the 31st May 1857. He was a vernacular teacher at Bareilly College but was thrown out of employment in 1857. He offered his services to the Nawab of Bareilly, Khan Bahadur Khan. During the revolt, he printed and published rebel proclamations against the British. He was arrested, tried, and sentenced to death by H. Vansittart, Special Commissioner of the Bareilly Division, on the 25th March 1859. Later, his sentence was commuted to transportation for life with the confiscation of property.[22]

Syed Akbar Zaman, son of Syed Ameer Zaman, a resident of Agra, was serving as Head Clerk in the military establishment of Agra Fort. He was tried for his anti-British activities and was sentenced to life imprisonment; however, he was released after twenty years.[23]

The website of Azadi ka Amrit Mahotsav features references to hundreds of patriots from across the country who were sentenced to transportation to Andamans after the First War of Independence in 1857. However, unfortunately, these names lack accompanying references, making it difficult to verify and collect more information about them. The description of some of the heroes of 1857 featured on the said website who were said to have been transported to the penal colony of the Andamans is reproduced below:

Abdul Latif Khan was the nephew of Azim Khan, the landlord of the Khanpur estate in Bulandshahr district. He was the second wealthiest landholder in the district, owning 225 villages and the headquarters of Barah Basti. During the Great Uprising of 1857, the District Magistrate called upon landholders, including Abdul Latif, to provide troops to suppress the revolt. Initially, Abdul Latif refused to assist the British. However, after Bulandshahr was occupied by British forces on 4th October 1857, he paid his land revenue but then shifted his allegiance to Bahadur Shah Zafar. Although he did not fight on the battlefield, he sheltered local revolutionaries, including Nawul Gujjar and Raheemoddeen. For these actions, he was tried by a military court and sentenced to life transportation to the Andamans. The British subsequently confiscated his family's Khanpur estate after the uprising was suppressed.

Abdul Kareem was in the service of the English East India Company Army. During the Uprising of 1857, he left his job and took an active part in the First War of Indian Independence. Abdul Kareem participated in attacking and plundering the British establishments. He also incited his fellow sepoys to disobey their British officials and take part in the struggle for freedom from foreign rule. He was captured in the course of a confrontation with the Company forces and charged with desertion and mutiny against the British authorities. Furthermore, he was sentenced to transportation for life on 19th June 1857 and was sent from Bombay to the Andaman Islands in April 1858. In the Andaman Islands, he and other convicts had to work under the command of the superintendent, who was known for his cruelty in dealing with rebels. Abdul Kareem was one of the convicts who tried to escape from the penal colony but was later recaptured. Unfortunately, he was one of the eighty-six convicts who were executed by Dr. Walker.

Jalahram Pandi was in the Army of the East India Company but left it during the uprising of 1857 to take part in the resistance against the British. He also incited his fellow sepoys to leave their service and join hands with the rebel forces to overthrow the colonial rule. He fought the Company troops at different places in Goozerat (Gujarat) and was finally captured while confronting the advancing Company army. He was charged with desertion and mutiny against the British authorities and sentenced to transportation for life with labour in irons in 1857. He was deported to the Andaman Islands in April 1858. While clearing jungles with other convicts, he escaped from the settlement. Unfortunately, he was recaptured and met his fate at the hands of Dr. J.P. Walker, along with Gomeen Khan, Gola Khan, Debedeen Panda, Chundra Singh, Gunga Singh, Hurddayal Misser, Jhowhuja Doobey, Meer Hussein Ally, Meer Modut alias Ruheem, Nassir Khan, Oomrau, Ooshur Singh, Ramasur Misser, Ramdial Misser, Ramzan Khan, Sheikh Chund,

Sheonarain Singh, Soobhan Khan, Ali Bux Khan, Badreeram, Boorzoo, Boodhan Pandey, Alum Khan and Balgobind.[24]

The book published by the Indian Council of Historical Research (ICHR) also acknowledges thousands of freedom fighters from every district and village across the country who were sentenced to transportation and sent to the penal settlement in the Andaman Islands. However, it is challenging to include all these names in this chapter; therefore, details of only a few heroes are provided here, while further research will be necessary for the others.

Echoes of Rebellion in 'South India' in 1857

There is a general notion that South India did not play a significant role in India's freedom struggle, but records defying this impression reveal that a large number of freedom fighters deported to the penal settlement of the Andamans in 1857 were from South India.

The different regions of South India began preparing for the uprising of 1857 as early as 1854. However, definite efforts were made, particularly in the last few months of 1856, by leaders like Rango Bapuji of Satara to recruit an army to fight against British rule. Similarly, in other areas, such as Kolhapur—Anna Phadnis and Tatya Mohite; in Hyderabad Nizam's Territory—Maulvi Syed Alauddin, Sonaji Pandit, and others; in Goa—Dipuji Rane; and in North Arcot—Syed Kusa and others were working towards uniting the general masses against the British. The Zamindars and Nawabs lost their earlier economic, social, and political positions, which paved the way for them to join the rebels.

The people of Nizam's Hyderabad strongly opposed the domination of the British East India Company. The subsidiary alliance, which was signed between the Nizam and the Company, worsened the situation as the Nizam handed over the districts of Berar, Osmanabad, and Raichur to the East India Company in lieu of the expenditure incurred on the Nizam's contingent. By June 1857, rebels consisting of Rohillas and Arabs under the leadership of

Cheeda Khan gathered in Mehboob Nagar to proceed towards Hyderabad. However, they were arrested by Salar Jung, the Prime Minister of the Nizam, and sent to the residents. This created widespread dissatisfaction among the masses.

On 17th July 1857, approximately two hundred Rohillas, under the leadership of Syed Alauddin and Jamadar Turabaz Khan, launched an attack on the British Residency in Hyderabad. The uprising was suppressed resulting in the loss of thirty-two Rohillas and a few Arabs. Turabaz Khan was arrested on 22nd July, but he was seriously wounded. Like Alauddin, Turabaz Khan was also tried and sentenced to transportation for life. However, he escaped from the confinement and later, while he was being arrested again, he was shot dead.[25]

Syed Alauddin, son of Hafizullah, born in 1824, was arrested from the house of Peer Mohammad at Mangalpally near Hyderabad and was sentenced to transportation for life with confiscation of property. On 28th June 1859, he was deported to the Andamans and registered as prisoner number 3807.[27]

The case of Syed Alauddin was placed before the Government several times. His release or transfer from Port Blair to the Indian mainland was always objected to by the Nizam's Government. The settlement officers recommended his release, but the Governor-General in Council did not sanction his absolute release despite several petitions submitted by Syed Alauddin himself.[28] He was physically weak by 1885 and suffered from chronic diseases. Surgeon Major Napier Keefer, Senior Medical Officer, in his medical certificate, recorded, "It appears to me that his health has lately begun to fail. Chronic… (?) has settled in his knees, ankles, and back, rendering him lame and bowing down his once powerful frame. His sight is growing dim. Obesity has come upon him with advanced age, hampering his movements and interfering with the functional actions of his heart and lungs. His right arm has long been crippled by a gunshot wound in the elbow and a deep sword cut over the shoulder; the cicatrices of these old wounds have latterly caused him much pain and suffering. He has long been most anxious to visit India, and I think the change to some station in Hindustan would improve his health and probably lengthen his life."[29]

The last letter, dated 9th August 1889, of Colonel Cadell, Superintendent of Port Blair, addressed to C.J. Lyall, Home Secretary to the Government of India, concluded with the following remarks, "The old mutineer is now very weak and will not last long even if released." However, this letter also could not attract the attention of the Governor-General in Council as the latter refused to allow the absolute release of Syed Alauddin. He died in the Andamans.[30]

Anti-British activities continued in the Hyderabad State after 1857. Abaji Damodar was one such rebel who entered into an anti-British agreement with the chief of Jamkhindi in North Karnataka. He was later sentenced on charges of treason and instigating treason in 1861 and was transported to the Andamans.[31]

The discontent of the common people of Hyderabad is evident from the fact that Ranga Rao Ratnakar Pagay, Patwari of a small village Narkhed, was among the principal leaders of the anti-British uprising in the area. He planned and organised the activities in South India with the letters and orders of Nana Saheb Peshwa. He was arrested at Ambalga where he was tried by Captain Bullock on charges of attempting to raise troops under instructions from Nana Saheb and sentenced to death in April 1859, later commuted to transportation for life. He died in the settlement in 1860.[32]

Indian soldiers of the 1st Cavalry of the Hyderabad Contingent stationed in Aurangabad openly revolted alongside the civilian populace. They refused to proceed to Delhi to fight against Bahadur Shah Zafar, resulting in the brutal suppression of their revolt. Approximately forty soldiers were sentenced to transportation for life, with thirteen reaching Port Blair by 6th January 1858. [33] Baladanda Das from Cuddapah and Syed Ahmed from the Hyderabad contingent emerged as the most courageous among these heroes.

The coastal areas of Andhra Pradesh—Rajahmundry, Machilipatnam and Guntur—were also affected by the anti-British uprisings. Kallu alias Yatim Shah and Hussain Shah, charged with *sedition* and *endeavouring to excite mutiny and sedition*, respectively, were sentenced on 9th September 1857 to transportation for life and forwarded by the Major General Commanding, Hyderabad Subsidiary Force, to Machilipatnam for onward transportation.[34]

Madras became an important centre in South India where anti-British activities took place, both in the army and civilian population. In September 1857, the Madras Government received copies of 'seditious proclamations' urging the people to rise against the British. Ghulam Ghouse and Sheikh Mannu were arrested in February 1858 for pasting these inflammatory wall posters. Later, they were sentenced by the Supreme Court at Madras to transportation. Another rebel, Ameer Khan, son of Lal Khan from Madras, was also transported for life.[35]

A few rebel leaders in the Karwar and Dharwad districts of Karnataka maintained close contact with Nana Saheb Peshwa. Under his guidance, they took a strong position at Darshangudda Hill on the Karwar border, which was attacked by the British on 24th February 1858. The revolt was suppressed, resulting in the deaths or arrests of the rebel leaders. Thirty-one were sentenced to transportation for life. [36] They were Bisai Bhiku Rawal, Rayu, Rowyo, Narajikar Bhiku, Jorekar Babi, Anajoe, Raghu Jadhav, Ganu Sakaram, Sant Sali Gopala, Gopala Bhandari, Ambala Nanu, Narayan Desai, Pancheli Govind Desai, Raghoba Desai, Vithu Gavali, Mahar Govinda, Jewahkitippah, Kupason, Ganesh Mirashi, Panjali Poku, Jogi Mallik, Konkankar Bombi, Mingali Kristun, Maun Appa Sawant, Tinajah, Nujakar Vithobha, Vithu Bava, Lakhsman, Vithu Bhava, Chaman Singh and Narayan Mirashi.

Bhaskar Bhave, also known as Babasaheb Bhave, served as the Chief of Nargund in Dharwad District and mobilised men and material for the planned attack against both the British and the Nizam. He beheaded C.J. Manson, the British Political Agent for the 'Southern Maratha Country', followed by a severe fight. Eventually, they lost, and Nargund was forfeited to the British on 3rd June 1858. The Chief of Nargund was publicly executed, and a large number of rebels were sentenced to transportation for life by the court at Nargund from 15th June to 16th July 1858 on charges of joining the Chief of Nargund in active and open rebellion against the British State. Chimnaji Yadav, Narsingh Mane, Narsing Shivappa, Fakira Lingappa, Vyankappa Sakarappa, Hatela Hussain, Abdulla Mohiudin, Raja Meera, Fakru, Narsa Linga, and Tukaram Krishnaji were sentenced on 17th June 1858.[37]

A court held by Lt. Col Malcolm at Nargund on 23rd June 1858 sentenced Bhikaji Ganesh Gokhale, lawyer of Bhaskar Bhave, the Chief of Nargund, on charges of aiding and abetting the rebellion, to transportation, where he later died. On 28th June 1858, the death sentence awarded to Timappa Mazumdar, Hanumant Ghatge, Vyankatrao Bhosle, Kallappa and Tammanna Lakshman was commuted to life imprisonment, and all of them were transported to the Andamans. Eight other persons, namely Budnya, Bhima, Bala, Raja Vyankat, Lingappa, Shivappa Sangappa and Gangaram, were also sentenced to 'transportation beyond seas with confiscation of their properties'.[38] In addition to the above rebels, Sheshagiri Rao, Ayuppa Hindulla, Faras Khan Imam Khan, Gulia Mudemiya, Bada Miya and Krishnaji Pant Joshi were deported to life imprisonment.[39]

Many rebels from the Halgalli region of Karnataka were also deported. Malya Yallappa and Malya Manjayya fought heroically against the colonial authorities during 29th-30th November 1857. They were sentenced on 18th September 1858 to transportation for 14 years by F. Schneider, Commissioner, Criminal Court at Dharwad, on charges of rebellion.[40]

After the British annexation of Khandesh in 1818, unrest spread throughout the region. The Bhils united under prominent leaders Bhima Naik and Kaji Singh. In September 1857, Bhima Naik declared himself the emperor's representative, leading to a fierce battle at Ambapani in April 1858 that continued for several months. The rebels seized treasure worth seven lakh rupees from sixty carts in the Sindhava Pass and cut telegraph wires. A prisoner named Tulia, son of Veria Naik, was arrested in connection with the battle at Ambapani and sentenced to death by hanging on June 9, 1858, for rebelling against the state. Later, the sentence was commuted to transportation for life on 28th October 1858. He was deported to the Andamans and registered as prisoner number 1407.

Twenty-one others were arrested in connection with the uprising in Yawal Taluka, and all of them were sentenced to life on 29th October 1858.[41] They were Adhuria, Bhai Khan, Bhikari, Arjun, Bhutia, Dama, Dharma, Jay Singh, Khiran, Narsingh, Mohan, Nassira, Ray Singh, Rohim, Sandu, Mharu, Rama, Suka, Supriya, Wazir, and Bhimaji.

Eleven rebels were arrested in the Nimar region of Madhya Pradesh, including Bahadur Singh, Devi, Futta, Gulab Khan, Jawahar Singh, Mahibullah, Qaim Khan, Manju Shah, Maya Ram, Noora, and Siraj-ud-din for their anti-British activities at Mandaleshwar, and they were collectively sentenced to transportation.[42] One Chaman Singh, alias Timan Singh, son of Shivdayal from Indore, was also sentenced to transportation for life.

Venkat Rao, the landlord of Arpally, organised an armed force consisting of Gonds, Marias, and Rohillas and joined forces with the Raipur rebels under Hanuman Singh to carry out attacks against the British positions. He was betrayed by the Raja of Bastar and subsequently captured by the British in 1860, then transported to Andamans, where he died.[43]

Bhima Naik, Bhil Chief of Dholi Bowlee, Nimar, joined hands with Bhils, Bhilalas, Mandlois, Naiks, and Tatya Tope against the British. He was defeated by British forces under Captain Keatings in 1859 and later arrested and transported for life to the Andamans, where he died.[44]

Hattee Singh, son of Madho Singh, Zamindar of Ghess, Orissa, fought bravely against the British attacks at Singhara Pass along with his father, brother, and friends. His father and brothers were executed, but he was sentenced to transportation for life, where he died.[45] Garbadas Patel, headman of Anand Village, Gujarat, joined Jivabhai, the Thakur of Khanpur, in the fight against British rule. He was sentenced to transportation for life and died in the Andamans. [46]

During 1857-58, uprisings occurred in various areas of the Bombay Presidency. Rango Bapuji Gupte emerged as the principal leader of the uprising in the Satara District, closely associated with the deposed Raja of Satara. A group of rebels attempted to attack the Mamlatdar's Office and the Government Treasury at Pandharpur in Satara on 13th July 1857. In this case, Kisan Santuram, Yadu Patlu Bagal, Kanhayya Veludi, Ganu Bapu Chavan, Hari Biru Chavan, and Dharma Subhana were arrested and transported. Bapu Naroji Thorat, Suznya Sattu, and Babun Jummal Khan were sentenced to transportation for life on 7th November 1857 on charges of *joining Rango Bapuji Gupte in 'waging war against the British Government'* in the Satara district. Sheik Ali was sentenced to transportation for life on 8th March 1858 on charges of *not giving information of concealed documents against the state* and transported.[47]

The Kolis and Bhils, two communities from the Nasik and Ahmednagar regions, were supported by the Peshwas. They made an attack on the 20th January 1858 against a British detachment at the village Mandusir in Patoda Taluka, Ahmednagar district. Three rebels, namely Jairam, son of Shivram, another Jairam, son of Rama, and Tulpia, were arrested and sentenced to death on the 27th August 1858, but were later commuted to transportation for life.

Babaji Balaji Kulkarni, Bhau, and Pandu were deported to the Andamans.[48] Penth, a small village in Nasik District, was an important centre of anti-British activities. The Kolis of the village, under the leadership of Raja Bhagwantrao, attacked Harsul tehsil and destroyed records in the Mamlatdar's office on the 6th December, followed by a grim battle in December 1857, resulting in the defeat of Kolis; subsequently, fifteen of them, Dhondu Kalu, Dhondia Birbal, Yesa Nathia, Kalu Rajia, Manya Koli, Santu Chandu, Sanu Bagal, Maoji

Arjun Patel, Trimbak Hari Patel, Arjun Mosya, Mahadu Kakdia, Ganga Eka Naik, Dhundai Maoji, Bhiwa Lakma, and Govinda Vithu, were sentenced to transportation.[49]

Tatya Mohite, also known as Gangaji Rao and the son of Dowlat Rao, was arrested in Kolhapur for instigating the sepoys of the 27th Native Infantry Regiment to revolt. On 26th July 1858, he was sentenced to transportation for life by the Special Commissioner's Court in Kolhapur, along with his companions Shridhar Sitaram Phadnis, alias Anna, and the younger brother of the Raja of Kolhapur. They were deported to the Andamans.

Anti-British activities among Indian sepoys in South India were notable. Following the British capture of Belgaum in 1818, there was significant unrest among the common masses. The newly raised 29th Native Infantry Regiment stationed at Belgaum planned an armed attack, but the plan was leaked, leading to the arrest of Havildar Major Devi Din, who was sentenced to transportation for life to the Andamans.[50] Additionally, the 10th and 11th Native Infantry Regiments in Bombay planned an attack during the Diwali festival on 15th October 1857, but the plan was exposed. Subedar Gulgar Dhobey, Havildar Subasing, and Sepoy Lakshman Thakur were sentenced to transportation for life.[51]

The sepoys of the 27th Native Infantry stationed at Kolhapur revolted on 31st July 1857. They established links with other prominent leaders and killed three British officers on their way to Ratnagiri. But the revolt was suppressed, and the Infantry was disarmed at Kolhapur and Ratnagiri. Sixty-six men were court-martialed and sent to the Andamans, but we have only a few names: Narayan Piraji Shinde, Rama Raghu Shinde, Dhaku Ghadi, Govind Gowda, Subhana Bapu Jadhav, Jagasesh Singh, Zillu Kochrakar, Gopal Karsowkar, Karim Khan, Girwar Kunbi, Krishnappa Gopal Chavan, Mendi Mochi, Ganu Sawant, Vithu Vaingankar, Trimbak Hari, Ramji Jagtap, Ram Parab, Ramsing Indrasing, Bhau Sathe, Gopal Salvi, Babji Sawant, Pandu Pade, Jivba Miru Pawar, and Bapu Poipkar.[52]

Ramdin Ahir, alias Mansa Singh, along with Ramdin Pasi, both sepoys of the 21st Bombay Native Infantry, were sentenced to transportation and sent to the penal settlement in the Andamans.

Sheik Ali of Srirangapatna, Mysore, Havildar of 22nd Native Infantry Regiment at Satara, was sentenced on 8th March 1858 on charges of 'not giving information of concealed documents against the state.'[53]

Heroes of 1857 in Official Letters

Few names of heroes of 1857 have come to light through official records and autobiographies. One such authentic source of information is the letters of Dr. J.P. Walker, the superintendent of the penal settlement, addressed to the Secretary of the Government of India. It provides us with information about a few freedom fighters who were transported at the beginning of the settlement.

Niranjan Singh, prisoner number 46, was deported on 10th March 1858 in the first batch. He committed suicide on 14th March 1858 by hanging himself at an isolated place on Ross Island. The other mutineer, Narain, prisoner number 61, was sentenced on 31st July 1857 to transportation for life *for having incited sedition in the Cantonment of Dinapore.* On the fourth day of his arrival, he attempted to escape from Chatham Island by swimming to the mainland but was recaptured, brought to trial, and executed.

In paras 8 and 9 of letter no. 242, dated 8th August 1858, Walker informed the Secretary to the Government of India, Home Department: "On the night of the 24th July, four convicts escaped from Ross Island: Prisoner number 836, Soobanah, a life-convict sentenced for rebellion, and received ex-Italian on the 1st July, prisoner number 762; Pandoo, a life-convict sentenced for mutiny and received ex-Sesostris on the 12th June, prisoner number 781; Kutt Beg, a life-convict sentenced for instigating rebellion, and received ex-Italian on the 1st July, prisoner number 834; Krishna Chowhan, a life-convict sentenced for treason and received ex-Italian on the 1st July. They were last seen on the night of the 24th July and were missing at muster on the following morning, one or two pieces of sawn wood used for railing posts and several small pieces of rope were found missing from the saw-pits on the sea-side. This induces the belief that the convicts used them to effect their escape. On the other hand, it is known that three out of the four missing convicts were weak men, and one was very markedly so, and as the wind was blowing fresh across the channel towards Ross Island, it is doubted whether they could have crossed."

"A case of suicide by drowning occurred this morning. Convict Mundraj Gir no. 901, landed on the 20th ultimo ex Coromandel, was admitted on the following day into the hospital with an ulcer of the leg and continued a patient therein until the time of his death. Between 6 and 7 o'clock this morning, he left the hospital and was seen to walk into the sea on the north side of Chatham Island and deliberately drowned himself. Several convicts endeavoured to induce him to return to the shore and threw in pieces of wood to aid him, but he refused to avail himself of them. Mr. Asstt. Apothecary J. Ringrow rushed into the sea to his rescue, but as the convict was evidently bent on drowning himself, he did not think it prudent to risk his life by placing himself in the grasp of such a person in deep water. The deceased was carried out into deep water, soon sank and disappeared. No cause is known for the act."

Dudhnath Tiwari, son of Thakur Tiwari and prisoner number 276, was a sepoy in the 14th Regiment of Bengal Native Infantry. He was arrested and sentenced to transportation for life on 27th September 1857 by the Commissioner of Jhelum, arriving at Port Blair on 6th April 1858. On 23rd April 1858, he escaped from the penal settlement with ninety other convicts. Though many were likely killed by aborigines, Tiwari gained the sympathy of the aborigines and lived with them for over a year. One day, he learnt of an impending armed attack on the Aberdeen convict station and found twenty canoes with two hundred and fifty aborigines preparing to leave. Along with another escaped convict, Sadloo, Tiwari waited until midnight to inform the authorities about the attack. This attack is known as the Battle of Aberdeen fought on 17th May 1859. His timely warning was appreciated by the authorities, and he was granted a pardon and subsequently released in 1860.[54]

A memorial has been erected for heroes of the Battle of Aberdeen in the Rajiv Gandhi Water Sports Complex. It was inaugurated by the then Lt. Governor of Andaman and Nicobar Islands on 15th August 1994 with the inscriptions, *This monument is built in the memory of those Andamanese Aborigines who bravely fought the Battle of Aberdeen in May 1859 against the oppressive and retaliatory policy of the British regime.*

Doolum, prisoner number 873, Horwan, Boorhana, prisoner number 2622, Sunker Kutwar, Shoo Dutt and Aga were a few other names that have come to light through official records. They escaped from the settlement but later returned during 1859, except for Sunker Kutwar, who was killed by the aborigines.[55]

During Walker's tenure, an incident occurred on 1st April 1859, in which convicts Nuzzer Mohammad and Sarvar Shah attempted to kill him and his associates. It is said that about 200 convicts conspired to seize control of the Andamans by killing them. However, a convict named Moti Ram warned Walker, allowing him to prepare for his safety. He was saved by other convicts who captured Nuzzer Mohammad and Sarvar Shah. Later, all other conspirators were also apprehended.[56]

Andaman-Assam Connection and 1857

The contributions of the eastern part of India during the uprising of 1857 are often overshadowed by the focus on Delhi, Lucknow, and Meerut.

Earlier, the Treaty of Yandaboo in 1826 marked the subjugation of Assam by the British. Initially, the local population welcomed the British as saviours, unaware of their colonial mindset. The Ahom kings struggled to adapt to the new administrative system, while British rule brought Assam into direct contact with neighbouring Bengal, resulting in significant socio-economic changes. Within a few years, a revolt began as the people of Assam sought to restore their own Rajah, but this uprising was brutally suppressed.

By 1857, despite their geographical distance from the main centres of resistance, the rebels in Assam aimed to oust the British and reinstate the rule of the Ahom king.

While documentation on Assam's contributions during the 1857 uprising is limited, some lesser-known publications reveal that certain rebels were deported to Kala Pani. In this situation, the 'Azadi Ka Amrit Mahotsav' initiative successfully brought attention to the untold stories of resistance from the people of Assam during this period.

The 1857 revolt in Assam was led by Maniram Dewan, an adviser to the deposed Ahom King Purundar Singha, who recognised a prime opportunity to restore Ahom's sovereignty. He was supported by Piyali Baruah and several other notable rebels, such as Dutiram Baruah, Mayaram Nazir, Bahadur Gaon Burah, Gopen Roy, Benoy Laskar, and Sheikh Formud Ali. Maniram Dewan convinced the Ahom rulers and the sepoys of the Assam Light Infantry to join the uprising, but unfortunately, the British uncovered the conspiracy before it could take off, and later, all the rebels were arrested and tried. Maniram Dewan and Piyali Baruah were publicly executed by hanging at Jorhat Jail on 26th February 1858.[57]

One of the prominent freedom fighters deported to the Andaman Islands was Bahadur Gaon Burah, also known as Sheikh Bahadur. Under the leadership of Maniram Dewan, Piyali Baruah, and other rebels, he played a crucial role in organising secret meetings to mobilise resources and plan future actions. His home became a hub for anti-British activities. On 25th January 1858, Bahadur Gaon Burah was arrested, and the Jorhat Court sentenced him to transportation. He was finally transported to the Andaman Islands on 2nd September 1859. After completing four years of exile, he was released from Andaman on 16th September 1863 along with other rebels.

Dutiram Barua was a key figure in the First War of Independence in Assam, participating in the 1857 revolt against the British alongside Maniram Dewan. He was an associate of both Maniram Dewan and Piyali Baruah and actively participated in all anti-British activities. Following his involvement in the anti-British uprising, Dutiram was tried, sentenced to life imprisonment, and deported to the penal settlement. He was released in 1863, along with others.

All other rebels, Sheikh Formud Ali, Gopen Roy, Benoy Laskar, and Mayaram Nazir, were subsequently tried along with Dewan and others in Jorhat in 1858 and sentenced to life imprisonment to the penal settlement in Andamans. In addition to these heroes, Madhu Mallik was also transported to the Andamans, but nothing definite is yet known about his fate.[58]

All the above-mentioned rebels were deported to the Andamans for their heroic deeds, and all of them share a similar story of valour and courage.

Heroes in Oral Histories and the Aftermath of 1857

The heroes of 1857 are often celebrated in oral histories, which serve as narratives that preserve the memories of those who fought against colonial rule.

The oral histories and radio interviews of old residents and their memoirs are available with the All India Radio, Port Blair. These radio interviews are repositories of records that reveal the names of several freedom fighters – Mangal Singh Dogra, Devi Prasad, Honaji, Itu Patel, Sadashiv Narayan Parulkar, and Lalai, mostly soldiers of the Dogra battalion and the platoon of Rani Lakshmi of Jhansi. They were brought to the Andamans on life terms after 1857 and were settled in various convict stations as self-supporters. [59]

The details of the above freedom fighters have also been mentioned on the website of Azadi Ka Amrit Mahotsav and are supported by an extract from a newspaper article written by Shri Madan Mohan Singh, a family member of Shri Mangal Singh Dogra. It is worth mentioning that Shri Madan Mohan

Singh has made significant contributions to educating and inspiring young generations about the rich heritage of the Islands. The other eight names of freedom fighters, which have come down to us through oral history, have already been mentioned in the story on Musai Singh stated above.

There were many others whose names did not appear in the above-mentioned anti-British activities, but they were also deported to the penal settlement in the Andamans in the aftermath of 1857. They include Lakshman, prisoner number 20, Ram Prasad, sentenced on 20th March 1876 after 19 years of 1857, and Vithoba, prisoner number 36, son of Kondaji, who was sentenced in May 1867.[60]

Bhalki village, District Bidar of Maharashtra, was one such area where anti-British activities continued till May 1867. Balakrishna, son of Bankatt Rao, and Bhim Rao, son of Guruji, along with Rama Rao, nephew of Chhatrapati Shahu of Satara, raised men and material for anti-British activities. They were arrested on the charges of inciting people to rise against both governments—the Nizams and the British. They were sentenced to life and deported to the Andamans.[61]

Though the First War of Independence was brutally suppressed, the everlasting flame for achieving freedom could not be put out, and the struggle continued with the same dedication and commitment. The events following the 1857 uprising significantly influenced India's historical journey, laying the groundwork for future movements against colonial rule.

Wahabi Movement

There is a strong connection between the Wahabi Movement and the Andamans, as a few of the key leaders of the movement were transported and even died in the Andaman Islands.

The term *Wahabi* applies to the disciples of Abdul Wahab of Najd (Arabia). The Wahabis of Najd had challenged Turkish authorities in Arabia and opposed British control in North Africa. [62]

The Wahabi or the Tariqah-i-Muhammadiyah movement was a significant Islamic reform movement that emerged in the early 19th century, primarily in the areas in present-day Uttar Pradesh, Bihar, and Bengal. Led by Syed Ahmed of Rai Bareli, it initially sought to bring social and religious reforms to Muslim society but later transformed into a strong resistance against British rule. The movement became particularly active during the 1857 uprising and continued until 1868.[63]

Syed Ahmed encouraged his followers to engage in physical training and learn to use weapons, often appearing in military attire and organising parades.[64] After his death, his legacy was carried on by two brothers, Wilayat Ali and Enayet Ali, from the Sadiqpur family in Patna, who continued anti-British activities in regions like Rajmahal, Malda, and Chittagong. By 1847, the Wahabis were ready to wage war against the British from their base camp in Sitana under the leadership of Wilayat Ali.[65]

All possible measures were taken to suppress the movement. A large number of Wahabis were arrested and tried in the Ambala trial of 1864, Patna trial of 1865, Malda and Rajmahal trial of 1870, and sentenced to transportation to the Andamans until 1872. The book '*Kalapani-ya-Tawarikh-e-Ajeeb*' by one of the Wahabi rebels, Mohd. Jaffar Thanesari is an important source that describes the life of the following Wahabi rebels in the penal settlement.[66]

Ahmedullah, son of Illahi Bakshi, Sadiqpur, was the principal leader in Patna. He was arrested on 5th November 1864 on the charge of *conspiracy to wage war against the Queen* and deported on 15th June 1865. He died on 21st November 1881 at Viper Island at the age of eighty and was buried at Dundas Point.

Abdul Rahim Sadiqpuri, son of Furhat Hussain, Patna, was appointed as Ghat Munshi in Andamans and later became Muharrar at the settlement hospital. After nine years, he got a ticket to leave and opened a shop to earn his livelihood. He was released on 3rd March 1883.

Amir Khan was a banker and leather merchant in Calcutta. He was released in 1878 after six years.

Amiruddin, hailing from Bengal and serving as a teacher in a Madrasa, played a pivotal role as the principal agent of Mobarak Ali in Malda District. His commitment to the cause led to his imprisonment for 11 years. He was released on 3rd March 1883.

Hasmatdad Khan, a well-known banker and leather merchant of Patna, was sentenced and deported in 1872. He was released in 1879.

Ibrahim Mondal of Islampur, Bengal, was convicted in the Raj Mahal trial of 1870 and sentenced to transportation for life but was released in 1878.

Tabarak Ali of Pabna, Bengal, who was deported in March 1872, was appointed station Muharrar and later released in 1883.

Mohammed Jafar Thanesari was tried in Ambala and sentenced to death. However, on 2nd May 1864, the Chief Court of Punjab changed his sentence to transportation for life. He arrived on the Islands on 11th January 1866 and lived on Ross Island with other Wahabi leaders. Here, he worked as an assistant clerk and taught Urdu and Persian to officers, including Major Protheroe. Jafar married a Kashmiri prisoner and later remarried after his first wife passed away. He was released on 9th November 1883 after serving 18 years in penal servitude. After his release, he wrote his autobiography titled 'Kalapani-ya-Tawareeke-e-Ajeeb'.

Yahya Ali, brother of Ahmedullah, mobilised thousands of people into the movement. Following his arrest and trial in 1865, he was sentenced to death, which was later commuted to transportation for life, and deported to the Andamans in January 1866. He passed away on 20th February 1868 and was buried at Aberdeen in South Andaman.

Masud Khan, Mohd. Shafi Hussaini, Mohd. Shafi Lahori, Abdul Karim from Ambala, Abdul Gaffar of Thaneswar, and Abdul Gaffur of Patna were also transported to the Andamans.

The Kuka (Namdhari) Movement

The Kuka or Namdhari Movement began in Punjab as a response to the new political system imposed by colonial rulers after 1849. Under the leadership of Satguru Ram Singh, the movement gained strength, driven by his belief that "Political Freedom is my religion."[67] Recognising the importance of empowerment, Satguru Ram Singh provided military training to his followers, which contributed to the movement's popularity. By 1863, around forty thousand people had joined him, attracted by his teachings that emphasised protecting cows and supporting the poor, as well as simplifying rigid religious practices. Tensions escalated between the Kukas and the British over the issue of cow slaughter by Muslim butchers, thus hurting the religious sentiments of Hindus. In June 1871, there were violent clashes in Amritsar, resulting in four deaths. The situation intensified with a raid on Malerkotla on 15th January 1872, "where Muslim Officers had displayed a revengeful attitude in permitting cow slaughter in the very presence of the Hindus and the Sikhs."[68] The movement was ultimately met with brutal suppression, with sixty-six Kukas killed by cannon fire.

In March 1872, Satguru Ram Singh was exiled to British Burma. Several key figures, including Constable Lal Singh Namdhari, Lehna Singh, and Lahiya Singh, were sentenced to life transportation and deported to the Andaman Islands in 1873.[69]

Sher Ali - the Assassin of Mayo, the Viceroy of India

No chapter on the Andamans would be complete without the mention of Sher Ali, the Pathan convict who attained martyrdom in the settlement.

Sher Ali, son of Wulli, was born in 1842 in the small village of Pakhree in Kabul. At the age of fifteen, he was recruited into the Punjab Mounted Police by Major James in 1857, where he served as an orderly for several British officers, including Colonel Teylor, Becher, and Pullock. However, his life took a drastic turn when he was convicted on 2nd April 1867 by Colonel Pullock, the Commissioner of Peshawar, for the murder of a man named Hyder. He was sentenced and deported to the Andamans in June 1869 via Karachi and Bombay, where he was registered as prisoner no. 15557.

Based on Sher Ali's good conduct in the settlement, he was granted the status of a ticket of leave convict. On 15th May 1871, he was placed at the Hope Town convict station to work as a barber. However, Sher Ali had a strong desire to return home, and his distress deepened when he received a letter from his family describing their dire circumstances. The letter also mentioned a man named Abdullah, who had assassinated Justice Norman in Calcutta. It was likely on this day that the idea of killing a high-profile British officer took root in Sher Ali's mind.

On 8th February 1872, Lord Mayo, the Viceroy of India, arrived at the penal settlement. That same evening, Sher Ali stabbed him to death when he was returning from Mount Harriet (now renamed Mount Manipur). Sher Ali was arrested immediately, and after a trial, the High Court in Calcutta confirmed his death sentence on 21st February 1872. He was executed at the Viper Island Gallows on 11th March 1872.[70]

This was a significant historical event—an ordinary convict assassinated Lord Mayo, the highest-ranking British officer in India. This chapter has not received proper recognition in history books for unknown reasons. It marks the only instance during British rule in India when a Viceroy was killed, and notably, it happened in the Andaman Islands. The reasons for keeping this incident confidential remain unclear and are better known to those in power, pre- and post-independence.

There is another angle to this, and it is really hard to believe and understand that a monument has been erected at the same site, but it is dedicated to Mayo, not to Sher Ali. This reflects the colonial mindset that persists among our people, valuing colonial figures over those who fought against their rule.

Phadke's Followers in Andamans

Several followers of Vasudev Balwant Phadke, a revolutionary from Pune, faced transportation on various terms of imprisonment.

Phadke believed that colonial rule was causing suffering to the common people and harming local industries. This was the time when there existed a political interlude as Ranade was propagating Swadeshi, and Tilak was waiting to enter active politics. In response to the oppressive policies of colonial rule, Phadke turned to armed resistance against the British and engaged in anti-British activities. On 3rd November 1879, Phadke and his fourteen companions were tried in Pune for charges including committing dacoities, conspiring to wage war against the Queen, and gathering men and weapons for rebellion. Following the trial, Phadke was arrested and sentenced to life imprisonment in Aden, where he reached on 9th January 1880. Later, he died there on 17th January 1883. His fourteen associates received life transportation and were likely deported to the Andaman Islands, though their names are yet to be unearthed.[71]

Maharaja Divyasingh Dev III in Viper Chain Gang Jail

There are a few prisoners whose names are not associated with any significant movement, but they deserve a special mention.

For quite some time, it was believed that the Raja of Jagannath Puri, Maharaj Brij Kishore Singh Deo, was exiled to the Andamans and died on Viper Island in 1879. However, recent revelations have brought to light that it was actually his adopted son, Maharaja Divyasingh Dev III, who was deported to the Andamans and died as an ordinary convict in 1887.

Maharaja Divyasingh Dev III belonged to the royal family of Puri and was popularly known as Maharaja Jagannath Puri. He was exiled to Andaman, where he was kept in a hospital for lunatics at Haddo. He was treated like an ordinary criminal convict. Whenever he could not finish his assigned arduous tasks, he was punished by caning, confinement, and other inhumane torture.

He was alive till 1887, contrary to the date given by Thanesari in his book, who mentioned that he was imprisoned in Viper Island jail.

During the British occupation of Odisha in 1803, the authorities were concerned and showed sensitivity towards the religious beliefs of the people, especially those linked with the Jagannath Temple. Raja Divyasingh Dev III was the adopted son of Raja Birakishor Deva III, the Superintendent of Sri Jagannath temple, who died childless in 1859 when the former was only 4 years of age. After the Raja attained the required age, he took over control of the temple in 1872. Soon after this, problems relating to the management and maintenance of the temple were noticed. Some Sevaks of the temple made allegations of financial mismanagement by the Raja.

The following description is an extract from an article titled "Maharaja Dibyasingha Deva III and British Crown in Odisha" by Dr. Janmejay Choudhury, published in June 2017. The author has given a detailed account of the circumstances which led to the Maharaja's exile to the Andamans and his death in 1887. The relevant extract from the article is reproduced below:

"Two festivals, Govinda Dwadasi and Dola Yatra, which came in close proximity in early 1877, brought a large number of pilgrims to the temple. The crowd was not properly controlled, and in the rush which occurred at the gate, at least eleven persons were crushed to death on two occasions. Such a lamentable loss of life aroused much criticism against the management of the temple, and especially Raja Dibyasingha Deva III, the superintendent, was held responsible for the accident. His apathy, neglect, and lack of control over his subordinates, the Lieutenant-Governor believed, were the main causes of the disaster. The displeasure of the government was shown by temporarily withholding the title of Maharaja, which was to be conferred on him according to the notification issued in January 1877. The local officers were also blamed for their lack of foresight and unpreparedness. They did not take proper notice of the large crowd in Puri and also failed to take sufficient measures to control the internal arrangements, which led to the loss of life. The Commissioner of Odisha was required to submit a scheme for regulating the large number of pilgrims to the temple. But before any scheme for better management of the temple affairs could be fully implemented, Raja Dibyasingha Deva III was arrested on a criminal charge of murder. Dibyasingha Deva III was charged with the murder of Siva Das, an old sadhu, the Mahanta of a Math at Damadarapura, six miles off from Puri. On the 11th March 1878, the Raja and his servants were committed to trial under section 302 of I.P.C. The special trial was held at Cuttack by the session judge who sentenced the Raja and four of his servants to transportation for life. The Calcutta High Court also confirmed the sentence of transportation for the Raja and his two servants. Thus, Raja Dibyasingh Deva III, the superintendent of the temple, became a convict and spent the rest of his life in the Andamans."[72]

Raja Dibyasingh Deva III was deported and arrived at Port Blair on 4th September 1878 by SS Satara. It is believed that he breathed his last in the Andamans in 1887.

Unsung Heroes from Mizoram

The Azadi Ka Amit Mahotsav website reveals the names of two brave warriors of Mizoram who spent their lives in Andaman for raising their voices against the injustice caused to their people in Mizoram. Their brief description is given as follows:

Dokulha, the son of Taihmunga, was a tribal leader from Chinzah in the Lushai Hills, now part of Mizoram, India. After his brother Hausata, the Chinzah Chief, was executed for killing British Survey Officer Lt J.T. Steward in 1889, Dokulha took over as chief. He gained power by defending his village boundaries against British encroachment. Along with his friend Hnawncheuva, he fought against British officers who exploited the villagers. They killed a British officer, which led to their arrest. Both were sentenced to transportation to the Andaman Islands. During their journey, they attempted to escape multiple times, facing brutal treatment by their captors. Dokulha was sent to the Tezpur Lunatic Asylum and later to the Andamans. After serving his sentence, when the time came for him to go home to Mizoram, Dokulha was arrested again after killing a British man, resulting in spending the rest of his life in detention until his death in the Andamans. Hnawncheuva returned home upon completion of his imprisonment.4

Manipur Maharaja in Andamans

As discussed earlier, the Manipuri prisoners, sentenced to transportation after the Anglo-Manipur Conflict of 1891, were confined in the Andaman Islands under Regulation III of 1818. As per the report of the Indian Jail Committee, pages 242-43, para 467, "the term 'State prisoner' is generally used to denote a prisoner confined under Regulation III of 1818 or the corresponding regulations in force in the Madras and Bombay Presidencies. These prisoners, when in jail, are detained in special enclosures or buildings separate from all other prisoners; they are granted such indulgences as books, writing materials, tobacco, betel nut and the like and are subjected to no more restraint than is necessary for their safe custody. The arrangements made appeared to us to be as satisfactory as is possible in the case of persons who have to be confined within a jail, and we received no complaints from any state prisoner regarding his treatment by the jail authorities. In many cases, facilities have been provided to enable prisoners of this class to play badminton or lawn tennis."

Though there is inadequate documentation on the Anglo-Manipur War of 1891, which supplied heroes of the princely state to the penal settlement, serious efforts were made as part of the Azadi Ka Amrit Mahotsav initiative serious efforts were made to document the unsung heroes of Manipur.

The Anglo-Manipur War of 1891 initially arose from discord among the princes of Manipur and ultimately worsened into a conflict against the British colonial rulers. Following the death of Maharaja Chandrakirti Singh, his eldest son, Surchandra, ascended to the throne in 1886, which led to a split within the royal family. On one side, Jubaraj Kullachandra, Tikendrajit, Angousana and Zillanamba united against King Surchandra. The rivalry among the royal brothers had been brewing for some time but became public on 21st September 1890, in an event that would later be known as the "*Palace Revolt.*" This revolt marked a significant turning point, setting the stage for the subsequent war against colonial rule. Under these circumstances, Surchandra and his brothers sought help from the British authorities. Meanwhile, Kullachandra became the king, and Tikendrajit became the Jubraj of Manipur. Taking advantage of the internal conflict, the British Government openly interfered in their affairs.

To exploit the situation, the British devised a plan, but their efforts failed when Manipuri forces launched an attack on the British residency. Under the orders of Jubraj Tikendrajit Singh and General Thangal, they assassinated several high-ranking British officers. In retaliation, the British initiated a large-scale military operation against the rebels from March to April 1891. On 24th March 1891, British forces suddenly assaulted the residence of Jubraj Tikendrajit, escalating the conflict further.

On 27th April 1891, following the occupation of the Manipur palace by British forces, the administration of the state was placed under British military authority. A proclamation on 19th April 1891 announced the end of Raja Kulachandra Singh's rule and the assumption of governance by the British Military Command.

After the Anglo-Manipur War, prominent figures Jubraj Tikendrajit and General Thangal faced significant consequences for their roles in the conflict. Both of them were publicly executed on 13th August 1891. A few others, Niranjan Subedar, Kajao Singh and Chirai Naga of Mayangkhang, were also executed during June-October 1891. Twenty-three Manipuris, including Maharaj Kulachandra and his nobles, were sent for life to the Andamans.[73]

They, being 'state prisoners', were detained under Regulation III of 1818 and under its provisions, they were housed in a bungalow on Mount Harriet.

They were granted land for cultivation, including facilities to carry on some kind of business to maintain themselves.

This was the first time in the history of the penal settlement in Andamans "that prisoners charged for waging war against the Queen were treated differently, which was later questioned by the political prisoners of the Cellular Jail. They demanded a similar kind of treatment for themselves. Hrishikesh Kanjilal, a political prisoner convicted in the Alipore Conspiracy case, in his representation dated 16th September 1912, expressing displeasure over the official concept that they are not 'political', observed that "They (the Manipuris) represent only a part of India, while the whole of India spoke through us. Theirs was a voice of an individual fighting for his own interest, while ours was the voice of the people, the voice of God."[74]

As per the details available, the following were deported to Andaman. They reached the penal settlement on 23/11/1891 by the ship S.S. Shahjahan and were released as per the details mentioned against each.[75]

	Name	Date of release/death
1.	Maharaja Kulachandra Dhaja	26/05/1896
2	Prince Angou Singh, Senapati	23/07/1896
3	Lokendra Birjit Singh, Wangkhairakpa	29/07/1896
4	Samu Singh, Colonel, alias Luwang Ningthau	26/05/1896
5	Chongtham Nilamani Singh, Major Ayapurel	26/05/1896
6	Chongtham Mia Singh, Major	12/05/1896
7	Uru Singh Usurba	July 1906
8	Abungjao Yengkhoiba, Lalup Singba	Died
9	Chauba Hida, Machahal	July 1906
10	Ghun Singh, Kongdram, Lalup Chingba	July 1906
11	Kumba Singh, Laisram	Died on 17/12/1904
12	Dhaja Singh, Mayengba	July 1906
13.	Noni Singh, Nepra, Machahal	1906

(Contd.)

	Name	Date of release/death
14.	Trilok Singh, Nongtholba Satwal	No information is available after 1903.
15.	Dhon Singh, Sagolsenba	
16.	Ghun Singh, Indujamba, Jamandar	1901-02
17.	Ningthauba Singh Chingsuba, Jamadar	
18.	Thaoba Singh, Phanjao, Jamandar	
19.	Tonjao Singh Mangshataba Jamandar	
20.	Chaobatol Singh Haigrujamba, Subedar	
21.	Paradhumba Singh, Havildar	No information is available after 1903.
22.	Chowkami Naga, Mayangkhang	1901-02
23.	Gowho Naga, Mayangkhang	

Note:

- *Ayapurel: Officer-in-Charge of the Maharaja's escort and responsible for the area between the capital and Burma*

- *Jubraj: Crown prince*

- *Jemadar: Highest-ranking native officer in the army*

- *Wangkheirakpa: Second in rank to the Senapati and chief judicial officer of the state*

- *Satwal: Superior Officer*

- *Luwang Ningthou: King of the Luwang yek, a high official*

- *Lalup Singba (chingba): Officer-in-charge of the Lalup or Levy*

- *Senapati: Commander-in-chief of the army, usually the third eldest prince*

- *Subedar: Native officer-in-charge of a company of sepoys*

However, there is also a mention of Prince Sana Chahi Ahum, alias Prince Narendrajit, alias Prince Ranjit of Manipur, who was arrested in connection with the 1857 war of independence in Manipur and deported to the Andamans. He is said to have been released in 1862-63. However, no more details are available on this matter.

As a gesture of appreciation and tribute to the Manipuris who bravely fought against colonial rule, Mount Harriet was renamed Mount Manipur on 16th October 2021. This peak was originally named after Harriet Tytler, the wife of the Chief Commissioner. The renaming serves to honour the sacrifices made by the Manipuri people and acknowledges the legacy of Maharaja Kulachandra and other freedom fighters who resisted colonial rule.

NOTES AND REFERENCES

1. Singh, Ujjawal Kumar (hereinafter referred to as Singh) *Political Prisoners in India*, Delhi: Oxford University Press, 1998, p. 51.

2. Majumdar, R.C., *Penal Settlement in Andamans*, Gazetteers Unit, Department of Culture, Ministry of Education and Social Welfare, Government of India, New Delhi, 1975, p. 81.

3. Divekar, V.D. South India in 1857 - War of Independence, Lokmanya Tilak Smarak Trust, Pune, 1993, pp. 405-412.

4. *Home Department Proceedings*, Government of India, Port Blair, June 1907.

5. News about Musai Singh's arrival in Rangoon published in 'The Tribune' on 5th July 1907 was reproduced in its issue dated 5th July 1972.

6. Based on an oral transcript by Madan Mohan Singh published in the souvenir of Homfraygunj Martyrs' Memorial Committee.

7. Shahabi, Mufti Intezam-ullah, *Gadar Ke Chand Ulema*, Urdu, Deeni Book Depot, Bazar Jama Masjid, New Delhi, p. 29.

8. Mujtaba, M. Ahmed, *Some Freedom Fighters of 1857*, Port Blair, p. 26.

9. Sherwani, Maulana Shahi Ahmed Khan, *Baghi Hindustan*, Al-Majma-Al-Islami, Mubarakpur, District Azamgarh (U.P.), 5th Edition, 2001, pp. 249-253 & 256-258. This book is a collection of Al-Surat-ul-Hindia written in Arabic by Fazal Haq Khairabadi in the Andaman Islands. Further translation of Al-Surat-ul-Hindia in Urdu and biography of Fazal Haq is added by Maulana Shahi Ahmed Khan Sherwani. This book was first published in 1947 at Madina Press, Bijnor. The second edition was in 1974, Lahore, the third edition in 1978, Lahore, and the fourth edition was published in 1985.

10. Chopra, P.N., Who's Who of Indian Martyrs, Vol. III, Department of Culture, Ministry of Education & Social Welfare, Government of India, New Delhi, 1973, p. 83.

11. Thanesari, Maulana Mohammad Jafar Ali, *Kala Pani —ya- Tawareek-e-Ajeeb*, Reprinted, 1969 Maulana Waheedudin Qasmi, All India Dini Talimi Board 1505-Gali Qasimjan, Delhi, p.6. (Thanesari was sentenced to transportation for life in the Wahabi Movement. He was in Andaman from 1866-1883. After his release, he wrote the book wherein he mentioned that he offered the last Namaz along with Maulavi Liaqat Ali on Friday, the 9th November 1883, before his departure from Port Blair after 18 years of servitude.)

12. Sherwani, p. 280.

13. Mujtaba, pp. 77-8 & 84.

14. Chopra, p. 55 & 79.

15. *Ibid*, p. 83.

16. Nagar, Amrit Lal, *Gadar Ke Phool*, Rajpal & Sons, Hindi, 1991.

17. Mujtaba, p. 115.

18. *Ibid*, pp. 78-81.

19. *Ibid*, p. 75.

20. *Ibid.*, pp. 97-98.

21. F. No. 158, *Central Records Section*, Secretariat, Port Blair.

22. Mujtaba, pp. 91-92.

23. *Ibid.*, pp. 84-86.

24. The execution of over eighty freedom fighters in May 1858 is a dark moment in history, and we should know their names. However, there is no information or reference about the names on the website.

25. *The Freedom Struggle in Hyderabad*, A Connected Account, Vol. II 1857-1885, published by The Hyderabad State Committee appointed for the

compilation of a History of the Freedom Movement in Hyderabad, 1956, pp. 1-3, pp. 51-52

26. *Ibid.*, p. 64.

27. *Divekar*, pp. 115-116.

28. *HD-P*, September 1882, Nos. 58-50.

29. *HD-P*, December 1887, Nos. 72-73. The medical certificate was forwarded to the Secretary to the Government of India by the Superintendent of Port Blair via a letter dated 3rd December 1887.

30. The exact date of death of Hyderabad mutineer Syed Ala-ud-din is not known, but it can well be presumed that he died after 9th August 1889, the date of the last letter seeking his release.

31. Divekar, p. 72.

32. *Ibid.*, pp. 24-25.

33. *Ibid*, p. 110. (However, the date of arrival mentioned in the reference appears to be incorrect or a technical error, as the first batch of prisoners reached the Andamans on 10th March 1858.)

34. *Ibid.*, p. 125.

35. *Ibid.*, pp. 49-50.

36. *Ibid.*, pp. 147-158.

37. *Ibid.*, pp. 251-257.

38. *Ibid*, pp. 258-9.

39. *Ibid*, pp. 383-8.

40. *Ibid*, p. 200.

41. *Ibid.*, pp. 201-207.

42. Kulkarni, Narayan H., *Andaman and 1857*, an article published in Mukti-Tirtha-Andaman, Ex-Andaman Political Prisoner's Fraternity Circle, Calcutta, 1976. p.3.

43. *Ibid.*

44. *Ibid.*, pp. 104-105.

45. *Ibid.*, pp. 53-4.

46. *Ibid.*, p. 113.

47. *Divekar, pp. 5-15.*

48. *Ibid.*, pp. 215-6.

49. *Ibid*, pp. 221-7.

50. *Ibid.*, pp. 81-2.

51. *Ibid.*, pp. 189-192.

52. *Ibid.*, pp. 162-7.

53. *Ibid.*, pp. 383-388.

54. Majumdar, pp. 83-4. (He writes that "opinion differed widely both as regards the nature of the fight as well as the object of the attack. Some regarded it as an insignificant attack of the ordinary type, which the savages often made for plunder.")

55. Portman, pp. 280-6.

56. Mathur, L.P., *Kala Pani - History of Andaman and Nicobar Island with a study of India's Freedom Struggle*, Eastern Book Corporation, Delhi, 1985, p. 133.

57. S.K. Bhuyan, Studies in the history of Assam, Smti Lokeshwari Bhuyan, Gauhati, 1965, pp. 168-170.

58. *Ibid*,p172.

59. Oral transcript by Madan Mohan Singh published in the souvenir of Homfraygunj Martyrs Memorial Committee.

60. *Divekar*, pp. 383-8.

61. *Ibid.*, pp. 300-2.

62. Balkhi, Fasihuddin, *Wahhabi Movement*, Classical Publishing Company, New Delhi, 1983, p. 5.

63. Singh, Ujjwal Kr., p. 51, footnotes.

64. Balkhi, p. 4.

65. Ray, Santimoy, *Freedom Movement and Indian Muslims*, 1983, pp. 12-14.

66. *Thanesar*, pp. 1-119.

67. Bali, Yogendra and Kalika, *The Warriors in White, Glimpses of Kooka History*, Har-Anand Publications, New Delhi, 1995, p. 20.

68. Aggarwal, S.N., *The Heroes of Cellular Jail*, Rupa & Co, New Delhi, 2006, p. 49.

69. *Ibid*, pp. 48-49.

70. Sen, Shatadru, *Disciplining Punishment, Colonialism and Convict Society in Andaman Islands*, Oxford University Press, 2000, pp. 56 & 67-8.

71. Aggarwal, pp. 49-51.

72. Extract from the article titled "Maharaja Dibyasingha Deva III and British Crown in Odisha" by Dr. Janmejay Choudhury and published in June 2017.

73. Parratt, John & Saroj N. Arambam, *Queen Empress Vs Tikendrajit, Prince of Manipur - The Anglo Manipur Conflict of 1891*, Har-Anand Publications, 1992, p. 172.

74. Singh, Ujjwal Kr, pp. 68-9.

75. *Shukhdeba Sharma Hanjabam & Aheibam Koireng Singh, Unsung Anglo-Manipur War Heroes at Kalapani, National Book Trust, New Delhi, 2021, pp. 53-57.*

CHAPTER IV

The Making of Cellular Jail - A Fortress of Isolation

10th March 1858 stands out as a significant milestone in the Indian freedom struggle, representing both the spirit of struggle and the sacrifices made by those who fought for India's independence. On this day, the first batch of 200 freedom fighters arrived in the Andaman Islands, marking the beginning of the present settlement. Similarly, the construction of the Cellular Jail represents a significant chapter in the history of India, symbolising the struggles endured within its solitary cells by the heroes of our nation. Several stories of valour and courage displayed by our revolutionaries are hidden within its walls and are still waiting to be told. This chapter will address the circumstances surrounding the construction of the Cellular Jail, especially since the Andaman Islands were already functioning as an open jail. It will explore the extensive planning undertaken by the colonial rulers to turn life into a living hell for India's firebrand revolutionaries.

The construction of the jail was taken up with the purpose to "build a place through which every convict sent here was to pass on arrival so that he might carry away with him a vivid impression of what deterrent punishment meant and secondly, as a place where those convicts, whom the ordinary settlement system failed to keep in order, might be confined on occasion with a view to coercing them into good behaviour."[1]

In fact, the purpose of constructing a jail in the settlement was to prevent the spread of revolutionary ideas by isolating the prisoners. The conditions of transportation to the Andamans were designed to be so severe that they were viewed as a punishment almost equivalent to capital punishment.

As per the existing system of convict management in the penal settlement, the only jail in the settlement was that on Viper Island where transported prisoners and those under local sentences were confined, but it was not very large for the purpose. All the other prisoners were housed in wooden barracks scattered over the settlement. These barracks were closed at night by only grilled doors and were not surrounded by any security walls. Some of the barracks were situated at considerable distances from police stations, and none were properly guarded by the police. The prisoners were controlled by their petty officers, and the police only interfered in cases of crimes.[2] These prisoners worked outside by day and were locked up in the cells by night. New arrivals during this period landed on Ross Island to have their tickets prepared, but this system was discontinued with the construction of the Cellular Jail at Atlanta Point.

Capital punishment was also imposed on the prisoners, but no prisoner with capital punishment was deported to the penal settlement. This was "inflicted in the case of those prisoners who, being already under severe sentence, attempt the lives of their fellows, their warders, or the officials of the settlement."[3]

In 1885, Alexander Mackenzie, Home Secretary to the Government of India, inspected the Islands and advocated a number of measures for the improvement of the penal settlement.

Lyall-Lethbridge Commission

In order to get a more detailed report on the working of the penal settlement, the Secretary to the Government of India, via his letter no 7 dated 6th January and no. 80, dated 15th January 1890, directed C.J. Lyall, Surgeon of Bengal Civil Service, and Major A.S. Lethbridge to visit and report on the working of the settlement of Port Blair. In pursuance of the directions, the *Lyall-Lethbridge Commission* visited Alipore and Presidency Jails before leaving for Port Blair aboard the ship *S.S. Peshwa*. After their inspection of the Alipore and Presidency Jails, they found that "the confinement within the walls of an Indian prison is now a much more severe form of punishment than transportation, as a number of prisoners waiting to be transported to the penal settlement of Port Blair."

After inspection, they submitted their detailed report and stated that "the system of treatment has had the most beneficial effect. Of 12,549 convicts at the end of 1888-89, 9,093 were life convicts. Of these, 3,285 were self-supporters; that is, they had attained the status almost of free persons within the settlement, living a domestic life in their villages, cultivating the soil and earning money by trade, service, or agriculture." This system contributed towards the reformation of transported prisoners, with some exceptions. However, the Lyall-Lethbridge Commission expressed dissatisfaction over the prevailing conditions in the Andamans and noted that "it was aimed that the place for transportation should be second only to capital punishment, but the transportation to the Andaman does not fulfil this intention."[4]

They reported broadly three causes for the attitude of prisoners on the mainland towards the penal settlement. Firstly, the information with regard to the life of a prisoner in the Andamans reached all parts of the country due to the release of certain prisoners from the jails of the districts in which they were convicted. This helped them to spread this information among a large number of prisoners in the jails through which they had passed before release. Secondly, the strict confinement of prisoners within jails made jail life in India much more penal than it used to be. On the contrary, prisoners in the Andamans spent their days in the open air and were shut up in barracks only at night. Thirdly, the journey from Calcutta or Madras to Port Blair, though three and a half days by steamer, was now performed under conditions of little hardship compared to the early days.

The Commission observed that the existing system is open to improvement and recommended increasing the discipline and penal character of the settlement by adopting various measures. First of all, they advocated that transportation should be for life only and suggested discontinuing the transportation of male term convicts. While giving justification for these recommendations, the report observed that "…it is impossible to make life at Port Blair sufficiently penal or deterrent for these men (term convicts). They are not allowed to become self-supporters and thus are not brought under what is certainly the most wholesome and successful part of the transportation system, viz. the reformatory character of the ticket of leave rules, by which a prisoner is encouraged to start life afresh, and gradually train himself to habits of self-reliance, industry and thrift…". Secondly, it was recommended that the settlement of released prisoners at Port Blair should be encouraged. Thirdly, the rules for the release of prisoners returned to India should be altered, and the prisoners should be released either at Port Blair or on arrival at Calcutta or Madras.

The most important proposal of the Commission was to increase the 'penal character of discipline' in its earlier stage to further improve the discipline and make imprisonment more deterrent by the introduction of a preliminary stage of separate confinement. The Commission suggested organising the second stage of confinement in associated jails. It was also recommended to replace the existing tin ticket with the wooden neck ticket for all prisoners. The main intention of the Lyall-Lethbridge Commission was to isolate the jail as much as possible from the rest of the settlement and to maintain in it a degree of discipline till then unknown in Port Blair.

In order to make the earlier stages of transportation more severe, the Commission recommended the introduction of a preliminary stage of separate confinement in cells and observed that "…to enable the authorities to carry out this system, a Cellular Jail containing six hundred cells should be constructed without delay. Even if the system was unsuitable for the transportation of prisoners, the jail could take the place of Viper as a jail for the ordinary purpose of the settlement. If six hundred cells were available, it would be possible to carry out six months of separate confinement in the case of six hundred prisoners, which is about the number of life prisoners that we receive yearly from India."

The most difficult task before the Commission was to locate a suitable site near the seashore for the construction of the Cellular Jail. The suitability of promising sites on the seashore, such as Perseverance Point, Navy Bay, South Point, and Minnie Bay, was discussed but dropped due to being unhealthy because of low-lying areas. They recommended identifying a suitable site at Aberdeen, which was considered the healthiest location of the settlement.

While the Commission recommended the site at Aberdeen, the settlement officers were of the view that the reclaimed land on Viper Island should be selected for the construction of Cellular Jail. But this proposal was rejected on two grounds. Firstly, most of the sites in Viper Island were reclaimed land; hence, it was difficult to place a strong foundation for two-storied masonry buildings in newly made soil. Secondly, there was a lack of adequate space to build a massive jail on Viper Island. Other than these two objections, the location at Viper Island was considered a better choice until a final decision was taken.[5]

In order to find a suitable land, a topographical survey was ordered, and only two sites were found to be appropriate from all points of view: one site between Pahargoan and Protherapur and the other at Aberdeen near Atlanta Point, a place about sixty feet above sea level.[6]

Taking all the advantages and disadvantages of promising sites into consideration, it was concluded that Aberdeen is the most suitable site for the construction of the jail. The only negative aspect of this chosen site, being located on the top of a hill, was the transportation of building materials. The road was too steep for a heavily laden cart to be easily drawn up by bullock power. But finally, it was decided that the site at Atlanta Point had more advantages than drawbacks.

The selected site was not only the most permanently healthy site, but it was within a short distance of the police lines and of the houses occupied by various officers and subordinates so that in the event of disorder, immediate information could be given, and responsible officers and their men could be on the spot in a shorter time compared to other sites. The site, located just opposite the Ross, was more suitable as an alarm could be quickly signalled to Ross, and, if necessary, the troops could reach there in a short time. The supplies and materials for labour could be transported more easily than to other probable sites. The site was also suited in terms of the security of the jail, as more than half of the outer wall was bounded by the sea.[7]

The construction of the Cellular Jail in Port Blair was an important project for the British Government, and they attached a lot of importance to this. Therefore, all precautions were taken at the planning and execution stage, even for the smallest detail related to the construction of the jail building. It was earlier planned to have two stories, which was later dropped on the grounds that it would only provide forty-five cells instead of six hundred cells, which were then required.[8]

The initial plan for the Cellular Jail was prepared by Mr. Davies, Executive Engineer I, Calcutta Division, in consultation with Dr. Lethbridge. Before the final plan of the Cellular Jail was approved, a number of modifications were made based on the suggestions and recommendations of various officers to make the Cellular Jail self-contained.

As the road from the site at the Cellular Jail to Aberdeen was too steep for a heavily laden cart to be easily drawn up by bullock power, a tramway was obtained in the year 1893 from M/s Fowler & Co.'s patent 'portable' railways with a two-foot gauge to facilitate transportation of construction materials.[9] Later, in 1895, a tram was also purchased from M/s T.E. Thomson for Rs 4,010/- for the Dundas Point brick kilns to convey the clay from the spot where it is dug to the place where the bricks were moulded.[10]

A Panopticon Prison

The design of the Cellular Jail was based on the' Pennsylvania System 'or separate confinement wherein complete isolation of prisoners is ensured.

The first prison built in the United States based on this system was the Eastern State Penitentiary ,established in 1829 in Philadelphia, Pennsylvania.

All possible measures were taken to build a jail that could be strong enough to resist the earthquake shocks in view of the earthquake, which shook Andamans on 31st December 1881, causing severe damage to the buildings in the Islands, particularly the European Infantry barrack on Ross Island. Keeping this in mind, while preparing the plan, the dimensions of the Cellular Jail were accordingly proposed. It was suggested that in the case of a double-storied building, it should be 27' high and 38'3" feet high in the case of a three-storied building. The size of the cells and the addition of more cross walls were planned to make the jail stronger than other structures of the settlement.[11]

Mr. McQuilan was appointed the Sub-Engineer of the Cellular Jail, and an extra allowance of Rs 100 a month was sanctioned to him in addition to his salary of Rs 400 per month. However, McQuilon left for the Public Works Department of the Central Provinces in the year 1896, and most of the construction of the Cellular Jail was undertaken under the supervision of other Sub-Engineers, Mr. Tuson and Mr. Booley.[12] Mr. Dobson was appointed as the overseer of the construction.

The total cost of the Cellular Jail was estimated at Rs 5,17,352/-. Out of this, Rs 2,58,764 was earmarked for the purchase of local materials and Rs 1,62,707/- for engaging convict labour.[13] This was sanctioned, and the plan and estimates were approved by the Government of India vide letter dated 29th July 1893.[14] The expenditure was debitable to *45-Civil Works-Imperial.*[15]

The building of the Cellular Jail was unique in its own way. The site at the centre of the Cellular Jail building was 67 feet above the level of the Aberdeen Jetty. Based on the star principle, it had a Central Tower with seven radiating blocks, with three stories each, like the spokes of a bicycle. The blocks were not positioned at equal angles from the centre to ensure each block was placed on the best site while minimising the need for filling and excavation as much as possible.

The jail got its name from its unique design, as there were no dormitories, and it contained only cells for solitary confinement. Each cell measured 13 ½ x 7 ½ ft with only a ventilator. The doors of the cells faced the northeast and were protected by a verandah running along the whole length of the building. The entrance to each cell was confined by iron-grated doors. The doors were made in such a way that they opened in one direction only, and thus, the prisoner in one block is unable to see those in the opposite one. As such, the petty officer walking up and down the verandah was able to check the prisoners communicating with each other. All entry and exit were controlled by the Central Tower. The locking system of each cell was made as per the system that existed in the Viper Jail, the locks being quite beyond the reach of the prisoners.[16] The first room on each floor was larger and served as the guard room.

In six of the seven blocks of the Cellular Jail, the arches of the ground floor corridors, which opened to the yards, were not closed with iron bars as had been done in the case of the upper tiers of corridors, but later in 1908, in order to prevent the convict warders from acting as a channel of communication between the prisoners and friends outside, the corridors on the ground floor were permanently closed by using iron gratings.[17]

Red bricks manufactured mainly in the Minnie Bay and Dundas Point brick kilns were primarily used for the construction of the Cellular Jail. It is estimated that about three hundred lakhs of bricks made out of broken corals from Dundas Point and Navy Bay brick kilns were used to construct this colossal structure. Instead of cement, a unique mixture of jaggery and lime called surkhi was used as binders. A large number of labouring prisoners engaged in Viper, Dundas Point, and other areas were diverted to the brick kilns for the production of bricks required for its construction. Rolled iron beams and joists were used for the construction of the building. About 2000 labouring prisoners were engaged in construction, from brick manufacturing to earth cutting and other works, at different times and locations.

There is a debate over the exact number of cells in the Cellular Jail. Published books on the Cellular Jail and autobiographies of the political prisoners give different numbers, ranging from 663 to 698. This is mainly due to the fact that a number of changes were made in the original plan and design of the Cellular Jail during the course of its construction and thereafter.

Official records reveal that by 1895, Blocks 1 and 2 were ready, work on numbers 3 and 6 was in progress, and Blocks 4 and 5 were untouched. It was decided in 1896 to build an additional block by converting Block 4 into two blocks. Hence, the star-shaped jail with seven blocks came into existence.[18] The inspection note on Port Blair settlement by Mr. J.P. Hewlett, Secretary to the Government of India in January 1896, also confirms that by 1895, Blocks 1 and 2 of the Cellular Jail were ready with one hundred and thirty-eight cells. It was also proposed in 1896 that there should be at least seven hundred and five cells, but the proposal was turned down as it was thought that six hundred and sixty-three cells would be sufficient.[19] Mr. C. Boden Kloss, who visited the Andamans in 1901, mentioned in his book 'In the Andamans and Nicobars' that "*Passing first close by the suburb of Aberdeen, which is on the mainland just opposite Ross, we obtained a good view of the Cellular Jail, a huge building of red-brown bricks, with long arms—three storeys in height—stretching from a common centre like the rays of a starfish. It has been built almost entirely from local resources, with local establishment and labour, and holds 663 cells and the accompanying jail buildings.*"

In 1909, Lt Colonel H.A. Browning, Chief Commissioner of Andaman and Nicobar Islands, proposed to provide thirty additional cells in the Cellular Jail by prolonging Block 3 in three tiers of ten cells with an estimate of Rs 23,945. This was sanctioned by the Government in March 1909.[20] With the construction of thirty additional cells in the Cellular Jail, the total number of cells rose from six hundred and sixty-three to six hundred and ninety-three.

By 1895, a total of 138 cells were ready to be occupied, comprising seventy-eight cells in Block 1 and 60 cells in Block 2. By March 1900, all the blocks of the Cellular Jail were completed, except Block 5, which was finished in 1901 along with the main entrance and the Central Tower, whereas the Gallows were erected by 1907. However, there is some confusion regarding the numbering of the blocks and the exact number of cells in these blocks. Taking into consideration old records, memoirs of freedom fighters, views, and photographs published in the brochure "Uphold Cellular Jail National Memorial" by the Ex-Andaman Political Prisoners' Fraternity Circle in 1978, the exact number of cells, including later additions, is mentioned below:

Block	Cells on each floor	Total Cells	Remaining Cells as of today
Block No1.	35x3	105 Cells	105 Cells
Block No2.	35x3	105 Cells	--
Block No3.	52x3	156 Cells30) additional cells built in(1909	--
Block No4.	22x3	66 Cells	--
Block No5.	26x3	78 Cells	---
Block No6.	19x3	57 Cells	52 Cells
Block No7.	42x3	126 Cells	126 Cells
Total Cells		693 Cells	283 Cells

The jail authorities took all possible measures to prevent the prisoners, so far as possible, from mixing with each other during food and exercise time as well as during the hours of work. Convict warders were put in charge of supervising them. These warders were chosen as carefully as possible by the Medical Superintendent, but the Government always viewed them with doubt on the grounds that, after all, they were convicts and hence took all possible measures to keep a check on them and made communication from outside the jail almost impossible. Special precautions were taken to manage the corridors and staircases and minimise communication among the prisoners. During the routine affair of taking the prisoners to the exercise yard and back again, two warders visit each cell together and ask the prisoners to come out of the cell. . The implements in the cell, such as the utensils, blanket and other items, were counted and locked in the cell. The prisoner was then asked to stand at *attention* while the warders unlocked the remaining cells. When the full gangs of twenty-five men were taken out, they marched down the corridor and staircases in a single line; one warder led the gang, and the other brought up the rear.[21]

In later years, several modifications were made to the original plans regarding the beds and latrine accommodation for inmates of the jail.[22] Initially, there was a proposal to provide an earthen bed to all prisoners in their cells, but this was later substituted with wooden beds. It was believed that the earthen bed would take a long time to dry thoroughly, readily absorb dampness, and, if cracked, would constantly require repair. There was also a fear that the bed may be used as a weapon since sun-dried bricks would be used to build it. Therefore, it was decided to use wooden beds, which had none of these drawbacks and were successfully used in Viper Jail.

The actual latrines in the original plan were too large, but they were also altered on the grounds that large latrines would collect too many prisoners at one time. The number was reduced by providing seats in the latrines at the rate of one to every six prisoners instead of one to every three.[23] However, by 1896, a huge latrine building with twenty-six seats for each block, which had seventy-eight cells with a ratio of one to every three prisoners, was completed.[24]

Saline water from the nearby sea was made available to the inmates of the Cellular Jail using a donkey pump. Drinking water was supplied through the condensing plant installed at the Cellular Jail. Later, when the plant failed to supply the required quantity of two thousand gallons of water, a plant installed at the women's jail in South Point was used to fulfil the requirement.[25]

A hospital was also constructed within the premises to make the jail self-contained and independent of the ordinary settlement hospitals. It contained forty-two beds, three wards of fourteen beds each. It was a wooden building and consisted of an operating theatre and morgue.[26] There were four other hospitals for prisoners in various convict stations in the settlement at Bambooflat, Middle Point, Haddo and Viper Island.

A two-storey building at the entrance gate of the Cellular Jail was constructed to be used as an Administrative block. This building contained accommodation for two European masters of the jail—the jailor and assistant jailor on the upper floor—and godowns on the ground floor along with rooms for police guards, offices, and a central passage to the main jail building. The Administrative block was also built of brick and rolled iron joists like the jail building.

In order to secure the jail and to avoid any escape, boundary and enclosure walls were also built.

Cellular Jail - a White Elephant for Settlement Officers(?)

The British Government of India attached a lot of significance to the project of construction of the Cellular Jail, but the settlement officers were not at all interested in this project and showed negligence in keeping the expectations of their masters.

Dr. Lethbridge strongly urged the necessity of completing the jail within three years from November 1894 so that the jail building would be ready to receive the first batch in October 1896. Later, it was thought that it would be finished within five years, but it took much longer than expected.[27]

The attitude of the settlement officers towards the construction of the jail was not very positive. This is evident in the following unofficial remarks recorded in the Home Department dated 5th September 1895: "The Cellular Jail was ordered in 1891, but Colonel Horsford did little to start the work. All the settlement officers were opposed to it or lukewarm about it, and when Major Temple joined in August 1894, he was told locally that it was a *white elephant* but had to be done. He was not impressed with the urgency that the Government of India attached to the project until he came to Calcutta in January 1895, long after his budget had gone in. On his return to Port Blair, he set himself energetically to consider what could be done to meet the demands and has ever since been loyally shaping all the labour schemes of the settlement to push on the jail. It is natural enough that in a big business of this kind, second thoughts should sometimes be better than the first, and Major Temple now finds that he will have great difficulty in carrying out the building work planned for this cold weather unless his labour force is supplemented by appliances for economising it and enabling him to get his fuel and clay for bricks more easily to the site. He, therefore, proposes to spend Rs 4,010/- on a tramway, which has been purchased in Calcutta."[28]

Questions were also raised on Temple, the Superintendent of Port Blair, who "had made an estimate or undertaken a big building without any definite plan; he did not even make any provision for this tramway in his budget, which he prepared before his visit to Calcutta." An irritated Alexander Makenzie, on the question of the proposal for the purchase of a tramway submitted by Temple, went to the extent of noting that, "The finance department, however, would prefer to see the work on the Cellular Jail hindered, or possibly even for a time stopped, rather than allow the Government of India to exercise the power, which it undoubtedly has, of sanctioning Major Temple's proposal for the tramway." But the matter was brought to a little cool with the justification that refusal to allow the purchase of this tramway would create *serious inconvenience to the public service.*[29]

Mr. J.P. Hewlett, Secretary to the Government of India, in his inspection note on the settlement of Port Blair during January 1896, justified the displeasure of the government and reported that "No doubt the Government of India had great reason to complain about the delay in the earlier stages of this work. The estimate was sanctioned on 29th July 1893, and work commenced on 25th September 1893, but only 100 men were employed until April 1894 (the best months for building are January – April). All the coolies were removed, and only artificers were left who could not work properly without coolies. The brickwork was not started until May 1894. Again, from

January to the end of April 1895, the coolies were taken off the jail for brick-making operations, owing to the scarcity of labour, and only twenty-eight bricklayers and twenty-seven coolies were kept in the jail during these four months."

Except for the reduction of labouring prisoners and the not-so-positive attitude of settlement officers, the main reason behind the delay in the construction of the Cellular Jail was the shortage of the required number of bricks. This shortage occurred because, in fact, a number of other big construction works, which were not so urgent, such as the Aqueduct at Hope Town Jetty and Phoenix Bay workshops, were undertaken by the settlement officers at almost the same time as the Cellular Jail. The Aqueduct had consumed more than nine lakh bricks and thus caused a delay in providing bricks for the Cellular Jail.[30] It was thought that if these two works had not been undertaken, and a regular plan of brick burning had been put in hand as per the wishes of the Government, the Cellular Jail building could have been completed in a time-bound manner and as per expectations.

It was thought that as soon as the work on the Cellular Jail was finished, a local jail having a hundred cells should be built on Viper Island to take the place of the Viper Jail and the chain gangs to prevent the association of new prisoners with those who have experience of the settlement. The Lyall-Lethbridge Commission proposed to imprison the prisoner at the Cellular Jail for the first six months on arrival and the next eighteen months in an associated jail, for which Viper Island was selected as the best locality. Dr. Lethbridge demi-official, dated 22nd October 1890, to Mr. Lyall states that "Viper should be selected as the island on which 1200 to 1500 prisoners serving the second stage of imprisonment should be located. All the buildings on this island, with the exception of the police barracks and the residences of the Assistant Commissioner of the southern district and overseer, should be occupied by these prisoners. With the jail and hospital buildings included in the accommodation, there would be ample room for 1500 prisoners on this island."

The new arrivals in Port Blair during 1900-04 are detailed below.[31]

Year	Number of convicts received	Prisoners with life terms	Prisoners locally sentenced to solitary confinement
1900	1137	710	44
1901	1483	894	27
1902	1687	881	31
1903	1724	860	19
1904	1197	507	10

After the construction of the Cellular Jail, the deportation of term prisoners to Port Blair was stopped. This decision was revised in the year 1910 after the Alipore Bomb Case judgement, and once again the penal settlement was opened for both life and term convicts.[32]

Meanwhile, the Cellular Jail was completed during the early part of 1905-1906.[33.] Subsequently, Viper Jail was closed on 1st February 1907 with the shifting of the last batch of eighty prisoners to the Cellular Jail on both moral and medical grounds.[34] These prisoners were awarded separate confinement in the Cellular Jail in lieu of chain gang punishments.

In the beginning, it was estimated that the Cellular Jail would cost an amount of Rs 5,17,352, but actually, an expenditure of Rs 7,83,994 was incurred. Out of this, only Rs 2,25,378 was spent in cash expenditure; the remainder accounted for expenses related to the cost of labour and local materials. The construction of the associated jail, as proposed by the Lyall and Lethbridge Commission, was postponed and later suspended.[35]

The Cellular Jail was built within the penal settlement to ensure the complete isolation of our patriots, but despite this, political prisoners found ways to convey their sufferings and inhuman atrocities by the colonial authorities to the leading newspapers in the mainland, resulting in strong criticism of the Government. The Cellular Jail has become a significant landmark, greatly changing the perception of transportation to the penal settlement in the Andamans. It stands as a powerful symbol of India's revolutionary struggle for freedom, inspiring generations to remember the sacrifices made in the quest for independence.

NOTES AND REFERENCES

1. *Home Department Proceedings*, GOI, Port Blair Branch, July 1895.

2. *HD*-P, PB, January 1886.

3. Kloss, C. Boden, *Andaman and Nicobars*, Vivek Publishing House, Delhi-7, October 1902, p. 27.

4. *HD-P*, PB, June 1880.

5. *Ibid.*

6. *HD-P*, PB, February 1892, No. 1903.

7. *HD-P*, August 1892, No. 711.

8. *Ibid.*

9. *HD-P*, PB, July 1893.

10. *HD-P*, PB, September 1895.

11. *HD-P*, PB, August 1892. (The question also considered whether, because of the earthquake of 31st December 1881, the building should be only double-storied. This severe earthquake shock damaged the European barrack at Ross and lightly affected the church on Ross, doing little damage to the jetties at Aberdeen and Junglighat.)

12. *HD-P*, PB, January 1896.

13. *HD-P*, PB, March 1893.

14. *HD-P*, July 1893, No. 689.

15. *HD-P*, May 1893.

16. *HD-P*, PB, January 1892, No. 1578.

17. *HD-P*, December 1908, No. 374/VIII.

18. *HD-P*, February, No. 1691.

19. *HD-P*, February 1896.

20. *HD-P*, March 1909, No. 3167-VIII-2.

21. *HD-P*, March 1896, No. 259.

22. *HD-P*, January 1896.

23. *Ibid.*

24. January 1896, Inspection Note by Mr. J.P. Hewlett, Secretary to the GOI.

25. *HD-P, PB*, February 1907, No. 2903.

26. January 1896, Note of inspection by M. J.P. Hewlett, Secretary to the Government of India, on his visit to Port Blair. The original building plan of the hospital was revised by Mr. Finnimore, Ex. Engineer, 1st Class division, Calcutta. He suggested that it is not a convenient arrangement to have the operation room on the ground floor, as patients would have to be carried up and down, but his suggestion was rejected on the grounds that "as there will be very few operations and the room on the ground floor will be well lighted by six windows. The GOI, therefore, considers that it will be better to adhere to the original plans."

27. *HD-P, PB*, March 1893.

28. *HD-P, PB*, September 1895.

29. *Ibid.*

30. January 1896, Inspection note of Mr. J.P. Hewlett, Secretary to the Government of India, on the settlement of Port Blair during January 1896. The Aqueduct began in 1892 and finished in September 1893. It conducts water to fill a tank about 30 feet square at the jetty (Hope Town) where Lord Mayo, the Viceroy of India, was assassinated on 8th February 1872 by a convict, Sher Ali.

31. *HD-P*, June 1905.

32. Singh, Ujjwal Kumar, pp. 51-52 footnotes.

33. *HD-P, March 1907 and December 1908.*

34. *HD-P,* March 1907, Nos. 28-29.

35. *HD-P*, March 1907, No. 107-8.

CHAPTER V

Revolutionary Prisoners 1909-38

Revolutionary Movements: an Overview

The twentieth century in India began with the revival of the spirit of nationalism for freedom from colonial rule.

As the British continued to impose harsh policies, dissatisfaction across various segments of society intensified; as a result, anti-British revolutionary activities gained momentum. The latter part of the century was marked by key developments that roused the Indian freedom movement. The establishment of the Indian National Congress in 1885 was a milestone that provided a platform for Indian leaders to raise their demands for political rights and engage with the colonial Government. Simultaneously, a wave of discontent among the youth ignited a spirit of revolutionary fervour, leading to organised efforts that sought to challenge colonial rule. The emerging extremists in the Indian National Congress also advocated armed struggle. To quote Tilak, "Political rights will have to be fought for. The moderates think that these can be won by persuasion. We think that they can only be obtained by strong pressure."[1]

A major cause of the discontent among the common Indian masses, particularly in Maharashtra, was the outbreak of the famine of 1897, which affected almost twenty million people. This was followed by the outbreak of plague in Bombay. W.C. Rand, the Plague Commissioner, was cruel in his dealings with the affected people. Instead of paying attention to the relief of the affected people, the British Indian Government was busy with the Diamond Jubilee Celebrations of Queen Victoria. The discontent of the people reached its peak when Rand and his associate, Ayerst, were assassinated by the Chapekar brothers—Balkrishan, Damodar and Hari—on 22nd June 1897.[2]

The revolutionary organisations were formed, mainly in Maharashtra and Bengal, which trained their members in the use of firearms. The formation of *Anushilan Samiti* by P. Mitra in 1902 and the *Abhinav Bharat Society* by the Savarkar brothers in 1904 in Bengal and Maharashtra (Bombay Presidency), respectively, contributed greatly to organising anti-British activities. The partition of Bengal in 1905 added to the discontent among the people, which led to widespread agitation not only in Bengal but also in other parts of India.[3]

The young revolutionaries were inspired by the lives of great social and religious leaders, and they targeted unpopular British officials and their Indian counterparts. Numerous unsuccessful assassination attempts were made on the Lt Governor of Bengal and Viceroy Lord Minto. In April 1908, a bomb aimed at a judge in Muzaffarpur mistakenly killed two European women. One of the assassins, Prafulla Chaki from Rangpur, shot himself, while Khudiram Bose was tried and executed on 9th August 1908. Following the raid on the Manicktala Garden House, many revolutionaries were arrested.[4] However, the execution and arrest of these young revolutionaries did not demoralise young patriots, and organisations like the Anushilan Samiti of Dacca, led by Pulin Behari Das, continued to inspire Indian youth.

The Indian Revolutionary Freedom Movement is marked by various milestones of glory. Numerous actions took place in India, where revolutionaries were either killed during encounters, hanged, or sentenced to various jails. However, the main focus of this chapter is specifically on those revolutionary actions that led young revolutionaries to Cellular Jail. The chapter will highlight some of the significant political cases in which freedom fighters were sentenced to transportation to Cellular Jail during 1909-1921 and 1932-1938. The rebels and peasants deported to the Andaman Penal Settlement between the two phases will also be discussed here.

Manicktala Conspiracy Case or Alipore Bomb Case

The Manicktala Garden House in Calcutta became the centre of revolutionary activities, where bombs were made, and shooting practices were conducted. This group of revolutionaries became known as the Jugantar Group. They launched a newspaper of the same name, which played a crucial role in shaping revolutionary activities and motivating the masses to take up arms against British rule.

The political prisoners convicted in the Manicktala Conspiracy Case, also known as the Alipore Bomb Case, were the first batch of political prisoners to experience solitary confinement in the infamous Cellular Jail. The prisoners convicted in this case were tried between 14th October 1908 and 4th March 1909, and the verdict was delivered on 6th April 1909, wherein Barindra Kumar Ghose, Ullaskar Dutt, Bibhuti Bhushan Sarkar and Upendra Nath Banerjee were sentenced to death. Their sentence was commuted to transportation for life on 23rd November 1909, along with Hem Chandra Das (Kanungo). Others, namely Indu Bhushan Roy, Hrishikesh Kanjilal, Sudhir Kumar Sarkar, Abhinash Chandra Bhattacharjee and Biren Chandra Sen, were sentenced to transportation for various terms of imprisonment.

All prisoners of the Manicktala Conspiracy Case were repatriated from Port Blair to jails in mainland India in 1915, except Hemchandra Das, Ullaskar Dutt, and Indu Bhushan Roy. Hemchandra Das was repatriated in 1920.[5] As a result of torture inflicted on the bodies and minds of these political prisoners, Indu Bhushan Roy committed suicide on 28th/29th April 1912, and Ullaskar Dutt became insane and was repatriated in 1913. Indu Bhushan Roy was the first martyr of Cellular Jail.

Editors of Swarajya in Cellular Jail

Notably, newspapers such as Swarajya, launched in November 1907, propagated revolutionary ideas in northern India. Seditious articles encouraged Indian youth to rise against oppression, with contributions from prominent writers awakening the younger generation. During the two-and-a-half years of its existence, from 1907-1910, all editors of Swarajya—Ladha Ram Kapur, Hoti Lal Verma and Babu Ram Hari—were prosecuted and sentenced to long terms of imprisonment and deported to the Cellular Jail. Pandit Ram Charan Lal Sharma, an eminent writer and editor of *Yugantar* newspaper from Etah district, was convicted and sentenced to ten years transportation on 3rd March 1909 on the charges of his association with the Swarajya paper.[7] All of them were deported to the Cellular Jail in 1910 and repatriated in 1915.

Prisoners from North-East and North-West

Two political prisoners, namely Ghulam Sarwar and Mohammed Akram Khan, from North-West Frontier, were also deported to Andaman in 1910.[8]

Matmur Jamoh and his assistant, Namu Nonang, were significant figures in the fight against British colonial rule in Arunachal Pradesh during the early 20th century. Their actions were driven by a sense of insult and a desire for justice. This led to a violent confrontation with British officials, resulting in their capture and punishment. Matmur was tried by a military court on 2nd April 1912. He was convicted and sentenced to life imprisonment in Cellular Jail. However, his fate remains unknown to this day.

Namu Nonang was arrested in February 1912, and the military court found him guilty. However, due to his young age and the fact that he acted under Matmur's influence, he was awarded ten years of rigorous imprisonment in the Cellular Jail. After serving his time in Cellular Jail, Namu Nonang returned home in 1922.

Veer Savarkar and Nasik Conspiracy Case

In July ,1906 Vinayak Damodar Savarkar left for London to become a Barrister and stayed at India House ,established by Pandit Shyam ji Krishna Varma to offer housing for Indian scholars .Here ,Savarkar founded the Free India Society ,which served as a recruitment branch of the Abhinav Bharat

Society ,aiming to foster pride and nationalism among Indian students .The British authorities attempted to suppress Savarkar's activities.

Meanwhile, the Society was engaged in writing, printing, packaging, and distributing explosives and revolutionary literature, with pistols being smuggled into India concealed within books. Savarkar's associates Bapat and Hem Chandra Das learnt bomb-making techniques and copies of the bomb-making manual were sent back to India. Additionally, Savarkar authored a leaflet titled "O Martyrs" in commemoration of the heroes of the First War of Independence. On the 10th May 1908, a large number of students from various parts of Europe gathered at a meeting in Highgate, where these pamphlets were distributed.

Savarkar continued revolutionary activities, both in India and London. He sent pistols with his associates, Mirza Abbas and Sikandar Hyat Khan, and also smuggled twenty Browning pistols into India through Chaturbuj Amin, a member of the Society who worked as a cook at India House. Amin was tasked with delivering these weapons to H.A. Thatt, the President of the Society in Maharashtra, but he could not do so as he was under police surveillance, and finally, these weapons reached the hands of revolutionary groups.[9]

On 1st July 1909, Madan Lal Dhingra shot Curzon Wyllie as revenge for the atrocities being committed by the British in India. He was tried and sentenced to death. Back in India, his elder brother Ganesh Savarkar was arrested in Nasik for publishing patriotic poetry and sentenced to transportation for life. Following this, the local collector, A.M.T. Jackson, known for his brutality, was killed by Anant Kanhere on 21st December 1909 with the pistol sent by Savarkar. Finally, Savarkar's involvement in the matter was detected, and as expected, a warrant was issued against him in London on 22nd February 1910 on various charges, including waging war against His Majesty, the King Emperor of India, procuring and distributing arms, and abetting the murder of Jackson among others. He was arrested on

13th March 1910. While he was being shipped to India on the S.S. Morea, he jumped into the sea and reached Marseilles harbour. However, he was arrested and handed over to the British Police by the French authorities. He was tried under the Nasik Conspiracy case along with several other revolutionaries and, after a long trial, sentenced to two life imprisonments of twenty-five years each and transported to Cellular Jail, where he arrived on 30th June 1911. By this time, his eldest brother, Ganesh Damodar Savarkar, was already undergoing his imprisonment. Waman Daji Narayan Joshi, arrested on 30th December 1909 in connection with the murder of Jackson, was also sentenced to life imprisonment. They were repatriated in May 1921.

Nangla-Khulna Conspiracy Case

Revolutionary activists of Anushilan Samities formed in different parts of Bengal continued their activities. A group of such revolutionaries committed political dacoities in the Khulna and Jessore districts. On 16th August 1909, a political dacoity was committed in the Nangla district of Bengal. During the search operation of the houses of revolutionaries, revolutionary literature was found. The revolutionaries were convicted in the Khulna Gang (Conspiracy) Case and sentenced on 30th August 1910 to various terms of transportation. Nagendra Nath Chandra, Abani Bhushan Chakraborty, Bidhu Bhushan Dey, Sachindra Nath Mitra, Kalidas Ghosh, Prem Nath Kinu Pal, Ashwani Kumar Bose, and Sudhir Kumar Dey were sentenced to transportation and deported to the Andamans.[10]

Dalhousie Square Bomb Case

Nani Gopal Mukherjee, alias Jogendra Nath Mukherjee, was only sixteen years of age when he threw a bomb on the running motor of a senior-level police officer at Dalhousie Square.[12] He was sentenced to transportation for fourteen years on 27th March 1911 under Sections 307 and 4 of the Explosive Act of the Indian Penal Code. He was deported to the Cellular Jail, Andamans, in 1911.

Rajendrapur Political Dacoity Case

During this period, Suresh Chandra Sengupta of Dacca was also deported to the Cellular Jail. He was a member of the Dacca Anushilan Samiti. He took part in a political dacoity committed to raise funds for the revolutionary activities at a railway station in Rajendrapur, in which a sum of Rs 23,000 was looted.[13] He was arrested and convicted on 8th August 1911, in the Rajendrapur Political Dacoity Case and sentenced to transportation for life. He was deported to the Cellular Jail in August 1912.

Dacca Conspiracy Case

Pulin Behari Das, a revolutionary and an active activist of Dacca Anushilan Samiti, was arrested and convicted in the Dacca Conspiracy Case and sentenced to transportation for life. On appeal, his sentence was reduced by the High Court to seven years' transportation on 2nd April 1912. He was deported to the Cellular Jail. Another revolutionary, Jyotirmoy Roy, was also convicted and sentenced to transportation for six years in the Dacca Conspiracy Case. He was transported to the Andamans along with Pulin Behari Das.[11]

Arrival of Ghadar Heroes

The Government decided in April 1914 to discontinue the deportation of political prisoners with term sentences to the Cellular Jail, and in pursuance of this decision, a major number of the political prisoners were repatriated to different jails in mainland India by September 1914.[14] However, this decision could not last long, and the Cellular Jail was again opened to deal effectively with the growing revolutionary activities in India. This phase of deportation was dominated by the young Punjabis convicted in the First Lahore Conspiracy Case.

The main feature of revolutionary activities during this period was its wider stage. It was no longer restricted within the Indian borders.

The revolutionaries who settled outside India also challenged the colonial power in their own way. These firebrand revolutionaries, mostly Sikhs, were either part of the Ghadar Movement or moved by its ideology.

The origin of the Ghadar movement dates back to 1905. The British policies, followed by repeated droughts and epidemics towards the end of the nineteenth century, had left Punjab in a very miserable state. Under this situation, the poor peasants started migrating to other countries in search of livelihood. They found America and Canada most favourable.[15] The social and economic status of emigrant Indians, consisting of Bengali students and Sikhs, mostly unskilled workers in the United States of America and Canada, led them to unite and fight against their oppressors. In America, being British Indian subjects, they were called slaves by the workers of other countries like Japan and China. The British officials did not show much concern for their grievances. In Canada, an ordinance passed by the Government in 1910 restricted the entry of Asians into Canada, and this law was largely enforced against Indians. This law made it difficult to bring their families. Despite several representations, they could not get relief.[16] This humiliation and unfair treatment meted out to the Indians abroad, particularly in America and Canada, led to an intense desire to unite and fight for the freedom of India. Under this prevailing situation, the Indians working in America formed an association called the *Hindustani Association of the United States of America* in Seattle, Washington, in 1906, with branches in other countries.

Hardayal, a professor, was the chief promoter of the Ghadar movement. He was the man behind uniting unorganised Indians working abroad. One of his close associates, Tarak Nath Das, published a newspaper by the name *Free Hindustan*. This paper was widely circulated not only in America and Canada but was also sent to some of the prominent leaders of Bengal and Punjab through the mail, in spite of a ban.[17] Activists like Sohan Singh Bhakna, Bhai Harnam Singh Tundilat, Bhai Udham Singh Kasel, Ram Rakha, Bhai Isher Singh Marhana, and Bhai Parmanand were a few prominent leaders of the movement.

A group of twelve men under the leadership of Jatindra Nath Lahiri was sent to Germany to learn the art of bomb-making. Master Udham Singh trained the youth in guerrilla warfare. Kartar Singh Sarabha joined a German Air Service Company and learnt flying and repairs of planes.[18]

In 1910, the *Hindustan Association* was formed in Canada. A meeting was organised in Vancouver where it was decided to send three delegates to India and England to report their grievances to both the authorities and the general public. The delegates consisted of Nand Singh, Bhai Balwant Singh, and Narain Singh. They reached Lahore and organised public meetings besides meeting the authorities.[19]

A third association, named the Pacific Coast Hindi Association, was formed by Hardayal to bring all Indians under one roof. Hardayal won the faith of the labouring class of India working in the United States of America and collected sufficient money to establish a press for spreading revolutionary ideas. He started the publication of the newspaper *Ghadar*. The first issue was published in Urdu on 1st November 1913. The Ghadar press also published other revolutionary pamphlets and leaflets such as *Ghadr di Gunj, the Ilan-e-Jang, the Nia Zamana,* etc. [20] These associations were formed in Canada and America, and the Ghadar paper did commendable work to keep the Indian workers united in the United States of America, Canada, Malaya, and Shanghai. Through the paper, the organisation gained wide publicity, and in due course, it became known as the *Ghadar party* or the *Ghadar movement.*

Germans had promised to support the movement as both had a common enemy - the English. By this time, the war between the English and the Germans was inevitable, and the outbreak of the First *World War* offered these revolutionaries a long-awaited opportunity to fulfil their mission. The Ghadar paper "advocated going to India with the express object of starting a rising in conjunction with the enemies of the empire, and advocated the murder of all Europeans and loyal Indian subjects, the overthrow of the existing Government and laying the foundation of a Republic." In order to achieve this, it was planned to incite sedition among Indian troops, looting of treasuries, breaking of jails, propagation of seditious literature, arms procurement, forming of secret societies and destruction of railways and telegraphs.[21]

It was decided that Germans and Indians would jointly attack Burma under the leadership of the exiled king of Burma. They also made a plan to send three ships loaded with arms, with five hundred German officers and a hundred soldiers, to India. It was planned that out of these ships, one would release the political prisoners of the Cellular Jail and take them back to Calcutta. The others would go to Bengal and the Western Coast. It was also planned that with the attack on Burma, simultaneously, there would be revolutionary outbreaks in Bengal and Punjab.[22] A meeting was held on 15th February 1914 at Stockton, which was largely attended by all Indians. Immigrant Indians were so excited that there was a rush to return to India by the first available ship.

Meanwhile, as a result of the law passed by the Canadian Government, large numbers of Indians were held up in Hong Kong, Shanghai, and Manila, waiting for an opportunity to enter Canada. About two hundred Indians on board the ship SS Minnesota reached Seattle from the Philippines, but they were not allowed to disembark. A granthi of the Hong Kong Gurudwara who landed in Canada under a false name was deported. A Japanese ship, *S.S Komagata Maru*, was chartered, and about three hundred emigrants from Manila, Hong Kong, Shanghai, and Yokohama reached Canada, but immigration was not allowed for these Indians. The ship, with infuriated Sikhs on board, arrived at Diamond Harbour, Calcutta, on 27th September 1914. [23]

The outbreak of war between England and Germany in 1914 provided an excellent opportunity for Indians living abroad to intensify their activities. A large number of Indians aboard six ships returned to India. Seven hundred and seventy-two passengers from America, Hong Kong, and the Straits

Settlements were brought by *S.S. Korea, S.S. Siberia, S.S. Mexico Maru, and S.S. Canada Maru*, and another ship formed the first contingent of Ghadar heroes who reached India during 1914-15.

Meanwhile, in order to check conspiracy against the Government in the wake of the First World War, the British Indian Government promulgated legislation in the name of national security such as the *Ingress Into India Ordinance 1914* and the *Defence of India Act IV of 1915*. The Ingress into India Ordinance (1914) authorised the Government to indefinitely detain and compulsorily domicile suspects, while the Defence of India Act (1915) allowed suspects to be tried by Special Tribunals sitting in camera whose decisions were not subject to appeal. Eight thousand returned emigrants during 1914-1916 were dealt with under the provisions of this legislation.[24]

In India, these returned emigrants had no organisations to unite them. Many groups were formed by individuals, and they wandered from village to village to meet other returned emigrants and organise gatherings for their activities. On arrival in India, some of the Ghadrites were restricted to their homes, but others assembled in Amritsar in October 1914, where plans were made to continue their activities. The Ghadarites were instrumental in seducing the Indian troops stationed in Lahore, Faizabad, Benaras, Kanpur, Allahabad and Agra. They also committed political dacoities in Ludhiana, Malerkotla and Amritsar to raise funds for their activities. Unsuccessful attempts were also made to loot the Government Treasury at Moga on 27th November 1914. Arms were collected, and Ghadar literature was distributed. Secret meetings were organised. Dates were fixed for the outbreak of the revolt, and men were recruited by visiting towns and villages and motivating the people to join the noble cause.[25] However, the plan of the emigrants could not materialise and culminated in failure as the ships carrying arms were intercepted by the Allies.[26]

In spite of its failure, the contribution of the Ghadar movement to the Indian freedom struggle cannot be overlooked. Acknowledging its contribution, Dr. Ved Prakash Vatuk has remarked, "Ghadar Party and Ghadar paper both declared the movement aimed to attain complete freedom for India and establish a democratic rule based on equality, economic and social justice.

Ghadar was truly a people's movement. It consisted of people from all walks of life with equal contributions. Its outlook was 'work for the freedom of the country where you are living, work for the masses'. It was completely a secular movement. Unity was its strength. Equality was its goal along with social and economic justice."[27]

First Lahore Conspiracy Case

Lahore was the main centre of revolutionary activities of the Ghadar heroes and accordingly, the trial began here under the name Lahore Conspiracy Case. A special tribunal was constituted under the chairmanship of Major Irvine and Mr. T.P. Ellis, Session Judges, and Rai Bahadur Pandit and Sheo Narain as Commissioners. This trial against eighty-two listed accused began on 26th April 1915. During the trial, unprecedented security arrangements were made. The general public was not allowed to witness the trial. The proceedings of each day were reported to the press officially. The special tribunal, after hearing the case in Central Jail Lahore, delivered its judgement on 13th September 1915. "They were accused of waging war against the Crown, of conspiring to do so in and out of India, seducing troops to that end, committing dacoities, two of them with murder, abetting murder, attempting murder, abetting the mutiny of troops, etc. Some were further accused of offences under the Explosives Act." An idea of its magnitude could be gained from the fact that the case record covers seven hundred and four pages of printed matter.[28] During the trial, the prosecution witnessed four hundred and four persons.

From Ludhiana district, Rulia Singh, Chuhar Singh, Gurumukh Singh alias Anoop Singh, Indar Singh, Kesar Singh and Nand Singh were sentenced to transportation for life, whereas two Ghadrites, namely Bhan Singh and

Kirpal Singh were sentenced to transportation for ten years. The majority of the Ghadar heroes who belonged to Amritsar district, namely Sohan Singh Bhakna, Sawan Singh, Lal Singh, Bishen Singh, Kushal Singh, Bishen Singh, Hazara Singh, Kehr Singh, Mangal Singh, Wasakha Singh, Udham Singh, Wasawa Singh, Sher Singh and Kala Singh were also sentenced to transportation to the Cellular Jail.

Indar Singh, Jawand Singh, and Kala Singh from Lahore were sentenced to transportation for ten years. Others who were sentenced to various terms of transportation include Gurdit Singh, Jwala Singh of Beas, and Chattar Singh.

Harnam Singh, Jagat Ram, and Piara Singh, alias Karam Singh, were sentenced to transportation for life, and Shiv Singh was sentenced to transportation for ten years from Hoshiarpur.

From Mandi State, Hirde Ram, son of Gajjan Singh, was transported for life. Others who were transported for life in the First Lahore Conspiracy Case include Nidhan Singh of Ferozepur, Pandit Parmanand of Hamirpur, Bhai Parmanand of Jhelum, Prithvi Singh Azad from Patiala, Ram Saran Das from Kapurthala, Roda Singh and Rur Singh of Ferozpur.

It is worth mentioning here that forty-five persons convicted in the Supplementary Lahore Conspiracy Cases, Padri Murder Case, and Mandi Conspiracy Case were also sentenced to transportation. Out of them, 18 were sentenced to transportation for life, and twenty-seven were sentenced to transportation for terms varying from 2 to 14 years. The deportation of these prisoners to Andaman became a major concern for the authorities as the Andaman settlement officers were not in favour of *receiving any more seditionist type of prisoners.* The Madras Government also regretted receiving and accommodating these prisoners in their jails. Finally, it was decided to imprison them in the Hazaribagh Jail. This decision of the Government was based on the numerous representations received in the past from the settlement officers of Andaman, stressing the *need to transfer the already confined seditionist and cautioning the Government that it would not be safe to allow men of this class to Andaman at large.*[29]

Mandalay Conspiracy Cases

Many Ghadarites were sentenced to transportation in the first and second Mandalay Conspiracy Cases, also known as the Burma Conspiracy Case. Ghadar leaders, on their arrival in Burma, kept themselves busy spreading the Ghadar message and seducing the troops. They secretly read and distributed Ghadar literature. However, after the failure of the Ghadarites' plan in India, a thorough search was conducted in Burma, and a large amount of Ghadar literature was found. Persons involved in this conspiracy were arrested and convicted in the First Mandalay (Burma) Conspiracy Case by a special tribunal set up under the Defence of India Act in Mandalay.

In the First Mandalay Conspiracy Case, judgement was delivered on 27th July 1916. Hardit Singh of Ludhiana, Kirpa Ram of Gujarat, Chet Ram of Sialkot, Jiwan Singh of Gujranwala, and Kapur Singh of Ludhiana were sentenced to transportation for life, whereas Budha Singh of Gujranwala and Gian Chand of Lahore were sentenced to transportation for ten and seven years respectively.[30]

In the second Mandalay (Burma) Conspiracy Case, the judgement was delivered on 6th July 1917, and four persons, namely Mujtaba Hussain alias Mulchand alias Mohammed Mujtaba of Jaunpur, Amar Singh of Ludhiana, Ali Ahmed Siddiqui of Faizabad, and Ram Rakha of Hoshiarpur, were sentenced to transportation for life.

Rebel Sepoys of the 23rd Cavalry Platoon

The sepoys of the 23rd Cavalry Platoon also experienced solitary confinement in the Cellular Jail.

"You go and fight for the sake of the whites… You always attack other countries. Why do you not take your own country into your charge?" These were the extracts of *Ghadar* inspiring the Indian sepoys of the British army to join the revolutionaries in their fight against the colonial power. As stated earlier, *instigating mutiny among the sepoys of the British Platoons* was at the forefront of the programme of the Ghadar movement. In order to achieve this objective, many Ghadarites were sent to the frontier cantonments and other cantonments of northern India, but they could only succeed in involving Sikhs of the 23rd Cavalry Platoon. The Sikhs of this platoon, most of whom came from Manjha, were stationed near their homes, making it easier to achieve their goal. One of the most important witnesses in this case was Mul Singh, the granthi of the 23rd Cavalry. He stated that the Ghadarites returned by *Komagata Maru* were preaching in the villages from which the regiment drew a number of sepoys.[31]

During the shifting of the headquarters of the Cavalry, one bomb kept in the luggage of sepoy Wadhawa Singh exploded. A thorough search was conducted, and the conspirators were identified by the authorities. Most of them were summoned back from the battlefield, and without even giving them an opportunity to defend themselves, six accused were court-martialed at Dagshai (now in Himachal Pradesh) in 1915 and sent to the Andamans. They were Nand Singh (sepoy number 1327), Channan Singh (sepoy number 1775), Kehar Singh (sepoy number 1523) alias Kesari Singh alias Kesar Singh and Natha Singh (sepoy number 1393) alias Nathuwa Singh, Bishen Singh (sepoy number 1945), and another Bishen Singh from Amritsar.[32]

Orissa Conspiracy Case

Three conspirators of the Orissa Conspiracy Case, sentenced to transportation for life, were also deported to the Andaman on 29th October 1915. They were Artia Manjhi, Chhota, and Jagia Jaal.[33]

Benaras Conspiracy Case

In the Benaras Conspiracy Case, Sachindra Nath Sanyal was transported for life. He was the second in command of the revolutionary movement in Benaras. He worked as a link between the Ghadarites and Rash Behari Bose.[34] His arrest was the result of a lack of coordination among the revolutionaries in planning the revolt in Benaras. He was deported to the Cellular Jail in August 1916.

The revolutionary activities in Bengal gained momentum with the passage of time. The revolutionaries conducted political dacoities to raise funds and procure arms and ammunition. They also learnt bomb-making. A large number of young revolutionaries were arrested and tried, and some of them were deported to the Andamans.

Raja Bazaar Bomb Case

On 27th March 1913, a bomb was thrown in Maulvi Bazar, also known as Raja Bazar, in Sylhet, Assam. The accused—Amrit Lal Hazra, Dinesh Chandra Sen Gupta, Chandra Sekhar De, and Sarda Charan Guha—were arrested in November 1913 during a search operation. Later, three others were also arrested from different locations and convicted in the Raja Bazar Bomb case. Except for one, all were sentenced to varying terms of transportation; however, on appeal, only Amrit Lal Hazra was sentenced to transportation for fifteen years and deported to the Cellular Jail. Hazra was a student at the Bengal Technical Institute of Calcutta and a member of the Dacca Anushilan Samiti and Kartick Datta's Jugantar Party.[35]

Barisal Supplementary Case

In Barisal (now in Bangladesh), the revolutionaries formed an organisation known as Barisal Samiti, modelled after the Dacca Anushilan Samiti. The samiti was well-organised and aimed primarily at overthrowing British rule in

India. Its leaders recruited young boys into the organisation and also collected arms. To raise funds, they conducted about fourteen political dacoities from 30th September 1910 to 14th November 1912.

Forty-four accused were tried in the Barisal Conspiracy Case, which was registered on 12th May 1913, but none of them were transported. The absconders in the case were later arrested and tried under the Barisal Supplementary Case. Trailokya Nath Chakraborty, one of the earliest members of the Anushilan Samiti, along with Madan Mohan Bhowmick and Khagendra Nath Chaudhary, was sentenced to transportation for life and deported to the Andamans.[36]

Baleswar Case

Jyotish Chandra Pal of the Baleswar Case was sentenced to transportation for life on 16th October 1915. He developed signs of insanity in the Cellular Jail and hence transferred to a mental hospital, and later died in Berhampur Jail on 4th December 1924.[37]

Shibpur Political Dacoity Case

The Shibpur Political Dacoity Case was the result of a political dacoity committed by twenty-two armed revolutionaries on 30th September 1915. The revolutionaries raided the house of one Kristo Biswas and looted cash and ornaments worth Rs 20,689. One policeman was killed during the encounter. All the accused were convicted in the Shibpur Political Dacoity Case.[38] The court of the Special Commissioner delivered the judgement on 15th February 1916, and Naren Ghosh Choudhary, Nikhil Guha Roy, Surendra Nath Biswas, Sanukal Chatterjee, Satya Ranjan Basu, Jatindra Nath Nandi, Kalicharan Das, Bhupendra Nath Ghosh, Harendra Nath Bhattacharjee, and Sachindra Nath Dutta were sentenced to transportation.

Pragpur Political Dacoity Case

In Pragpur, a political dacoity was committed on 30th April 1915, at the shop of Harinath Saha in the village of Pragpur, during which arms were used. The revolutionaries arrived by boat. Cash and ornaments valued at Rs. 7,000 were looted. On their way back to Calcutta, an encounter took place between them on one side and the villagers and the police on the other. Sushil Sen died, and others were arrested and convicted in the Pragpur Dacoity Case, including Ashu Lahiri, Gopen Roy, Kshitish Chandra Sanyal, and Phanindra Bhushan Roy. All of them were sentenced to transportation and deported to the Cellular Jail in the Andamans.[39]

Bengal Arms Act Case

During a revolutionary encounter, Sub-Inspector Haridas Maitra was killed by the revolutionaries. Later, they were arrested and tried under the Bengal Arms Act Case. The Special Tribunal of Pabna Court awarded them transportation for seven years on 17th August 1918. Gobinda Chandra Kar of Mymensingh and Nikunja Behari Pal of Tippara, Bengal, were transported to the Andamans.

Martial Law Prisoners

The First World War was over, and Indians were hoping for some relief from the Government. Instead, the Government enacted the Rowlatt Act to curb the national movement, particularly in Bengal, Maharashtra, and Punjab. A few days later, Martial law was imposed in several districts of Punjab. British officers like General Dyer, O'Dwyer, and Johnson used repressive methods and established a reign of terror throughout the entire state.[40]

A large number of arrests were made in various cases from Punjab, the North-West Province, and Gujarat during the martial law regime. Out of these, nineteen martial law prisoners were transported in 1919. They included Deena, Girdhari Lal, Jalaldeen, Karamchand, Mehardeen, Mohd. Akram

Khan, Mohammadi, Ratan Chand of Amritsar, Sadiq, Sandhi, Wilayati, Sunder Singh, Jayram, Manohar Singh, Ala-ud-din, Dair Ali Shah and Raja Ram.[41]

Mainpuri Conspiracy Case

Another group of revolutionaries sent to the Andaman belonged to the Mainpuri Conspiracy Case of 1919. The youth of the Mainpuri district of Uttar Pradesh had been restless for some time. As a result, revolutionary activities in the district gained momentum when Dammi Lal, Karori Lal Gupta, Sidh Gopal Chaturvedi, Gopinath, Prabhakar Pande, Chandradhar Jauhri, and Shiv Kishan joined hands with Genda Lal Dixit of Etawah, one of the prominent revolutionary leaders who organised Matrivedi. The group organised revolutionary activities, and a few members were also trained in bomb-making. Their activities spread to Lucknow, Agra, Farrukhabad, Kanpur, Fatehpur, Benaras, and other areas. They also established contact with prominent revolutionary leaders outside the state and conducted political dacoities to raise funds. The news of these activities reached the authorities, who arrested the prominent leaders and brought them to trial in Mainpuri in what came to be known as the Mainpuri Conspiracy Case. Various terms of imprisonment were awarded to these revolutionaries on 1st July 1919. Ten of them, namely Kishori Lal Vaishya, Gopinath Brahman, Sidhgopal Brahman, Chandradhar Kayasth, Prabhakar Brahman, Mukund Lala Baniya, Rajaram Brahman, and Fatehsingh Thakur, were sent to the Andamans.[42]

Indian Jails Committee 1919-20 and Repatriation

The settlement officers' repeated requests regarding the unsuitability of the Andamans for accommodating revolutionaries and other prisoners in large numbers, coupled with reports of inhuman treatment of the political prisoners, raised significant concerns for the authorities. Under pressure from all sides, the Government of India appointed the Indian Jails Committee on 28th April 1919 under the Chairmanship of Sir Alexander Cardew.

When the Indian Jails Committee visited Andaman in January 1920, the political prisoners submitted a memorial to the Jails Committee outlining their common grievances regarding the unsuitability of Port Blair for the habitation of prisoners. They cited several reasons, including the unhealthy climate, high mortality rates, high maintenance costs of the settlement, corrupt petty officials in the jail, unrealistic work quotas, lack of medical treatment, and a limited number of female prisoners, among various other issues. The Indian Jails Committee also expressed grave dissatisfaction with the conditions they found in the Andamans in 1920.

The Committee, in its exhaustive report, has observed on page 280, para 557 that 'The fundamental difficulty in the way of the retention of the present system in the Andamans lies in the enormous size of the convict population which is collected there and the varied and incongruous sources from which that population is drawn. The number of prisoners in the Andamans has risen as high as 14,000 and is now about 12,700. These criminals are drawn from every part of the Indian Empire. There were Pathans from the North-West Frontier Province and Nagas from the hills of Assam. The population receives contributions from Ceylon and Madras at one end of the chain and from Sind and the Punjab at the other. The settlement has, in fact, been used as a receptacle for criminals from all parts of India without regard for race, religion, or language. The difficulty of dealing with a heterogeneous collection of this sort is inherently very great. We are inclined to the opinion that such an admixture of races, castes, and religions would never be likely to work well. On this ground alone, we are strongly disposed to deprecate the continuance of the existing system." The Committee further observed that "the old prejudice against crossing the sea has largely disappeared. As Sir Reginald Craddock observed, "The mere terror of crossing the Kala Pani is an exploded bogey."[43]

The Committee recommended that deportation to the Andamans should cease except in regard to such prisoners as the Governor-General in Council may, by special or general order, direct. The Government accepted the recommendations of the Committee and announced 'to end the use of the Andaman as a penal settlement'. Accordingly, a major part of the political prisoners confined in the Cellular Jail were released in pursuance of this decision.

In spite of this, the Government encouraged the system of deportation of convicts to the Andamans on a voluntary basis. Accordingly, two hundred and seventy-six men and thirty-one female convicts from Indian jails, who offered their willingness, were deported to the Andamans during 1924-26 along with a large number of Moplah prisoners.[44] This was mainly allowed in order to avoid the overcrowding of Indian jails.

Moplah Rebellion - 1921

The Mappillas, commonly referred to as Moplahs, are a distinct group of Muslims residing along the Malabar Coast of Kerala. They trace their ancestry back to Arab traders who arrived in India centuries ago, establishing a rich cultural and commercial legacy. Historically, the Moplahs primarily engaged in agriculture, but they faced significant exploitation at the hands of their landlords, which led to social and economic challenges within their community.

According to R.M. Palat, the Moplah Rebellion of 1921 has its roots in history. "The ancient custom was that the Jenmi, the Kanakaran, and the Verumpattakaran shared between them the produce of grains. When the Mohammedans invaded the country, they took a certain share of the produce, which the Moplahs maintained was the Jenmi's share. This did not cause any great confusion, as most of the Jenmis had fled from the country. The Jenmis returned when the British took over the country, and the British recognised them as the true owners of the soil and allowed them to recoup themselves from the tenantry on condition that they guaranteed the proper payment of revenue. This led to frequent outbreaks, which culminated in the murder of a Collector. The consequence was the passing of the Moplah Acts, which penalised the whole community for the outbreaks of the individuals."[45]

Under the new land revenue system of the British, the landlords were authorised to evict tenants. The landlords, chiefly Namboothris and Nairs, took advantage of the situation and evicted a large number of poor, illiterate Mappilla tenants from their lands. This led to numerous Moplah outbreaks from 1836 to 1873 and thereafter. "Annual famines had been almost a regular feature of Malabar in those days, and perhaps it was not an accident that the Mappila outbreaks also took place during periods when the worst famine conditions prevailed."[46]

The early decades of the twentieth century marked a period of national awakening, and the Moplah uprising was certainly influenced by the rising tide of nationalism. While the uprising was primarily a result of agricultural discontent, it gained momentum through the Non-Cooperation and Khilafat movements. From July 1920, regular meetings of the Non-Cooperation and Khilafat movements were organised in districts where the Moplahs were concentrated. The Moplahs were made to believe that their struggles against exploitation by the British and local landlords would soon come to an end. At the Kerala Ulema Conference held in April 1921, the Moplahs passed a resolution endorsing Non-Cooperation with the Government. Prominent Muslim and Hindu leaders, including M.P. Narayana Menon, Manikanth Gopala Menon, and K.V. Raman Menon, actively engaged in various Moplah centres and played key roles in forming committees at various places. Finally, the Kerala Provincial Khilafat Committee was formed on 3rd July 1921 at Calicut. In the ensuing days, numerous meetings drew thousands of Moplah attendees, with Ali Musaliar, a key leader, tirelessly working to mobilise the Moplah community in major centres.[47]

Under these circumstances, the uprising of August 1921 began with the incident at Pookottoor and Tanalur when unsuccessful attempts were made by the British to arrest some of the Khilafat leaders on false charges. But they could not do so in view of the gathering of a large Moplah crowd with arms. In order to avoid mass protest, all the Khilafat and Congress leaders of Pookottoor were arrested on false charges at midnight by Thomas, the District

Collector, and were sentenced to imprisonment for various terms. However, the arrested leaders were soon released as a result of a strong agitation by the Moplahs, and this was followed by celebrations all over. Meanwhile, meetings and activities against the British continued with full vigour.[48]

To address the escalating situation, a contingent of special troops was dispatched to Tirurangadi on 20th August 1920. A large number of Moplahs sought refuge in the local mosque, but the British forces, disregarding the religious sentiments of the Moplah community, forcibly entered the mosque. This inflammatory action incited the Moplahs' anger, leading approximately five thousand of them to surround the British troops. With great difficulty, the District Collector and his soldiers could manage to escape. This news reached every corner of Malabar, highlighting the intense and explosive atmosphere of the uprising, and there were general risings in the taluks of Ernad, Valluvanad, and Poonani. Other principal leaders, Valian Kunnath Kunyahamad Haji and Seethi Koya Thangal of Kuamaranpatoor, took control in their hands in a number of areas. By 28th August 1921, the British administration had virtually come to an end in Malappuram, Tirurangadi, Manjeri, and Perinthalmanna, which were in the hands of the rebels. The rebels did not spare British planters and the local landlords.[49]

It took about six months for the British to bring the old order to Malabar and suppress the revolt. More than seven thousand Moplahs were killed. Special Tribunals were set up for speedy trials. About six thousand four hundred and ninety-two Moplah rebels were dealt with under martial law by December 1921. More than twenty-four thousand Moplahs were convicted during and after the uprising.[50] Three hundred and one Moplahs were sentenced to death. In addition to these atrocities, about sixty Moplahs died due to suffocation while being transported in a closed luggage van from Tirur to Podanur during the period of martial law on the 19th of November 1921. To keep the Moplah rebels in total isolation, the Government decided to deport Moplahs to the penal settlement of the Andamans.

In conclusion, while the Moplahs ultimately lost the battle, their uprising posed an unexpected challenge to the British Government. The Moplah Rebellion was undoubtedly rooted in economic grievances, reflecting the broader struggles of the community against exploitation and injustice. Panikkar, justifying the movement as more than communal and agrarian in nature, writes, "The rural poor as a whole lived and worked in extremely oppressive conditions. Yet the Hindu peasantry, who were by no account less exploited than their Mappilla counterparts, refrained from following a violent path. Similarly, despite sharing the same religious beliefs, a substantial section of the Mappilla had held back from a militant course. Obviously, neither economic discontent nor religious resentment in them was sufficient to generate action."[51]

In 1922, the Government of India permitted, as a special measure, the transfer of Mappilla convicts to the Andamans to relieve the congestion in jails in the Madras Presidency, which were packed to their utmost capacity by the large number of convictions in the Malabar rebellion.[52] In pursuance of this decision, five hundred Moplahs were transported to the Andamans in 1922, where they were kept in a closed prison, obviously the Cellular Jail.[53] However, the first batch, comprising 160 Moplah prisoners, reached Port Blair on 22nd April 1922, and the group included a Namboodri and four Nairs as well. It is generally believed that about three thousand Moplahs were deported to the Andamans.

In the Andamans, after spending a brief period in the Cellular Jail prison, they were allowed to settle down in the villages of South Andaman as part of the 'Moplah Colonisation Scheme'. They built huts of bamboo thatched with palm leaves on the lines of the huts found in Kundungal and Valayil in Calicut of Malabar.[54] Initially, out of 1,133 Moplah convicts, 258 were provided with agricultural tickets and were asked to bring their families and other relatives from India, resulting in the arrival of 468 relatives.

In the following years, the Government faced criticism over the pitiable conditions of the Moplah settlers in the Andamans. Under this situation, the

Government appointed a committee consisting of Mahmud Schamnad, Syed Murtaza, Mir Abbas Ali and Dr. K.D. Mugaseth directed them to proceed to the Andamans and see for themselves the conditions of the Moplah settlers. At last, the Government decided that their future policy on the 'Mappilla Colonisation Scheme' in the Andamans would be based on certain principles.

Firstly, the Mappilla colonisation scheme would continue on its present lines but on a voluntary basis. Secondly, any of the Mappilla settlers in the Andamans who wished to return to jails in India or send their wives and families back to Malabar would be allowed to do so. Thirdly, long-term Mappilla prisoners now in jails in India would be given the option to either remain in Indian jails or lead the free life of a settler in the Andamans. Prisoners who may volunteer hereafter to go to the Andamans would also have the option, after they had been in the Islands for one year, to return to jails in India and send their wives and families back to Malabar. Fourthly, where Mappilla convicts, who would prefer life in the Andamans with their wives and families, the Government would arrange to convey their wives and near relatives to the Islands. It was also decided that physically fit relatives would have to earn their own livelihood after the first month of their arrival.[55]

The Andaman Moplah Service Organisation (AMSO) is an association formed by the descendants of the Moplahs. As part of the year-long celebrations, AMSO organised a series of events to celebrate the centenary year during 2022-23. A souvenir was also published to commemorate this milestone, which also included a list of 229 Moplah Freedom Fighters with their prisoner number.

Manyam (Rampa) Rebellion of 1922-24

During this period, many heroes from Manyam, who took part in the Rampa Rebellion of 1922-24 under the leadership of Alluri Seetaramraju, were also deported to the Andamans.

Frequent disturbances took place in the agency areas of Andhra Pradesh since the introduction of the permanent settlement of the land revenue in 1802. Alluri Sitaram Raju prepared his ground in the agency area to start a revolt against the prevailing land revenue and judicial system, which caused great dissatisfaction among the residents of the area. Raju, on finding the situation favourable, planned attacks on the police stations. Accordingly, the first attack was organised on Chintapalli Police Station on 22nd August 1922, along with his three hundred followers armed with country guns and swords. They attacked Rajavommangi police station and, having freed Veerayya Dora, a prisoner at the police station, looted arms and ammunition. Within three days, the rebels collected a large number of arms. On 24th September 1922, the rebels shot two British officers, namely Scott Coward and Hayter, dead and seized their arms. However, the British suppressed the rebellion, and Raju was shot dead on 7th May 1924.[56]

The followers of Raju were convicted and sentenced to various terms of imprisonment. The heroes who were deported to the Andamans include Korrabu Kotayya, Bonangi Pandu Padal, Golivilli Sanyasayya, Kunchatti Sanyasi, Vegiraju Satyanarayana Raju, Taggi Veerayya Dora and Gam Mallu Dora.[57] However, Dr. Pala Krishna Moorthy, in his book titled '*The Grand Rebel*', writes that Bonangi Pandu Padal, one of the rebels, in his affidavit of 18th May 1973, indicated that he, along with twelve other members of his party, arrived in the Cellular Jail by 1926.[58]

Cases and Deportations During 1932-38

The growing revolutionary activities after 1925 caused great concern for the Government. Such activities were suspended for a brief period as a result of the call given during the movement launched by Mahatma Gandhi during 1920-21. The failure of this movement after the incident at *Chauri Chaura* on 5th February 1922 paved the way for the resumption of revolutionary activities, particularly in Bengal and Punjab.

In order to deal effectively with the intense revolutionary activities during the period, the Government took repressive measures and armed itself with laws such as *Bengal Ordinances IX and XI of 1931*. These laws authorised the Government for *in-camera and in absentia trials* of revolutionaries by Special Tribunals and Special Magistrates. A large number of revolutionaries were arrested, tried, and transported to the Andamans as the Government was determined to isolate them. After a gap of nearly ten years, the transportation of prisoners to the penal settlement of Andamans was again started in 1932.[59]

Numerous organisations emerged during the period, and one such revolutionary organisation was the 'Hindustan Republican Association', which was later renamed the *Hindustan Socialist Republican Army* in northern India. This association is synonymous with the names of the great patriots Bhagat Singh, Rajguru and Sukhdev. The formation of the *Hindustan Socialist Republican Army* was a turning point in the history of the armed struggle for India's independence. The revolutionaries of the organisation were inspired by the Bolsheviks and Mensheviks of the Russian Revolution of 1917.

Kakori Conspiracy Case

The first major planned attack by the Hindustan Socialist Republican Army occurred on 9th August 1925 near Kakori Railway Station, during which the Government treasury was looted. Prominent revolutionaries, including Ram Prasad Bismil, Ashfaqullah Khan, Rajendra Lahiri, Chandra Shekhar Azad, Manmath Nath Gupta, and others, participated in this audacious act. All the accused were subsequently convicted in the Kakori Conspiracy Case, with the judgement delivered on 6th April 1927. On 19th December 1927, Ram Prasad Bismil, Ashfaqullah Khan, and Roshan Singh were executed, while the remaining revolutionaries were sentenced to various terms in different jails. Additionally, Vishnu Saran Dubey was deported to the Andamans as part of the repercussions of this case.[60]

Central Assembly Bomb Case and Lahore Conspiracy Case

The revolutionaries of the *Hindustan Socialist Republican Army* shot dead J.P. Saunders, an Assistant Superintendent of Police, on 17th December 1928, in Lahore as revenge for the death of Lala Lajpat Rai, who was brutally beaten up during the protest rally of *Simon Commission*. On 8th April 1929, Bhagat Singh and Batukeshwar Dutt threw two bombs in the Legislative Assembly of Delhi, and they surrendered after the incident. In this case, both were sentenced to life imprisonment. They were later shifted to Punjab Jail to face trial in the *Lahore Conspiracy Case*. Batukeshwar Dutt was transported for life to the Andamans in the *Central Assembly Bomb Case*. In the Lahore Conspiracy Case, Bhagat Singh, Rajguru, and Sukhdev were sentenced to death and were executed on 23rd March 1931. Dr. Gaya Prasad, Jaidev Kapoor, Kundan Lal, Mahavir Singh, Bejoy Kumar Sinha, Kanwal Nath Tiwari, and Shiv Verma were deported to the Andamans.[61]

Chittagong Armoury Raid Case

One of the most well-organised attacks and daring acts against the British took place on 18th April 1930 when the Chittagong Armoury Raid was conducted under the leadership of *Surya Sen*, President of the *Indian Republican Army*, Chittagong Branch. At 10.00 p.m., about a hundred young revolutionaries dressed as British Indian Army personnel marched in several groups. They destroyed the telephone exchange and telegraph office and cut off all communications connecting the town with Calcutta and Dacca. The Government could get support in Chittagong on 20th April 1930. On the 22nd April, fifty-seven revolutionaries were surrounded on the Jalalabad range by a British Regiment. Eleven revolutionaries were killed after killing sixty-four men of the British Regiment. The revolutionaries dispersed during the night and continued the guerrilla fights in different localities of Chittagong and Chandernagor.[62]

In July 1930, large-scale arrests were made, and all accused were booked under the Chittagong Armoury Raid Case. The special tribunal delivered judgement on 1st March 1932. Surya Sen was sentenced to death, and the others to various terms of imprisonment. Ganesh Ghosh, Anant Lal Singh, Loknath Bawl, Himanshu Bhowmick, Lal Mohan Sen, Haripad Bhattacharya, Faqir Chandra Sen Gupta, Kali Kinker Dey, Randhir Das Gupta, Sahay Ram Das, Subodh Kumar Choudhari, Subodh Roy, Sudhir Ranjan Choudhari, Subodh Chandra Roy, Kalipada Chakraborty, Saroj Kanti Guha, Anand Prasad Gupta, Phanindra Lal Nandi, and Sukhendu Dastidar were sentenced to transportation and deported to the Andamans on 15th August 1932.

Dalhousie Square Bomb Case

A bomb was thrown at the Calcutta Police Commissioner, Charles Tegart, on 25th August 1930 by Anuja Charan Sengupta and Dinesh Chandra Majumdar. In this case, Narayan Chandra Rai, Bhupal Chandra Bose and Surendranath Dutta were deported to the Cellular Jail. [63]

Hajipur Station Action Case

This event took place at Hajipur Railway Station on 15th June 1931. Located between Bihar and Orissa, five gunmen attacked and killed the station master while he was handing over a sealed bag to the guard. The revolutionaries involved in this incident drew inspiration from the Hindustan Socialist Republican Army. Ramdeni devised this plan to raise funds for the party's activities. The accused were sentenced on 30th March 1931. Chandrika Singh, who had connections with the renowned revolutionary from Bihar, Jogendra Shukla, was also convicted. [64]

Motihari Conspiracy Case

This case was initiated against individuals who assisted the revolutionaries of the Hindustan Socialist Republican Army by providing shelter to

Chandrashekar Azad and Bhagat Singh. Jogendra Shukla, Nanku Singh, Gulab Chand Gupta, and Kedarmani Shukla were arrested in connection with this case. They were sentenced to ten years of imprisonment and deported to Cellular Jail.

Attempt to Kill Watson

The revolutionaries were dissatisfied with the Statesman newspaper, as its editor, Sir Alfred Watson, regularly published articles criticising their activities. On 5th August 1932, Atul Chandra Sen, an intelligent student from Jadavpur Engineering College, reached the office of the Statesman and made an unsuccessful attempt to assassinate Watson. He was apprehended but later committed suicide. This incident inspired the revolutionaries of Bengal, leading to further unsuccessful attempts on Watson's life. On 28th September 1932, two young revolutionaries, Anil Bhaduri and Mani Lahiri, were shot dead by Watson's bodyguards while attempting to kill him. In response, the police initiated indiscriminate arrests of all revolutionaries associated with these incidents and also offered assistance to some of them. Haripad Choudhary, Sunil Kumar Chatterjee, Promod Ranjan Bose, and others were sentenced to transportation and deported to Cellular Jail as a result of this case.[65]

Patna Conspiracy Case

The Patna Conspiracy Case of 1932 was initiated against individuals involved in revolutionary activities in Bihar. A police sub-inspector, Ram Narayan Singh, was killed in a bomb explosion orchestrated by Hazarilal. Suraj Nath Chaubey was arrested on charges of assisting Hazarilal. Subsequently, other revolutionaries, including Mohit Chandra Adhikari, Shyam Krishna Agrawal, Mahavir Missir, and Kanhai Lal Mishra, were arrested on allegations of possessing illegal arms and explosives. All these revolutionaries were sentenced to various terms of imprisonment and deported to Cellular Jail in 1933.

Delhi Conspiracy Case

On 23rd December 1932, a high-powered bomb was planted by Dhanvantari on the railway track near Hazrat Nizamuddin Railway Station, Delhi, to blow up the incoming special train of Viceroy Irwin, but the Viceroy escaped unhurt. Dhanvantari was sentenced to life imprisonment in the Delhi conspiracy case. Dhanvantari was a member of the *Hindustan Socialist Republican Army* and a close associate of Chandrasekhar Azad and Bhagat Singh.

Ootacamund Bank Dacoity Case

In order to form a party in South India and create awareness among the youth to take up arms against the British, the revolutionaries of the 'Hindustan Socialist Republican Army' conducted a political dacoity on 28th April 1933 and looted Travancore National Bank in Ooty. This action is known as the Ootacamund Bank Dacoity Case. The absconded revolutionaries were arrested near Erode Railway Station. The accused included Shambu Nath Azad, Prem Prakash, Kushiram Mehta, and Hazara Singh. They were arrested and sentenced in July 1933 to life imprisonment and deported to the Andamans.

B.E.J. Burge Murder Case

The revolutionaries in Midnapore set unpopular British officials and their agents as their prime targets. After the murder of James Peddie and R. Douglas, B. E. J. Burge took over as the District Magistrate of Midnapore. He was known for his repressive methods used to suppress revolutionaries. A young revolutionary, Anath Bandhu Panja, shot him during a football match at the Town Club on 2nd September 1933. Anath Bandhu Panja was killed on the spot by the police. Later, Mrigendra Dutta, an associate, also died in the hospital. The assassination of the third consecutive District Magistrate of Midnapore, B. E. J. Burge, annoyed the British. Two revolutionaries were executed in this case, whereas Sukumar Sengupta and Kamakya Charan Ghosh were sent to the Cellular Jail in Andamans.[66]

Hilli Station Dacoity Case

The revolutionaries conducted a political dacoity on 28th October 1933 at Hili railway station (now in Bangladesh). During this action, a postal peon, Kalicharan Mahali, was killed. All the accused were tried under the Hill Station Dacoity Case. Hrishikesh Bhattacharya, Haripada Bose, Bijoy Krishna Chakraborty, Pran Krishto Chakraborty, Ramakrishna Sarkar, Prafulla Sanyal, Abdul Qadir Choudary, Satyavrat Chakraborty, Saroj Kumar Bose, and Ramkrishto Mondal were sent to the Andaman Islands[67].

Kamalpur Dacoity Case

The Kamalpur dacoity was conducted on 29th May 1933 by thirty-two young revolutionaries. Mohan Kishore Banik's house in Bajitpur was looted with the intention of raising funds for revolutionary activities. The revolutionaries used bombs and bullets during the action, resulting in many people being wounded. They also cut down the telegraphic line between Kithari and Sarachar Post Office. Eventually, the police arrested thirty-two people in the Dacoity Case. Dharni Mohan Baik, Dinesh Chandra Banik, Haribol Chakraborty, Jogendra Chandra Chakraborty, Prakash Chandra Sheel, Dinesh Chandra Saha, Bhuban Mohan Chandra, Manindra Chandra Sen, Indu Bhushan Das, Jankai Mohan Das, Birendra Chandra Lahiri, and Sudhangshu Kiran Lahiri were sentenced to transportation to the Andamans to undergo their sentences in the Cellular Jail.

Kakinada Bomb Conspiracy Case

In the Kakinada Bomb Conspiracy Case, Venkateshawar Rao Prativadi Bhayankara Venkatacharya was arrested on 11th September 1933 by C.I.D. Police, Madras, at the Kazipet Railway station. A 45-bore revolver was recovered from his custody. In addition, two more revolvers and fifty cartridges were also recovered from his belongings. He was arrested and tried in the Kakinada Bomb Conspiracy Case and sentenced to a fourteen-year prison term by the Sessions Judge, Madras, under Section 120-B of the Indian Penal Code and the 1920 Arms Act and the 4, 5 Explosives Act.

Lebong Governor Outrage Shooting Case

On 8th May 1934, two young men - Bhawani Prasad Bhattacharya and Rabindra Bandopadhyay, made an unsuccessful attempt to assassinate Sir John Anderson, Governor of Bengal, at Lebong Race Course near Darjeeling. He was engaged in suppressing the revolutionaries and accordingly made certain amendments to the Criminal Law Act. In this case, Madhusudhan Banerjee, Manoranjan Banerjee, Rabindranath Banerjee, and Fakir Chand Sen were transported to the Andaman. The assassin Bhawani Prasad Bhattacharya was arrested and executed on 3rd February 1935.[68]

Bathua Dacoity Case

On the night of 23rd February 1934, about fifteen armed revolutionaries looted the house of Parassann Mallaker. Police surrounded the area and conducted a search operation in which arms were found. The accused were tried by a special tribunal, which delivered judgement on 27th August 1934. Mahesh Chandra Bathua, Nirendra Barua, Saradindra Bhattacharya, Manoranjan Choudhary, Jibendra Kumar Das, Manmohan Shah, Ganga Chandra Dey, Arvind Dey, Kirti Majumdar and Priyada Ranjan Chakraborty were deported to the Cellular Jail.[69]

Rangpur Conspiracy Case

Fifteen revolutionaries belonging to the Jugantar party were arrested in connection with the Rangpur Conspiracy case on charges of collecting arms and distributing them to different places for revolutionary activities.[70]

In this case, Bimal Chandra Dey Bhowmick, Dhirendra Kumar Biswas, Biru Bhushan Chakraborty, Benoy Tarafdar, Narendra Nath Das, Nagendra Mohan Mustafa, and others were deported to the Andamans.

Interprovincial Conspiracy Case

After the Chittagong Armoury Raid in April 1930, several revolutionary leaders of Anushilan Samities were arrested. Conspiracy cases like the Interprovincial Conspiracy Case of 1933-35 were initiated, and many revolutionaries were sent behind bars. Persons against whom no definite charges could be made were arrested under the Bengal Criminal Law Act, which provided detention without trial.

This case was initiated against 40 accused on the charges of conspiracy against the Royal Government. Apart from Bengal, the centres of this conspiracy were extended to Punjab and Madras. The revolutionaries had planned to start a revolt in various parts of India. They also wanted to set up a bomb factory in the hilly areas of Ootacamund. Judgement was delivered on 1st May 1935 by the special tribunal, and various terms of imprisonment were awarded to the accused.[71] Bimal Chandra Bhattacharjee, Dhirendra Bhattacharjee, Dwjendranath Talapatra, Manindra Lall, Amulya Charan Sengupta, Jitendra Chand Gupta, Jyotish Majumdar, Provot Kumar Mitra, Provot Chandra Guha, Satyendra Narayan Majumder, Surendra Dhar Chaudhury and others were deported to Cellular Jail in 1935-36 and repatriated in 1937.

Revolutionary activities continued with increased strength and determination in Bengal and other parts of India. A large number of political prisoners were arrested and deported to Cellular Jail in the Andamans for charges including attempted murder, possession of illegal arms, involvement in political dacoities, adherence to revolutionary ideologies, and disobedience of Government orders. In Bengal alone, political prisoners were convicted in more than 30 to 40 cases, including notable incidents such as the Mechua

Bazar Bomb Case, Alipore Political Dacoity Case, Charmaguria Post Office Dacoity Case, Calcutta Arms Act Case, Itakhol Mail Dacoity Case, Tangail Political Dacoity Case, Naldanga Political Dacoity Case, Birbhum Conspiracy Case, Damodia Mail Robbery Case, Faridpur Arms and Explosives Conspiracy Case, Armenian Street Political Dacoity Case, and the Brahmanbaria Political Dacoity Case. All these freedom fighters were deported to Cellular Jail for their participation in various political actions.

NOTES AND REFERENCES

1. Singh, Ujjawal Kumar, p. 23, footnotes.

2. Mahajan, V.D., *Modern Indian History*, S. Chand & Company Ltd, New Delhi, p. 394.

3. *Ibid.*

4. Sinha, Bejoy Kumar, *Indian Revolutionary Movement*, Lokmanya Tilak Smarak Trust, Pune, 1994, pp. 22-32.

5. Aggarwal, p. 81.

6. *Ibid*, pp. 84-86.

7. *Majumdar*, p. 146.

8. *HD-P*, Political, July 1917, Nos. 462-48.

9. Keer, Dhananjay, Veer Savarkar, Veer Prakashan, Mumbai, Third Edition 2012, pp. 50-51.

10. Bhai Nahar & Bhai Kirpal Singh, *Struggle for Free Hindustan*, Vol. 2, Part I, Atlantic Publishers and Distributors, New Delhi, 1988, p. 26.

11. Aggarwal, p. 94.

12. Majumdar, p. 189.

13. Aggarwal, p. 100.

14. Majumdar, p. 235.

15. Aggarwal, pp. 163-4.

16. Singh, Bhai Nahar & Kirpal, Vol. I, p. 15.

17. Nahar & Kirpal, Vol. 2, pp. x-xi.

18. Aggarwal, p. 168.

19. Nahar & Kirpal, Vol. 1, *op. cit.*, pp. 15-21.

20. *Ibid*, p. 37.

21. Waraich, Malwinder Jit Singh & Harinder Singh, *War Against King Emperor, Ghadr of 1914-15*, Bhai Sahib Randhir Singh Trust, Punjab, 2001, p. 134.

22. Majumdar, p. 236.

23. Nahar & Kirpal, Vol. 1, p. 52.

24. Singh, Ujjwal, pp. 29-30.

25. Nahar & Kirpal, Vol. 1, pp. 279-284.

26. Sinha, p. 34.

27. Gadar Party – *Lahore Conspiracy Case – Judgement - 1915*, Archana Publications, Meerut, 2006, pp. viii-ix.

28. Nahar & Kirpal, Vol. 1, pp. 161-2.

29. *HD-P.* Political, July 1917, No. 462-48.

30. Aggarwal, 187.

31. Waraich, p. 212.

32. *HD-P, Pol.* July 1917, Nos. 462-48.

33. *Ibid.*

34. Aggarwal, 189.

35. Nahar & Kirpal, Vol. 2, p. 213.

36. Aggarwal, pp. 191-193.

37. Majumdar, p. 244.

38. Nahar & Kirpal, Vol. 2, p. 248.

39. Aggarwal, pp. 194-5.

40. Caveeshan, S.S, *The Non-Cooperation Movement in Indian Politics*, 1988, Discovery Publishing House, Delhi, pp. 17-20.

41. Aggarwal, p. 196.

42. Jain, Phoolchand, *Krantikari Aandolan, Suprasidh Prasang*, Institute of Social Sciences, New Delhi, 1999, pp. 181-186, Hindi, also see Jain, *Bandi Nama, Andaman Jail*, p. 24.

43. Report of the Indian Jails Committee, 1919-20, Pages 280 & 282, Paras 557 & 561

44. Mathur, L.P., *Kala Pani - History of Andaman and Nicobar Islands with a Study of India's Freedom Struggle*, Eastern Book Corporation, Delhi, 1985, pp. 61-62.

45. Choudhary, Sukhbir, *Moplah Uprising (1921-23)*, Agam Parakashan, Delhi, 1977, p. 99. (The statement of R.M. Palat on "Why the Moplahs rebelled?" was published in Indian Review (Madras) Vol. XXIII, January 1922, page 63, which was reproduced here.)

46. *Kerala District Gazetteer*, Kozhikode by A. Shreedharan Menon, 1962, pp. 174-5.

47. Choudhary, pp. 18-23.

48. *Ibid*, pp. 23-24.

49. *Ibid*, pp. 26-30.

50. *Ibid*, pp. 57-59.

51. Panikkar, K.N., *Against Lord and the State*, Oxford University Press, Delhi, 1992, p. 193.

52. No. F.188/24/Jails, GOI, *HD*, GOI, October 1926, Regional Archives, Kozhikode.

53. No. 2473, letter from the Secretary to Government, Law (General) Department to the Secretary to the GOI, *HD*, 9 October 1922, Regional Archives, Kozhikode.

54. No. F.188/24/Jails D GOI, HD, 4 October 1926, Regional Archives, Kozhikode.

55. *Ibid.*

56. Krishna Moorthy, Pala, *The Grand Rebel*, Kavitha Publishers, Hyderabad, 2006, pp. 16-31.

57. Xavier, Francis, *Manyam Heroes in the Cellular Jail*, published in the Souvenir of the Centenary Year of Cellular Jail, 2006, A&N Administration.

58. Moorthy, p. 67.

59. Singh, Ujjwal, pp. 111-3.

60. Aggarwal, pp. 244-246.

61. *Ibid*, pp. 250-254.

62. Sen, S.N., *History of the Freedom Movement in India (1857-1947)*, Third Edition, New Age International (P) Ltd. Publishers, 1997, pp. 251-252.

63. Jain, pp. 277-279.

64. *Ibid*, p. 291.

65. *Ibid*, p. 299.

66. *Ibid*, pp. 300-1.

67. *Ibid*, p. 305.

68. *Ibid*, pp. 302-3.

69. *Ibid*, pp. 303-5.

70. *Ibid*, p. 306.

71. *Ibid*, pp. 306-311.

CHAPTER VI

The Cellular Jail Story - Incarceration to Repatriation

The life of a political prisoner under the sentence of transportation, along with imprisonment in the Cellular Jail, portrayed the saga of sacrifice and heroism. The unending tale of torture and suffering began from the time he left the shores of India until his release or death in the penal settlement. The political prisoners not only suffered transportation but also solitary confinement in the Cellular Jail for the entire term of their sentence, which was meant to serve as a deterrent to Indian freedom fighters.

Autobiographies of political prisoners transported to the Andamans are important sources of information about their lives and struggles in the Cellular Jail. Political prisoners like Veer Vinayak Damodar Savarkar, Trailokya Nath Chakraborty, Bhai Parmanand, Bejoy Kumar Sinha, Baba Prithvi Singh Azad, and Sachindra Nath Sanyal have provided us with an insight into their lives and sufferings through their memoirs.

The following accounts relating to their life in the Cellular Jail are based on these autobiographies. Their account describes that life in the Cellular Jail remained more or less the same during 1910-1921 and 1932-1938. This chapter will focus on their life in the Andamans, right from deportation to repatriation, as presented by freedom fighters in their autobiographies, which are the primary source of information.

The Monotonous Days During the Ship Journey

The political prisoners were sent to the Andamans using three ports, namely Calcutta, Madras, and Karachi. They were transported to the Andamans on the ship SS Maharaja, where they had to spend three days and three nights at the bottom of the ship. Their miseries began on the day they had to embark on the suffocated and poorly ventilated ship bound for Port Blair. The monotonous days with seasickness and under 24-hour surveillance on board the ship made their journey to the Andamans an unpleasant one.

Bejoy Kumar Sinha, sentenced in the Alipore Bomb Case, recalls the ship's journey to Port Blair, "At night, sleep was not possible. The prisoners' blocks were big iron cages, just like the type in which animals are carried on railway wagons. These were around the boilers of the ship—quite dark, even during the daytime. Dim lights were burning there the whole time. The atmosphere was suffocating. It was a real blessing for us to stand turn by turn during the night hours at the ventilation hole and look out. The reigned stillness was broken only by the dull roar of the engines and the splash of the waves. The spray of seawater used to reach our faces sometimes. We would stand for hours together breathing in the freshness of the vast open sea and often forget our prisoner-selves in the engrossing thoughts."[1]

First Encounter

On their arrival at Port Blair, the political prisoners were taken to the Cellular Jail. The first person to meet the first few batches of political prisoners until 1920 was an Irish jailor of the Cellular Jail, David Barry. Barindra Kumar Ghosh gave this account of his first meeting with Mr. Barry:

"He (Mr. Barry) came and delivered a long speech, the gist of which was as follows: 'You see the wall around, do you know why it is so low? Because it is impossible to escape from this place. The sea surrounds it for a distance of 1000 miles. In the forest you do not find any animals other than pigs and wild cats, it is true, but there are savages who are called Janglis or Jarrawallas. If they happen to see any man, they do not hesitate to pierce him right through with their sharp arrows. And do you see me? My name is D. Barry. I am a most obedient servant to the simple and straightforward, but to the crooked,

I am four times as crooked. If you disobey me, may God help you, at least I will not. That is certain. Remember also that God does not come within three miles of Port Blair. The red turbans you see, there are warders. And those in black uniforms are petty officers; you must obey them. If they happen to molest you, inform me. I will punish them.

Then our fetters were broken. A half-pant, a kurta, and a white cap were provided for each."[2]

The dark dungeons of the Cellular Jail, specially meant for solitary confinement, remained their home from the first day until their departure from Port Blair. A low wooden bed in one corner was the only furniture in the cell. One of the most uncomfortable aspects of their life in the Cellular Jail was the total absence of urinals and toilets in the cells. Inmates were only allowed to answer the call of nature during specific times in the morning, at noon, and in the evening. If a political prisoner felt the urge other than the scheduled times, he had to use a small pot placed in his cell.

While narrating this horrible situation, Veer Savarkar writes, "...Of all the hardships of prison life in the Cellular Jail of the Andamans—gruelling work, scanty food and clothing, occasional thrashing and others—none was so annoying and disgusting as its provision for urinals and lavatories. The prisoners had to control the demands of nature for hours together, for want of these arrangements in the cell itself. Morning, noon and evening—these were the only hours when prisoners were let off for this purpose and at a stated time only. It was an outrage to ask the Jamadar for this convenience at any moment other than the stipulated hour. The prisoners were locked in their cells at six or seven o'clock in the evening, and the lock was opened only after six in the next morning. A sort of clay pot was given to them to use for that purpose during the night... During twelve hours of the night, the warders insisted that the prisoner shall have no occasion to ease himself. The pot was so diminutive in size that one could not discharge into it even once during the night. As for nature's call, one had to go down on his knees to the Jamadar to let him out. The warder may or may not take the call seriously. He may be reluctant himself, or he may fear the officer. The prisoner had, therefore, to check it till the morning. If the warder relaxed and carried the matter to the Jamadar, the Jamadar would severely berate the convict for the call at such an odd hour. He would severely reprimand the warder also for having heard the prisoner.

He would or would not report to the doctor as his fancy or memory may guide him. The doctor's report on the ailment was never made or made only in one case out of a hundred. That report had to go to Mr. Barrie, and Mr. Barrie would take action upon it at his own sweet will. Imagine the prisoner's condition during the night and during this process of red tape, particularly when the call was not normal but an abnormal and sudden ailment. In the morning, Mr. Barrie would sit in judgment upon it and rebuke the warder and the Jamadar sternly for their lapse of duty. When he brayed in this fashion, there was no answering him. The prisoner was also cross-examined by Mr. Barrie. And, if the former said that he could not help the call of nature, Mr. Barrie turned round upon him fiercely: 'Why the devil did you have it?' And, if the wretched creature had the courage to say, 'I got it because I got it,' the Jamadar would give a slap in the face and scold him for giving such an insolent answer. Usually, the prisoner was let off only with this cannonade of words. But Mr. Barrie's particular kindness to the prisoner always ended in an order to put him immediately on the grinding mill."[3]

Untold Stories of Suffering and Sacrifices

The food provided to them was not only inadequate but also unhealthy and unhygienic. The daily ration per person was insufficient. The wicked warders compelled the political prisoner to share this meagre food with them. In case of denial, the prisoner had to face torture by the Jamadars.

Barindra Ghose recalls his second day and the kind of food provided to him in the jail. "The next morning, we came out and washed our faces and then had for the first time the darshan of *ganji*, otherwise called kanji. It means boiled rice churned in water, say a sort of rice porridge. We were given a *dabbu* full of this. Dabbu is a kind of primitive spoon made of a broken half coconut shell with a cane handle fixed to it. Now, the *ganji* was saltless and therefore tasteless. Each prisoner was allowed only one gram of salt per day, and this being required for the dal and the vegetable, the ganji had necessarily to go without salt. However, we had to swallow the thing with the utmost perseverance, in spite of its tastelessness."[4]

Savarkar had no complaints about food. He was more concerned about the petty officers with whom he had to share the food. He narrates, "The quantity of daily food allowed to a prisoner in this jail, measured by prison regulations, was both sufficient and nutritious. But there was no end of trouble for the food to reach the mouth of the prisoner himself in quality as well as in quantity."[5]

The political prisoners were engaged in the hardest labour. They were yoked to the oil mill and engaged in coir pounding, rope making, brick making, etc., both indoors and outdoors. They were allotted a fixed quota of work with instructions to complete the same by evening. The number of tasks assigned daily to each prisoner was humanly not possible to finish, and failure to complete the task resulted in punishments in the form of flogging, wearing sackcloth uniforms, fetters, and so on. These tortures were beyond human endurance. Barindra Ghose, while mentioning the gruesome work connected with coir pounding, wrote, "To pound the coir and extract fibres out of it, to prepare ropes again from those fibres, to grind dry coconut and also mustard in the machine and extract oil, to make bulbs for hookahs from the shells—these formed the principal items of work for the prisoners, as has already been said before. Besides, there was a cane workshop where small boys were made to work.

The most difficult work was coir pounding and oil grinding. Barindra and Abinash were invalids among us and were given rope-making; all the rest had to do the coir pounding. We got up early in the morning, satisfied the demands of nature, and, swallowing the *kanji*, tucked up our *langoti* and sat down to business. Each one was given the dry husk of twenty coconuts. The husk had to be placed on a piece of wood and then beaten with a wooden hammer until it became soft. Then, the outer skin had to be removed. After that, it was dipped in water and moistened, and then one had to pound it. By sheer pounding, the entire husk inside dropped off, leaving only the fibres. These fibres then had to be dried in the sun and cleaned. Each one was expected to prepare daily a roll of such fibres weighing one seer."

Veer Savarkar gives the following account of 'picking oakum' (the technical name for rope making), "Though 'picking oakum' was a task hard enough, its tedium was relieved by the company of prisoners working in the same chawl. An educated man desires company and association with his equals, and therefore, this mode of working was a solace to him. One or two of these prisoners were ailing, and milk was provided for them. It was given to the Pathan warder as an offering to God. And the God—the Pathan—on that account was less cruel to them. All these factors made prison life for political prisoners less endurable than it is today. My elder brother was in the same chawl (Barrack)."[6]

Though rope-making was a difficult task, the political prisoners liked to be engaged in this work as it provided them with an opportunity to work in the company of their fellow prisoners. Questions were raised about such 'facilities' provided to the political prisoners. So, this work was replaced by oil grinding.

The oil grinding was the hardest work specified for the political prisoners in the Cellular Jail. Savarkar observes with reference to oil grinding, "We were to be yoked like animals to the handle that turned the wheel. Hardly out of bed, we were ordered to wear a strip of cloth, were shut up in our cells and made to turn the wheel of the oil mill. Coconut pieces were put in the empty and hollow space to be crushed by the wheel passing over them, and its turning became heavier as the space was fuller. Twenty turns of the wheel were enough to drain away the strength of the strongest coolly and the worst, brawny badmash. No dacoit past twenty was put on that work. But the poor political prisoner was fit to do it at any age. And the doctor in charge ever certified that he could do it! It was the medical science of the Andamans that had upheld the doctor! So the poor creature had to go half the round of the wheel by pushing the handle with his hands, and the other half was completed by hanging on to it with all his might. So much physical strength had to be expended on crushing the coconut pieces for oil. Youths of twenty or more, who in their lives had not done any physical labour, were put upon that labour. They were all educated young men of delicate constitution. From six to ten in the morning, they were yoked to the wheel, which they turned round and round till their breath had become heavy. Some of them had fainted many times during the process. They had to sit down for sheer exhaustion and helplessness. Ordinarily, all work had to be stopped between ten and twelve. But this *Kolu*, as the oil mill labour was called, had to continue throughout. The door was opened only when the meal was announced. The man came in, served the meal in the pan and went away, and the door was shut. If, after washing his hands, one were to wipe away the perspiration of his body, the Jamadar - the worst of gangsters in the whole lot - would go at him with loud abuse. There was no water for washing hands. Drinking water was to be had only for propitiating the Jamadar. While you were at Kolu, you felt very thirsty. The waterman gave no water except for a consideration, which was to palm off to him some tobacco in exchange. If one spoke to the Jamadar, his retort was, 'A prisoner is given only two cups of water, and you have already consumed three. Whence can I bring you more water? From your father?' We have put down the retort of the Jamadar in the most decent language possible. If water could not be had for washing and the drink, what can be said of water for bathing?"[7]

The political prisoners were not allowed to talk to each other, and strict vigil was kept on them to avoid any unpleasant incident. The unique jail building itself prohibited them from communicating with each other. Describing this situation where the political prisoners were not allowed to release their pain and agony by sharing with their fellows, Barindra Ghose had this to narrate: "The political prisoners are prohibited from talking to each other. So if more than one falls ill at the same time, they are not taken to the hospital but are kept locked up in separate cells. There is no arrangement for proper ventilation in these cells except through a very small skylight. One does not get proper food and nourishment but has to undergo physical labour to which one is not accustomed. One does not get proper treatment for illness but has to suffer punishment at every step. But the greatest infliction is to lead one's life under the orders of low and ill-bred people. It will unhinge any man, even in ordinary circumstances, not to speak of a prisoner, to be so hunted and insulted all the 24 hours. It is quite an inevitable eventuality that many should try to find release through suicide. Only those whose hearts have turned to stone can bury their pain and count their days in the hope of a future.

What is the meaning of this tragedy? Is it to be called just punishment or revengeful oppression?"[8]

Bhai Parmanand had recorded about the dull life of the Cellular Jail in these words: "This is the endless monotony of the life of this jail, which convicts have to undergo for days, months, and years or even a lifetime. There is absolutely no change or variety, for variety would mean pleasure and that is a thing prohibited in the jail code. The love for life, however, keeps a man alive in spite of all this and he even learns to go through this life with cheerfulness."[9]

Savarkar, accepting this monotonous life, observes: "In a prison, what happens on the first day happens always, if nothing worse happens. In fact, it seems to be the essence of prison discipline to avoid all novelty and all change. Like specimens and curios in a museum, here we are, each exactly in the same place and same position, belted and labelled with the same numbers with more or less just about us…"[10]

The prison life in the Cellular Jail became unbearable for the political prisoners. Bar fetters, handcuffs, standing handcuffs, penal diet, solitary confinement, and all sorts of punishment were imposed to demoralise them. Their life in solitary confinement added with hard labour and frequent punishments for minor indiscipline created unrest among them. They began to show strong resistance against the jail officials. One such incident has been described in most of the memoirs, which finally led to the first strike of the political prisoners of the Cellular Jail.

Nandgopal, editor of the *Swaraj* of Allahabad, was a strong-built person. When he was yoked to the oil mill, he refused to complete the fixed quota of work and even ignored the orders of the petty officers. Unlike the other political prisoners, he took his own time to finish his lunch and went to his cell for rest without showing any concern for completing his assigned task. He somehow managed to grind 15 lbs of oil instead of the fixed quota of 30 lbs. The jail officials made all possible efforts to threaten him with dire consequences, but he did not show any concern for their inhuman method of harassment. This situation continued for a month, which finally made the jail officials come to some sort of compromise with Nandgopal. He was asked to grind the full quota of oil for four days continuously to get released from the oil mill.[11]

Nandgopal's strong resistance against the jail officials inspired the inmates of the Cellular Jail to defy the authorities and go on a general strike. Political prisoners refused to work at the oil mill. As expected, this was followed by severe punishments. Barin Ghosh recalls, "Punishment continued unabated. When all kinds of fetters had been tried one by one, we were at last confined to cells. This latter affair also had a variety of forms. The ordinary convicts, when confined, could come downstairs to have their bath and meal. There was also no restriction on their talking to each other. But regarding ourselves, the orders were that we should not talk to each other and that anybody found speaking to us would be punished. So, although it was separate confinement in name, it was, in reality, solitary confinement. Many of us had to spend three months or more in this state."[12]

Suicide of Indu Bhushan Roy

The authorities resorted to all kinds of inhuman methods to put pressure on the political prisoners. Indu Bhushan Roy, a young political prisoner convicted under the Manicktola Bomb Case, could not tolerate the humiliation he had to undergo. As a result, he committed suicide on 29th April 1912 by hanging himself with a rope made of his own cloth. The authorities tried their level best to prove "that the deceased had developed a hallucination about his being killed by Noni Gopal Mukherjee and Ganesh Damodar Savarkar because these two persons believed that he had given some information about them to the authorities. It was on account of the fear of these two prisoners that he killed himself."[13]

One of the important documents is available in the form of a news article on the martyrdom of Indu Bhushan Roy published in the newspaper *Maharatta*, Poona, dated 28th July 1912 with the caption 'A Political Prisoner's Suicide in the Andamans'.[6] An extract of the same is reproduced below:

The suicide of one of the political prisoners named Indu Bhushan Roy throws a lurid light upon the whole situation regarding the treatment of political offenders in the Andamans. At 1 o'clock in the morning of 29th April last, he was found hanging in his cell by one of the warders during his rounds. An alarm was raised. The jailor hastened to the spot; the matter was telephoned four or five times, and a police orderly was sent to the Medical Superintendent's bungalow, which is situated only a few hundred yards from the jail building. We are informed that no response came before 8 o'clock the next morning. In the meantime, a Madrasi Hospital Assistant was sent for, but when he arrived, the body was found stiff and cold. The next morning, when the Superintendent, the District Magistrate, and the Police came to investigate, the jailor, Barry, gave his own version of the affair. Now, we would like to ask a question or two in this connection. Why did Indu

Bhushan commit suicide? If he was tired of prison life, one would expect that he would have committed suicide long ago, for he had already been in the Andamans for over three years. Was there nothing in anything that had happened recently in connection with him to account for his taking this fatal step? Was it not rather the act of a desperate man to whom life had become insupportable in the condition in which he found himself? Is it or is it, not the case that on the afternoon of the 28th April, only a few hours before his suicide, Indu Bhushan desired to see the jailor and was taken to his office, and there did he not, in the most entreating terms, request the jailor to change his work, as he was engaged in making white flax out of the 'rambash' plant? Did he not say to the jailor or, at any rate, address words to that effect, "See, my hands have become so blistered by the juice of the rambash that I cannot move my fingers freely, and it is so painful that I cannot get a wink of sleep the whole night. I cannot take my food to my mouth. The touch of 'dal' causes me so much pain that tears come to my eyes, and my food is left untouched. I will die of pain and starvation. Kindly change my work or allow me to go to the hospital for a few days to get my palms healed." Saying this, he stretched his hands to the full but met with a rebuff from the jailor. We will not reproduce the language that the jailor is reported to have used. Is it not the case that Indu Bhushan pleaded again, begging to be allowed to report himself personally and show his hands to the Medical Superintendent, but the jailor shouted, "You must carry out my orders." Then, after thinking for a couple of minutes, he again said, "All right, I will change your work," and ordered the warder in charge to engage Indu in the 'Kolu' oil mill from the next morning. Indu was so frightened that he told the jailor that he would simply die if he had to work in the 'Kolu' mill with those hands of his. The jailor was obdurate, and our information is that Indu was dismissed amid a shower of abusive language. This was the last straw on the camel's back, and before many hours, Indu was found dead, hanging in his cell.

Soon after the death of Indu Bhushan Roy, the insanity of Ullaskar Dutt, another prisoner of the Maniktala Bomb Case, created unrest among the political prisoners of the Cellular Jail. Ullaskar Dutt also became a victim of the inhumane tortures inflicted upon him in the Cellular Jail. These unbearable tortures led him to insanity.

Ullaskar Dutt has himself given a true picture of his life in the Cellular Jail. He wrote, "I was yoked to the oil mill similar to those we see in India for crushing oil from coconut and sesame. It is the bullock that is made to run the grinding mill in India. And even the bullock cannot turn out more than 16 lbs. of mustard seed oil during the day. In the Andaman jail, men were yoked to the handle of the turning wheel instead of bullocks, and it was imposed upon them to yield by their hard day's work 80 lbs. of coconut oil. Three prisoners were yoked to the handle of one mill. And they had to work continuously from morning to evening with a brief interval for their bath and morning meal. The interval actually given to us came to no more than a few minutes. We were made to run around the oil mill, unlike the beast, which could plod on slowly. We had the fear in our hearts that, otherwise, we would not be completing our daily quota of oil. If any one of us was found to slacken his pace, the Jamadar was in attendance to belabour him with his big stick. If that bludgeoning did not hasten the pace, there was another way of compelling him to do so. He was tied hand and foot to the handle of the turning wheel, and others were ordered to run at full speed. Then, the poor man was dragged along the ground like a man tied to the chariot wheel. His body was scratched all over, and blood came out from it. His head was knocked on the floor and was bruised. I have seen with my own eyes the effect of this mode of getting work done. What man can make of man? These words of the poet escaped my lips after watching the process and its torture. When I came back to my cell in the evening, I found myself completely washed out by the process. I was not sure that I would be alive the following morning to continue that harrowing work. Yet I remained alive and did the work all right during the day. For years together, it went on like this without respite and without a change of work. At last, a day came when I was ordered abroad. But the change was no better than from the frying pan into the fire. For I was sent to work in a district in a factory of bricks. I had to run for the whole day, to and fro, carrying bricks that were wet and not baked yet in the fire. This work was exhausting enough for an ordinary labourer…"[14]

At last, Ullaskar Dutt refused to work anymore. As a result of this, severe punishments followed. He was handcuffed and put in his cell continuously for a week. This state of affairs finally made him insane. His painful cries filled the atmosphere. Barin writes, "On that day, the real nature of a prison revealed itself to us. There was no hope for anyone to keep body and soul together and return to his country. Some would die by hanging; others would die by going mad. So, we asked ourselves, why should we tamely accept suffering if death was the only end."[15] Later, he was sent to Madras Lunatic Asylum in January 1913.

Voices of Revolutionaries

Meanwhile, the isolation of the Andamans was no longer a concern for the political prisoners. They found solutions to their problem and decided to inform the leaders in mainland India about the inhumane treatment of prisoners by the jail officials. Hoti Lal Varma was the first to dare it. He somehow managed to send a secret letter to the Bengal leader Surendranath Banerjee, giving the details of the inhumane treatment meted out to the political prisoners in the Cellular Jail. Surendranath Banerjee published the letter in *Bengalee* in its issues on 4th, 8th and 20th September 1911. This was followed by the publication of an extract of this letter in the *Tribune* of Lahore in its issue on 3rd May 1912.

After this news appeared in the newspapers, the Government decided to ascertain the facts behind the allegations. The Chief Commissioner of Andamans, in his false reply dated 30th May 1912, justifying the works being assigned to the political prisoners, wrote, "I have no doubt that according to the Bengalee's communicant, the only labour for the *seditionist* should be clerical work; this, however, it is obvious, could not be allowed. It is probable that none of these prisoners had ever done any manual labour or any other than clerical or scholastic work, and perhaps petty trading, prior to their arrival in the Andamans."[16]

Meanwhile, *Amrit Bazar Patrika* also published an article on the plight of political prisoners in the Cellular Jail. But the matter was not given due consideration, and the file was closed with the concluding remarks by R.H.C. Craddock, the Home member of the Governor-General in Council, that "there is no indication that these men are being treated in any way, which can give rise to reasonable complaint."[17]

General Strike of the Political Prisoners

The suicide of Indu Bhushan Roy and the insanity of Ullaskar Dutt, along with the unbearable tortures in the Cellular Jail, made other political prisoners very desperate. They decided not to do any work unless some special arrangement was made for them. They demanded three things: proper food, release from labour, and freedom to associate with each other. During this period, a new batch of political prisoners consisting of Nani Gopal Mukherjee, Pulin Das, and others arrived at the Cellular Jail. They also joined the general strike of the political prisoners. The agitating political prisoners were locked up in different cells, each separated from the others by four or five cells, in order to prevent them from talking to each other. Some of the prisoners were sent outside the jail for work.

Nani Gopal Mukherjee and Nand Gopal were sent to Viper Jail in order to break the spirit of others. Nani Gopal was brought back to Cellular Jail after four days as he went on a hunger strike in Viper Jail. Gradually, all the prisoners ended their strike except Nani Gopal Mukherjee. Under such a situation, the Government ordered Dr. Percy Lukis, Director of Indian Medical Services, to proceed to the Andamans to investigate the matter. However, no reports on the visit of Dr. Lukis were submitted. It can be reasonably presumed that there was some form of agreement between the political prisoners and the settlement officers regarding the allotment of work to prisoners. Finally, Nani Gopal ended his hunger strike after seventy-two days on 6th December 1912.[18]

However, Nani Gopal was again engaged in the oil mill. He was also segregated from others on the grounds that he *is only eighteen years of age and others are spoiling him.* But Nani Gopal's refusal to accept all such orders followed with repressive measures once again. When he declined to wash his clothes, he was given a sackcloth to wear. On his refusal, it was forcibly sewn upon his body, which he scratched during the night. He was put in chains but he managed to unlock it in the night. He asked the authorities to treat him as a political prisoner, but the Chief Commissioner informed him that this status would never be given to him. He was ordered to be put in the flogging stand for whipping but this also did not have any effect on him. Although, at the last moment this was withdrawn. He was shifted to another prison, where he again went on a hunger strike. He was brought back to the Cellular Jail, and on the request of Savarkar and others, he finally broke his hunger strike on 5th October 1913.[19]

Bomb Factory in the Settlement?

Meanwhile, in August 1913, the authorities were alarmed at the information provided by Lal Mohan Saha, a loyal prisoner to the settlement officers, regarding the working of a bomb factory in the settlement by the political prisoners working outside the jail.[20] There were also rumours that a bomb was found in an adjoining brook, and letters containing the plan of hiring boats to take the prisoners across the seas were intercepted. All prisoners working outside the prison were ordered to be removed from outside work and sent back to the jail. An Inspector of Explosives was called for investigation. All this made them alert, and thorough searches were made in each and every house of the colony by a party of European Officers. But all these exercises went in vain. Nothing could be found to substantiate the news. Barin Ghosh and Upendranath Banerjee, in their memoirs, also dismissed this news as baseless. Barin Ghosh had mentioned his interaction with Sir Reginald

Craddock during his visit to Port Blair. "We thought here was our most well-wishing patron. This time something would certainly be done for us. But no sooner had we begun to narrate our woes to him than he revealed himself in his true colours and told us point-blank: *You were hatching a conspiracy while outside.*" However, a simple sentence of Savarkar, while mentioning the 'noise and fury' of that particular day, points out a different theory. He writes… "And it was not altogether without foundation."[21] The records of the British are silent on the issue, and as such, it can be presumed that there was a conspiracy to prepare bombs, but its exact nature is not known.

The protest in the press, the rising of public opinion against the atrocities in the Cellular Jail, the general strike by the prisoners, and the news of a conspiracy of preparing bombs by the political prisoners brought pressure upon the Government of India and the Home Minister, Sir Reginald Craddock, paid a visit to the Andamans in October 1913.

Craddock, during his stay in the settlement, met and heard all those political prisoners who had any complaints to make. Five political prisoners, Savarkar, Barindra Kumar Ghosh, Hrishikesh Kanjilal, Nand Gopal, and Sudhir Kumar Sarkar, submitted their representations to him. The prisoners demanded, among other things, remission of sentences, as was granted to prisoners in Indian jails. Craddock's visit did not bring changes in the lives of the political prisoners until April 1914. As a result, they decided to go on strike for the third time. Savarkar writes, "In the manifesto about the strike, the prisoners had made three principal demands: (1) That, as political prisoners, we should have all the privileges of the first class, (2) that we should, otherwise, be put in the category of ordinary prisoners, given all the facilities accorded to them and the periodical visit to this jail be permitted to members of our families; or (3) we should be sent back to serve our term in the jails of India, so that we may get all the facilities of that jail life, including a reduction in the period of the sentence on a certificate of good behaviour."[22]

Except for one or two, all political prisoners stopped work. Once again, repressive measures were adopted to crush the zeal of the revolutionaries.

They were locked up under strict supervision, but this did not prevent them from communicating with each other through a device. According to Savarkar, "It went on splendidly for a long time. We had shackles on our feet, and they had manacles on their hands. We rang them on the bars of the doors according to a particular code. And the news went round not only through the three or four adjoining rooms but through all the stories of the nearby blocks. And in this mode of communication, there was no scope for the warders to betray us. We carried on the communication in English to start with. My brother remodelled it into Nagri. Thus, we had a pure Swadeshi telegraphic code and message to run through the whole building. We conveyed our messages through this device to all the political prisoners in our jail, and whatever we proposed to do, we did, all as one man."[23] During the general strike, a few prisoners resorted to a hunger strike, but Savarkar managed to convince them, except Nani Gopal, to put an end to their hunger strike. Later, Savarkar also declared a three-day hunger strike to persuade Nani Gopal. Finally, Nani Gopal agreed to break his fast.

Such a state of affairs in the Andamans compelled the authorities to issue a notification accepting their demands. It was decided, among others, that all prisoners on term sentences shall be repatriated to their respective jails in India. Prisoners with life sentences will be detained in prison for a period of fourteen years. Based on their good behaviour during their incarceration, they will be set free for light work. It was also assured that good food and decent clothing would be provided to the prisoners.

These promises satisfied the prisoners, and hence, they called off their strike. In pursuance of this decision, the first batch consisting of eighteen political prisoners with term sentences was repatriated to India between May and September 1914.[24] The concessions obtained from the authorities made the life of the remaining political prisoners of the Cellular Jail a little better than before.

In the next few years, Ghadarites convicted in the Lahore Conspiracy Case and other cases relating to the Ghadar movement were deported to the

Cellular Jail. Political prisoners from Bengal and other areas also joined the political prisoners of the Andamans. The life of a political prisoner during this period was also filled with bitter experiences like those of their predecessors.

The political prisoners of this period, namely Trailokya Nath Chakravorti, Bhai Parmanand, and Prithvi Singh Azad, have written their autobiographies, which provide us with important information from 1916 to 1920. These accounts give us a general idea that the authorities adopted two different ways of treatment. On the one hand, they gave concessions to the old batch of political prisoners but, contrary to this, followed a very tough policy towards the fresh batch of political prisoners of the period. This state of affairs in the Cellular Jail compelled the new arrivals to raise their voice against the authorities. They were demanding the same privileges that were provided to a few of the political prisoners. Trailokya Nath Chakravorti, describing this situation, observed, "This caused a split in the rank of political prisoners, and they were divided into *moderates and extremists*. The Savarkar brothers, Barin Babu (Ghosh), and a few others, who came long before us and suffered the same miseries, had wrung some concessions and privileges after a hard fight and were now favourites of the superintendent, so they were not prepared to renounce them and join us in our struggle. Only Pulin Babu (Das), who neither liked to create trouble nor tried to be a favourite of the superintendent, used to tell us, 'What is the use of making trouble and thereby incurring a new penalty? Rather, carry on somehow so that you may get out of jail and again serve your motherland.

However, the *extremist group* decided to violate the disciplinary rules of the prison by way of active protest against the treatment of the prisoners. The *moderate group* held aloof."[25]

The *extremist group* violated jail rules and disobeyed the orders of the authorities. The prisoners were tired of their lives filled with suffering and torture. They refused to do any work and protested against the inhuman conditions of the Cellular Jail. Again, flogging, confinement in cells, bar fetters, handcuffs, and a penal diet were imposed on the political prisoners for minor violations of prison discipline. The Ghadarites were men of strong build, and as such, they showed strong resistance against the malevolent treatment of the prisoners.

Martyrdom of Baba Bhan Singh and Pandit Ram Rakha

Describing one such incident, Prithvi Singh Azad gave this story in his autobiography, *Kranti Path Ka Pathik*, "One day, Bishen Singh (wrestler) annoyed the jail authorities. The superintendent ordered the officials to have him beaten up thoroughly. The prison warders advanced towards Bishen Singh with sticks in their hands. Bishen Singh had fetters on his feet. He tied the rope of the fetters to his waist and threw a loud challenge in Punjabi, 'Come on, whosoever wants death, I shall catch hold of your legs and tear you up into two.' Bishen Singh, of giant stature, was standing there, anger personified. He was six feet three inches tall and weighed 250 lbs. On seeing the infuriated giant, the Jamadars were convinced that whoever got caught in his hands would not come out alive. Barrie Baba was shouting from outside the enclosure, *catch him and beat him*, but who would dare go into the jaws of death? Barrie felt that discretion was the better part of valour and quietly left." [26]

The jail officials adopted repressive measures to tackle the situation. Bhan Singh, a Ghadar hero, was so mercilessly beaten up by the jail officials that he courted martyrdom in 1917. Chattar Singh, who had assaulted the superintendent, was given solitary confinement with fetters and handcuffs for five years.

About a hundred prisoners joined the strike. Two of the political prisoners submitted a memorandum to the authorities, but they did not show any concern for their demands. This made them furious. As per their plans, they resorted to a hunger strike, in which they were joined by Sohan Singh Bhakna and Prithvi Singh Azad, among others. Finally, after twelve days, the authorities surrendered to their demands. However, Prithvi Singh Azad continued his hunger strike for two more weeks until he was moved by the appeal of his fellow prisoners.[27] Finally, the general strike ended only after the authorities agreed to provide some concessions.

However, life continued to be very tough in the Cellular Jail. Pandit Ram Rakha, a prisoner of the Mandalay Conspiracy Case, resorted to a hunger strike when the jail authorities interfered with his right to wear the sacred thread. He breathed his last in 1919. Jyotish Chandra Pal, a prisoner of the Baleswar Case, became entirely mad as a result of cruelties in the Cellular Jail.

Repatriation of Political Prisoner - 1921

In order to put an end to all such troubles in the Cellular Jail and criticism all around, the authorities transferred the superintendent and the notorious jailor of the Cellular Jail. In addition, the Government of India Act 1919 was passed, and a general amnesty was declared, which was supplemented by the decision to repatriate the political prisoners of the Cellular Jail. Meanwhile, the Indian Jails Committee of 1919-20, led by Sir Alexander Cardew, Member of the Executive Council, Madras, was appointed to investigate the Indian prison system. The Committee visited the Cellular Jail in January 1920 and brought relief to the political prisoners. They were permitted to write letters within three months and keep the sacred thread. All these concessions were granted to the prisoners, but at the cost of many lives.

At last, most of the political prisoners, numbering about a hundred and fifty, were either released or repatriated to Indian jails in 1920. However, thirty political prisoners, including the Savarkar brothers, were still lodged in the Cellular Jail. On the basis of the recommendations of the Indian Jails Committee, Sir William Vincent, Home Secretary to the Government of India, declared on the 11th March 1921 in the Central Legislative Assembly to abolish the penal settlement from the Andamans. Accordingly, all the remaining political prisoners were released or repatriated by 1921.

Thus concluded the first phase of life in the penal settlement of Andamans. However, despite this decision of the Government, the Mappilla prisoners of the Malabar region were deported to the penal settlement of Andaman. This has been dealt with in detail in the previous chapter.

The Reopening of Cellular Jail

In order to restrain the growing revolutionary activities in India, the Government of India reopened the Cellular Jail for the political prisoners. About four hundred prisoners sentenced for taking part in various revolutionary activities, mainly in Bengal and Punjab, were deported to the Cellular Jail. One of the prisoners, Bejoy Kumar Sinha of the Lahore Conspiracy Case, in his autobiography, *In Andamans-the Indian Bastille*, narrated every aspect of life during the period.

The life in the Cellular Jail during 1932-38 remained more or less the same. Only the notorious jailor David Barry was not there to make jail life more terrible. Sinha experienced prison life from June 1933 to September 1937 and has given minute observations of each and every incident in the Cellular Jail. While mentioning his views on the life of his predecessors in the Cellular Jail, he observed, "The suffering and privations that were forced on them had no limits. Their number was about a hundred and as has been said earlier, they were accommodated in two different yards as Division Two and Division Three prisoners. The jail, as its name signified, was composed entirely of cellular blocks. The huge brick building was old and dilapidated with crevices in its walls everywhere. In all yards, the roofs leaked with extremely rough, uncemented, damp floors. Even in the daytime, it remained dark. Passing their day in these unsanitary and unlighted cells, many of the comrades had fallen victim to recurring malaria. The 'C' class comrades lying on their wooden boards on the cold floors of their cell were exposed to mosquito bites all through their sleepless nights. These tropical Islands were known for their heavy annual mortality from malaria. During the long hours of the night, the C-class prisoners felt extremely restless.

Despite repeated requests, lanterns were not allowed. These were considered articles of luxury. Dozing on their bare wooden sleep boards, the prisoners often woke up startled, as there were numerous scorpions and other insects inside the damp crevices, and these frequently crawled out in the dark and sometimes bit the prisoners. At such times, the only help that could be afforded was by the corridor warder who used to be on duty with the lantern. But these people took their cue from the ways and methods of their superiors..." [28]

The first batch, consisting of twenty-five political prisoners, was sent to the penal settlement of Andamans on 15th August 1932. By 1933, more than a hundred political prisoners from Bengal were deported to the Cellular Jail. In the following years, more political prisoners from Bengal, Orissa, Punjab, and Delhi were also deported. By 12th May 1933, the number of political prisoners was one hundred and twelve.[29]

The authorities did not keep the assurances they promised from time to time. The harsh treatment of political prisoners continued without any intervention. They were yoked to the oil mill and engaged in coir pounding. Severe punishments were awarded for minor indiscipline. Handcuffs and fetters were part of their daily life. Prison life almost remained the same as it was for the first and second batches. They were disgusted with their lives and finally decided to go on a hunger strike to obtain facilities of nutritious food, proper clothing, books, writing material and light in the cells, among others. Seven political prisoners, namely Bimalendu Kumar Dasgupta, Sushil Kumar Dasgupta, Probodh Chandra Roy, Prabir Goswami, Bimalendu Chakraborty, Barindra Kumar Ghosh, took the initiative in this regard.[30] They resorted to a hunger strike on 3rd January 1933, but this was withdrawn after the assurance given by the superintendent to look into the matter positively.

Hunger Strike and Martyrdom of Mahavir, Mohit and Mankrishna

Three months passed, but no facilities were provided. The political prisoners also submitted a representation demanding privileges for themselves. Being unheard, they decided to go on a hunger strike on 12th May 1933. Thus began the hunger strike, which continued for forty-five days. Describing the pre and post-hunger strike situation, Ram Chandra Das, a political prisoner convicted under the Charmugharia Post Office Robbery Case, in an interview, had this to say, "My prison life's experiences were very tough. In Cellular Jail also no facilities were provided to us. The food that was given to us was the worst. There was no light, no newspaper, no permission for moving outside, etc. We requested many times to improve the quality of food and to provide light for us. But no action was taken. Then we decided to achieve facilities through a hunger strike."[31]

Soon after the launching of the hunger strike by the political prisoners, the authorities started force-feeding in order to keep the hunger strikers alive. On the very first day of the force-feeding, Mahabir Singh, a close associate of Shaheed Bhagat Singh, convicted under the Lahore Conspiracy Case, died. Mahabir Singh refused to take food and resisted when the tube was being inserted into his stomach to pour the milk. He died on the midnight of 17th May 1933 at 12.24 a.m. The Chief Commissioner of Andaman and Nicobar Islands, in his telegram to the Government of India, informed, "Post-mortem examination shows that death was due to shock and not to any carelessness in the administration of food. Three other convicts show signs of serious weakness, but the condition of the remainder is quite satisfactory."[32]

The news reached the mainland across the seas. Rabindranath Tagore sent a telegram to the hunger strikers requesting them to call off their strike. However, there was a strong debate in the Council of State on the causes of the death of Mahabir Singh. Vinanyak Vithal Kalikar, a member of the Council of State, questioned, "We have seen people who go on hunger strike surviving for many days, and here what do we find? That a healthy and strong man goes on strike only for four days, and he collapses?" [33]

Mankrishna Nama Das,[34] a political prisoner convicted under the Netrokona-Sarikonda Action Case, died on 26th May 1933. During the hunger strike, he developed signs of pneumonia, which finally caused his death. The Chief Commissioner of the Andaman and Nicobar Islands tried his level best to assure the Government of India that "his death was due to natural causes and was in no way accelerated by his abstinence from food for one day."[35] Thirty-nine political prisoners were still on a hunger strike. Mohit Mohan Maitra, a political prisoner sentenced under the Arms Act, died on 28th May 1933 due to *double lobar pneumonia*. They both died due to force-feeding, but the Government of India denied this allegation.

Following the martyrdom of three political prisoners during the hunger strike, there was huge resentment all over the country, not only among the Indians but also in the government machinery. A protest meeting was organised on 30th May 1933 in Calcutta, which demanded an enquiry into the circumstances leading to the deaths of three hunger strikers.[36] The Chief Commissioner requested one extra assistant surgeon to deal with the situation. The press continued to criticise the Government for its attitude towards the hunger strikers and methods to deal with the situation. The Government of India deputed Lt. Colonel Barker, Inspector-General of Prisons of Punjab, who had experience in dealing with hunger strikers, to Port Blair to look into the ground situation. At the time of his visit to the Cellular Jail, fifty-five prisoners were on a hunger strike. In addition, twenty others refused to work but continued to take food.

Colonel Barker used his last weapon against the political prisoners to assess their strength. Sinha recalls, "That day, he ordered drinking water to be stopped. For twenty-four hours, none of the hunger strikers was given a single drop of water. Some of them were already lying in a precarious condition, and there were others who had blood pressure trouble. At the close of the period, two or three of them were moved to the hospital in an unconscious state."[37] Finally, Colonel Barker came to the conclusion that the strikers are very firm in their resolve, and nothing can frighten them to withdraw the strike.

At last, the Government surrendered before the strikers by accepting their demands. The strike was called off on 26th June 1933, forty-six days after its commencement. Sinha recalls, "Those of us who were in 'C' class were henceforth to be provided with bedsheets, mosquito nets, pillows and pillowcases, bathing towels, and wooden bedsteads. We could also, at our own cost purchase, shorts and vests. As for diet, the quality of rice, flour, and vegetables was improved. Provision was also made to vary dal daily and issue potatoes and onions as extra vegetables. Fish also was to be supplied whenever available, on alternate days. Kitchens were entrusted to us for proper arrangements and supervision. We were allowed to purchase some food articles barring luxuries… Maintaining the classification of the Indian jails, a new class for us was formed here. A term was coined for us - P.I., i.e., permanently incarcerated prisoners. We were so-called because, unlike ordinary Andaman prisoners, we were to be confined permanently within the Cellular Jail walls. For the ordinary convicts, the practice was three months of confinement, after the expiry of which they were taken out, to live and work on the settlement.

For our recreation, arrangements were made for both indoor and outdoor games. Carrom board, chess, playing cards, and ping-pong were provided. For outdoor exercise, we were given football and volleyball. Parallel and horizontal bars were fixed up for physical exercise.

What made our life most intolerable previously was the complete absence of any scope for intellectual and cultural development. Of the new facilities that we obtained, valued most, were those pertaining to this sphere. We had now the right to subscribe to magazines, both Indian and foreign, that were on the Government's prescribed list. We could also receive books in parcels from our friends and relatives, and also purchase them from our money deposited at the jail gate. The Government was to provide us with furniture for a prison library and reading room. Periodically books were also to be purchased by them. Lights were now being supplied in all cells until ten at night. At Government expense, the weekly overseas editions of *Statesman*, *Sanjibani* and *Bangabasi*, as well as the Hindi edition of the latter, were to be supplied.

All the punishments were withdrawn. Our Division II comrades went back to their yards, but henceforth we were not deprived of their association. Under new regulations, we could freely meet them as inter-yard communication was allowed. Our previous lock-up time had made any recreation in the evening hours impossible. Now the time was altered to 8 p.m."[38]

However, this attitude of the officials towards the political prisoners lasted only for a brief period, and once again the old story of torture and harassment was repeated in the Cellular Jail. On the other hand, the transportation of political prisoners continued until June 1937. During the next three years, there were clashes between the jail officials and the prisoners. There was a large number of prisoners who were suffering from one or other diseases. The deterioration in the quality of food, restrictions on communication, and denial of providing newspapers, books, and journals, restrictions on writing letters or meeting with relatives compelled them to raise their voices against the authorities.

The political prisoners submitted a representation to Sir Henry Craik, the Home Secretary to the Government of India, during his visit to the Andamans in 1936, requesting him to consider their repeated request for repatriation from the Andamans and uniform classification of political prisoners with equal facilities. On the contrary, Mr. Craik described the Andamans as a 'prisoner's paradise'. This comment by Craik met with strong criticism, and members of the Legislative Assembly demanded to be deputed to see the ground reality for themselves. The Government was compelled to depute two members of the Assembly, consisting of Raizada Hansraj, a member of the

Congress party, and M. Yamin Khan, a Muslim League Member, in October 1936. The political prisoners submitted to them a memorandum dated 13th October 1936, signed by two hundred and thirty-nine prisoners, describing in detail the sufferings and hardships of their prison life. A supplementary memorandum dated 18th October 1936 was also handed over to the two members in response to Craik's false statements in the Assembly regarding the 'health of political prisoners'.[39]

Last Hunger Strike and Repatriation

By July 1937, the Indian National Congress, which won the General Elections of 1936, formed governments in seven legislative assemblies. The Indian National Congress had been demanding the repatriation of political prisoners from the Andamans for a long time. Their cause was also supported by the non-official members of the other political parties, and numerous questions were asked in the Legislative Assembly about the inhuman treatment of the political prisoners of the Cellular Jail.

This was the time when the Indian masses were agitating for civil liberties. The political prisoners of Andamans, in an attempt to show their concern for their fellow countrymen, submitted a detailed representation dated 9th July 1937 to the Viceroy demanding the "declaration of general amnesty to all detenues, State prisoners and all convicted political prisoners; withdrawal of orders of internment; of a ban on exiles; of restrictions on workers and the repeal of all repressive laws."[40] The representation was followed by an ultimatum dated 18th July 1937 cautioning the Government that if these demands were not agreed to by 24th July 1937, the political prisoners would be forced to resort to a hunger strike on or about the same date. On 23rd July, they again addressed a representation to the Government, giving them a last chance to consider their demands. All of them were very firm and ready to sacrifice their lives for the betterment of their companions' lives. On the other hand, the Chief Commissioner visited the jail on 23rd July and informed them of the decision of the Government of India that "the Government had no desire to effect a wholesale release or repatriation and also cautioned them about the consequential punishments to the hunger strikers."[41] As decided, the last hunger strike of the Cellular Jail was launched by one hundred and eighty-seven prisoners on 24th July 1937.

In order to minimise the risk factor among the political prisoners as a result of a hunger strike, Sinha observes, "A new order was issued to keep us all open during the daytime in our corridors. Hot water was supplied in plenty for bathing. Extra blankets were issued. For the daily feeds, glucose, brandy and eggs were liberally used. By these steps, the authorities did succeed to some extent in checking the pace of general deterioration, but they failed in their main objective. The number of serious cases increased every day. The hospital was packed up. The whole of yard number five was transformed into an additional hospital."[42]

The hunger strike by the political prisoners created an unprecedented scene all over the country. The Government was unable to deal with the rising public pressure at various forums. A huge protest rally was organised in Bengal. Fazlul Huq, the Premier of Bengal, sent a telegram to the political prisoners requesting them to call off their strike. The Government of India, via their communique dated 12th August 1937, observed a favourable response, "... the Government of India desire to make it plain that so long as the hunger strike continues, they are unable to give any consideration to the demands put forward by the prisoners or by other persons on their behalf." Following this, leaders like Pandit Nehru, Bulabhai Desai, and Mahatma Gandhi, on behalf of Rabindranath Tagore and the Congress Working Committee, advised the strikers to abandon the strike. The strikers, 'touched by the nationwide appeal', finally decided to call off their strike on 30th August 1937 after thirty-six days.[43]

Immediately after this, the repatriation of political prisoners from Andaman began in September 1937. The last batch of political prisoners was repatriated on 18th January 1938, thus marking the end of the struggle of political prisoners in the Cellular Jail.

No one recognised that this marked the end of an era, leading to a dark chapter of terror and suffering as the Andaman and Nicobar Islands fell under the occupation of the Japanese Imperial Forces from 1942 to 1945.

NOTES AND REFERENCES

1. Sinha, Bejoy Kumar, *In Andamans, the Indian Bastille*, People's Publishing House, New Delhi, 1939, pp. 10-11.

2. Majumdar, pp. 148-9.

3. Savarkar, Vinayak Damodar, *The Story of My Transportation for Life*, English translation of the original Marathi book, *Majhi Janmathep* by V.N. Naik, pp. 124-5.

4. Majumdar, pp. 155-6.

5. Savarkar, p. 197.

6. Majumdar, pp. 158-9.

7. *Ibid*, p. 160.

8. Aggarwal, p. 206.

9. *Ibid.*

10. Keer, Dhananjya, *Veer Savarkar*, Popular Prakashan, Bombay, 1988, p. 113.

11. Majumdar, pp. 165-6.

12. *Ibid*, p. 167.

13. Mathur, p. 82.

14. Majumdar, pp. 184-5.

15. Aggarwal, p. 131.

16. *Ibid*, p. 136.

17. Majumdar, p. 77.

18. Mathur, pp. 83-84.

19. Mathur, pp. 84-5.

20. Majumdar, p. 192.

21. *Ibid*, p. 200.

22. *Ibid*, p. 216.

23. *Ibid*, p. 216.

24. Aggarwal, p. 154.

25. Majumdar, p. 238.

26. Aggarwal, p. 211.

27. Majumdar, p. 243.

28. Sinha, p. 20.

29. Promod Kumar, *Hunger strike in Andamans*, Martyrs' Memorial and Freedom Struggle Research Centre, Lucknow, 2004, pp. 9-10.

30. *Ibid*, p. 11.

31. Interview of *Ram Charan Das*, Martyrs' Memorial and Freedom Struggle Research Centre, Lucknow.

32. Promod, p. 15.

33. *Ibid*, p. 16.

34. The name of Man Krishna Nama Das has been erroneously mentioned as Mohan Kishore Nama Das in the Mukti-Tirtha Andaman, a book published by the Ex-Andaman Political Prisoners' Fraternity Circle and other printed materials. Promod Kumar, who has done extensive research on the hunger strike of the Cellular Jail based on the records available with the India Office and Records, London, indicates that there was no political prisoner in the Cellular Jail whose name was Mohan Kishore or Mohan Kishore Namodas. During the hunger strike, other than Mahavir Singh, Man Krishna Nam Das, and Mohit Mohan Maitra courted

martyrdom. For more details, please refer to the notes and references of Promod Kumar, No. 95, p.33.

35. Promod, p. 16.

36. *Ibid*, p. 17.

37. Sinha, Ujjawal, p. 35.

38. *Ibid*, pp. 39-41.

39. Majumdar, 303-8.

40. *Ibid*, p. 309.

41. Aggarwal, p. 281.

42. Sinha, p. 146.

43. Aggarwal, p. 285.

CHAPTER VII

The Reign of Terror - Island Under Japanese

The Andaman and Nicobar Islands are the only part of India that not only witnessed the inhuman atrocities by the British but also endured the barbaric tortures meted out to the locals by the Japanese Occupying Force during the Second World War.

The Japanese Imperial Force had occupied the Andaman and Nicobar Islands during World War II from 23rd March 1942 to 7th October 1945. During their reign, they killed hundreds of islanders in the most brutal manner because of the Allied bombings of the Islands. Many islanders (mostly educated) were rounded up on charges of espionage for the British. Many persons were picked up from their houses and arrested on the pretext of spy case charges. They were confined and tortured in Block 6 of the Cellular Jail. Various forms of torture were inflicted on them, forcing them to confess to being spies for the British. Many died due to the unbearable forms of torture, and several others were killed and shot dead, and their bodies were buried in mass graves at far-off places to cover up their war crimes against the civilian population.

The fall of Singapore was a turning point in the history of World War II. This marked the opening of the entire Indian Ocean to the Japanese Imperial Force. It was thought that the Andaman would be the next target shortly, and realising that they could not defend the Islands, the British Indian Government decided to evacuate.

And they left behind the local settlers—men, women, children, convicts, and free citizens—at the mercy of the Japanese Invading Force.

The Japanese force took control of the Islands without facing any resistance from the locals. Contrary to expectations, they established friendly relations with the islanders in the beginning. Some locals believed that the occupation of the island by the Japanese force marked the end of British domination. However, the time was about to change soon when the so-called saviours turned oppressors.

Just after the landing, CF Waterfall, the then Chief Commissioner, along with other subordinate officers, was arrested and made Prisoner of War. Colonel Bucho, a Japanese Officer, was appointed as the Civil Governor. He released all prisoners imprisoned in the Cellular Jail. Shortly after the release of prisoners, the Japanese tortured Ooty, the Officer-in-Charge of the Wireless and Telegraph Office, brutally. He was taken to the Deputy Commissioner's bungalow, where he was repeatedly thrown down the stairs until he succumbed to his injuries. Earlier, on the night of the landing of Japanese forces, Ooty successfully blew up the Wireless and Telegraph Office as planned. It was earlier decided that in case of the fall of the Islands, Ooty would blow up the two installations, the Wireless and Telegraph Office, whereas Shri Durga Prasad, the Divisional Forest Officer, would blow up the Chatham Saw Mill and Marine workshop. However, Durga Prasad was intelligent enough and hence did not use the button to blow up the two installations, thus saving the islanders. History will always remember his contribution to the islanders.[1]

The Story of Sunny

BB Lall, author of 'A Regime of Fears and Tears', referring to Master Kesar Das, an eyewitness, narrated the story of Zulfiqar Ali, alias Sunny. He writes, according to Master Kesar Das, "around 1:40 p.m. on 24th March 1942, he saw a few Japanese soldiers wandering the streets of Aberdeen. Rumours spread that the soldiers were entering homes and taking whatever they wanted. When Zulfiqar Ali saw the Japanese soldiers, he took a double-barrel gun and fired at one of them. The Japanese soldiers became angry and began searching for Sunny. Meanwhile, sensing the danger, Sunny's family escaped through the back door of their house. The Japanese soldiers threw hand grenades, and in no time, Sunny's house and the area around were set on fire. The people living in Aberdeen were frightened, and finally, the local Police Chief, Shri Narayan Rao, convinced Sunny's family to hand him over; otherwise, the consequences would be unimaginable. The next day, Sunny was brought by the Japanese officers to the Netaji Club ground. The firing squad killed him in a brutal way. Sunny was buried in the corner of the Netaji Club Ground."[2]

In the same manner, A.G. Bird, Private Secretary to the then Chief Commissioner, was assassinated on 5th May 1942 by Japanese Officers. It is believed that Pushkar Bagchi, the then Chief Naval Intelligence Officer, had some grudge against Bird and settled the scores in a more barbaric way.[3]

False Spy Charges Cases

Within two weeks of the Japanese occupation, a branch of the Indian Independence League was formed with Dr. Diwan Singh as its President. The Japanese Governor also established a Peace Committee aimed at maintaining law and order and encouraging the islanders to accept the authority of the Japanese Imperial Force. Sewa Samities were formed to provide assistance to the islanders in times of distress. The Japanese, sensing the world war scenario, made all arrangements for the fortification of the island.

By the end of 1942, Allied forces began targeting Japanese ships, which angered the Japanese. Some released prisoners from Cellular Jail started spreading false espionage claims. On 21st January 1943, the Japanese began arresting innocent people under the pretext of espionage, filling the 6th block of Cellular Jail. Many were forced to confess to spying for the Allies. On 30th March 1943, seven persons—Narayan Rao, M.A. Khalique, V. Gopalkrishna, Chotey Singh, Attar Singh, Dr. Surendra Nath Nag, and Suba Khan were taken out of Cellular Jail. All of them were killed by the Firing Squad of the Japanese at Dugonabad village.

As time passed, the Allied air force increased its air raids, which frustrated the Japanese. Under these tense circumstances, the second spy case began on 23rd October 1943 with the arrest of Dr. Diwan Singh, an active member of the Indian Independence League, Peace Committee, and Punjabi Literary Society. His close associates like Durga Prasad, Dr. Sher Singh, Laxman Singh Sankhwa, Rama Krishna, Gurumurthy Khan Sahab Nawab Ali, Ratnam Babu, Prem Shankar Pandey, Daulat Ram, Hira Singh Chawla, Pokhar Singh Chawla Rahalkar, Shakarkandi, and others were arrested to undergo a severe trial followed by inhuman torture. Many were forced to confess to spying for the Allies. "A suspicion also grew among the Japanese that all English-knowing locals were spying against them and would never assist them in tracing out the real culprits."[4] Dr. Diwan Singh attained martyrdom on 14th January 1944. The Gurdwara Dr. Diwan Singh at Port Blair is a tribute to this great and noble person who lived and died for the islanders.

Arrival of Netaji and National Tricolour Hoisted

Meanwhile, Netaji Subhas Chandra Bose, while in exile, launched a heroic struggle to free India from British rule under the banner of the Provisional Government of Azad Hind. This effort was supported by the Japanese. The Japanese Prime Minister, on 6th November 1943, at the Assembly of Greater East Asiatic Nations in Tokyo, declared that the Andaman and Nicobar Islands would be transferred to the Provisional Government of Azad Hind. Soon after, Netaji Subhas Chandra Bose visited the Andaman Islands as the Head of the State of the Provisional Government of Azad Hind from 29th to 31st December 1943. Islanders gave him a warm welcome on his arrival, and a guard of honour was presented by Azad Hind volunteers. During his visit, he stayed at the former British Chief Commissioner's official residence on Ross Island, now renamed Netaji Subhas Chandra Bose Dweep. Netaji hoisted the tricolour for the first time on Indian Soil on 30th December 1943, declaring the Islands as the first Indian Territory to be freed from colonial rule. After raising the Indian tricolour, Netaji addressed the crowd at the historic Gymkhana Ground and announced that the Imperial Government of Japan had ceded the Andaman and Nicobar Islands to the Provisional Government of Azad Hind. Netaji also expressed his wish to visit the Andaman Islands, stay in the British Chief Commissioner's bungalow, and fly the tricolour, which finally materialised. Shri Ramakrishna, Chairman of the Indian Independence League, read out the welcome address at the Gymkhana Ground and contributed a sum of Rs. 10,000/- for the league activities.

In the words of Netaji, "Like the Bastille in Paris, which was liberated first in the French Revolution, setting free political prisoners, the Andamans where our patriots suffered is the first to be liberated in India's fight for independence...." Netaji's visit symbolised his promise that the Indian National Army (I.N.A.) would be on Indian soil by the end of 1943. Before leaving Port Blair, he visited the Browning Club, later known as Netaji Club, to meet members of the Indian Independence League.

Netaji appointed Colonel Loganathan as the Chief Commissioner of A&N Islands. However, he took charge in February 1944.

Within a month of the departure of Netaji from Port Blair, the island witnessed the worst-ever crime against humanity. Forty-four islanders were taken out of the Cellular Jail to a village called Homfraygunj, and all of them were shot dead and buried in a mass grave.

With the untiring effort of Shri Gauri Shankar Pandey and members of the Homfraygunj Martyrs' Memorial Committee, a memorial stands at the holy place. Similarly, a small park with Saat Saput Memorial has been erected near the Marine Circuit House in memory of the seven martyrs. Shri Madan Mohan Singh and other Committee members contributed immensely to setting up the memorial.

These martyrs' memorials stand as silent witnesses to the atrocities faced by the islanders. They compel us to reflect on a crucial question: who is to blame for the suffering inflicted upon the islanders during this dark period?

Dasgupta has an answer to this question; he remarked, "Given the picture of popular resentment in the Andamans regarding Bose's total failure in alleviating the suffering of the local population, why was the Browning Club, the seat of the Local Born association and the hub of social life of the local population, renamed as Netaji Club, soon after his visit?"

NOTES AND REFERENCES

1. B.B. Lall, A Regime of Fears and Tears, Farsight Publishers & Distributors, Delhi, 1992, Page 23

2. *Ibid*, pp. 26-28

3. *Ibid*, pp. 33-35

4. S.K. Narang, Under the Shadow of Death, Prime Publishers, Delhi, 1988, page 83

5. Jayant Dasgupta, Japanese in the Andaman & Nicobar Islands, Manas Publication, Delhi, 2002

CHAPTER VIII

Cellular Jail - Surviving History

The term 'Kala Pani' has become synonymous with transportation to the penal settlement of the Andaman Islands. According to some interpretations, the expression 'Kala Pani' is derived from the Sanskrit word 'Kal,' which means 'Time' or 'Death.' Thus, the term 'Kala Pani' translates to 'water of death' or 'a place of death', from which none returned. Indian revolutionaries and freedom fighters were condemned to Kala Pani to endure this severe punishment; however, they immortalised the Islands through their sacrifices.

Cellular Jail is not merely a relic of the colonial mindset, but it stands today as a silent testament to the sacrifices and sufferings endured by our patriots to achieve freedom. It is a pillar of our freedom movement as it housed our bravehearts in its solitary cells for over five decades during the British and Japanese regimes.

In spite of inhuman treatment, the four walls of the prison encouraged them to fight until their last breath and always kept their morale high. Though we did not show much kindness to preserve their memories post-independence, this legacy remained not only neglected but also utilised in ways that demeaned the stature of the great monument. Many would not agree with the statement, but this is a fact that is hard to believe. We may have many excuses and reasons to justify the situation of that time, considering the priorities post-independence.

Damage Caused by Earthquake and Utilisation of the Jail Building

The Cellular Jail had already suffered damage during the earthquake of June 1941. The roof of the original brick-built Central Tower fell down, including the top part of both turrets of the Administrative Block. A few cells on the top floor of block number six were also damaged. The third and fourth blocks were damaged during the Japanese occupation of the island.[1]

After independence, the blocks and cells that had been home to our freedom fighters for a long period were allotted to different departments of the administration for their use. How can we be so rude to our freedom fighters? In the 1960s, the blocks of Cellular Jail were demolished, as they were said to have been damaged during the earthquake and were deemed unsafe. G.B. Pant Hospital now stands in the vacant space of Blocks 3, 4, and 5. Block 6, having fifty-two cells, was used as a Bachelor's Mess for Government servants entitled to rent-free Government accommodation, while Block 1, with 105 cells, was converted into a District Jail and placed under the Superintendent of Police, Prison, and continued as a District Jail until the construction of a new jail at Protheropur during 1992-93.

Block 7, with 126 cells, was utilised by the Directorate of Health Services as the central medical store. The entrance gate building, which served as an Administrative block during the British period, was used as an office and ward for the medical department until 1974. The Administrative Block was converted into a civil hospital, which continued until 1964, when it was shifted to the newly built hospital in the vacant space of Blocks 3, 4, and 5.[2] However, a few rooms continued to be used as their residence on the ground floor of the Administrative block by the jail warders and one staff nurse.[3]

Earlier, in a reply to the question raised in Lok Sabha, it was clarified that Block 7 is being used for the purpose of medical stores and the first and second floors are utilised for keeping stationery, forms, registers, etc., whereas the ground floor of the Administrative block is used as a mess for nurses and living quarters for them. The first floor is used as the office of the Director of Medical and Health Services.

The Andaman and Nicobar Regional Centre of the Anthropological Survey of India was initially started in 1951 with a small office at Cellular

Jail. Block No. 2 of the jail was used for a short time as a temporary rest camp to accommodate newly arrived refugees from Bengal. Block No. 5 was used as a widows' home and orphanage since 1946.

Today, Central Tower and Blocks 1, 6, and 7, consisting of 283 cells, remain.

Cellular Jail circa 1960s (PC: Madan Mohan Singh)

Ex-Andaman Political Prisoners' Fraternity Circle

We should be thankful to the Ex-Andaman Political Prisoners' Fraternity Circle who fought tirelessly to preserve this monument for future generations. After independence, the freedom fighters of Cellular Jail formed an All-India Association of All Living Ex-Andaman Revolutionary Freedom Fighters and named it Ex-Andaman Political Prisoners' Fraternity Circle. The association was formed with the main objective of taking up the issue with the Government to preserve and declare the Cellular Jail as a National Memorial. During their dedicated efforts which lasted for more than a decade, they fought numerous battles and faced difficulties, leaving no stone unturned to achieve their ultimate goal. However, they were supported by the then Members of Parliament, Freedom Fighters, islanders, and others in their fight to stop the demolition of the Cellular Jail, thus paving the way to convert it into a National Memorial. They fought many battles in this prison and sacrificed their lives, but they fought another battle after independence to preserve this legacy with the sole objective of giving a new meaning to this temple of freedom.

The issue of demolishing three blocks of the Cellular Jail was brought to the attention of the then Prime Minister Shri Jawaharlal Nehru by Smt. Illa Pal Choudhury, Member of Parliament from West Bengal. The then Home Minister of India, Shri lal Bahadur Shastri during his visit to the Islands in 1962 assured the islanders for the preservation of the Cellular Jail.[4]

The protest to preserve the memorial was raised in the Parliament for the first time in 1964 by Members of Parliament Shri N.C. Banerjee, Smti Renu Chakraborty, Shri Niren Ghosh and others who visited the Islands in connection with Refugee Rehabilitation Affairs, and the reply received stating that "the Cellular Jail was no longer a standing structure and hence building up of a humanitarian institution like Pandit Govind Ballabh Pant Hospital should in no way be adjudged to have adversely affected the interests of Cellular Jail, which happened to exist there 'once upon a time' but is now totally effaced due to Japanese bombardment."[5]

Meanwhile, Block 2 was demolished on 24th June 1967 during the course of objections raised by the Fraternity Circle.

The Fraternity circle got support from the islanders, too. In a letter dated 24th June 1967, addressed to the then Prime Minister of India, Smt. Indira Gandhi, freedom fighter Shri B.L. Banerjee, along with 300 individuals from the Andamans, expressed their concern over the situation. At that time, only twenty-three names of freedom fighters were written on a blackboard in the Cellular Jail. Later, marble plaques were installed on the first floor of the Central Tower in 1968, but all those names were full of mistakes—surnames changed, names misspelt, and many freedom fighters found no mention in the plaques.[6]

The Fraternity Circle first submitted a representation in April 1968 to the then Prime Minister of India for the preservation of the Cellular Jail, and thereafter, a delegation comprising five members from the Fraternity Circle, Vishwanath Mathur, Samarendra Ghosh, Bangeswar Roy, Bejoy Bannerjee, and Benoy Bose, was deputed to Andamans to see the ground reality. Landed at Port Blair airport on 20th March 1969, the team first visited the Cellular Jail and then offered their floral tribute to all freedom fighters near Aberdeen jetty.[3] During this visit, it was informed to the Committee that some parts of the Jail were destroyed during the Japanese bombing; however, this was not true. They also met locals, municipal councillors, jail employees, and islanders who suffered during the Japanese occupation of the island. The team met about thirty islanders at the central school hall, which was attended and presided over by the Deputy Commissioner of Andamans. During the meeting, the locals informed them that the Japanese demolished one of the blocks of the Cellular Jail and another partly to get bricks to make their pill-boxes. The team members were felicitated by the municipal councillors and were invited to the prize distribution ceremony of the Government College and cultural groups such as the Tamil Club, Atul Smrity Samiti, and Port Blair Club.

In February 1968, a committee of Rehabilitation works from West Bengal consisting of Members of Parliament Shri NC Chatterjee, Renu Chakravorty, Niren Ghosh, and others visited Port Blair. During their visit, the old jail hospital (now the Martyrs' Column) was being demolished. On their return, they issued a statement appealing to the Prime Minister to stop the demolition of the Cellular Jail. This news was also published in the Hindustan Standard dated 28th February 1968. Meanwhile, Mrs Renu Chakravarty made an appeal to the then Prime Minister to preserve the Cellular Jail and informed her about the discussion she had with the Chief Commissioner of Andaman and Nicobar Islands, who had informed her that all records of the Cellular Jail had been destroyed by the Japanese. She also mentioned that, as per the Chief Commissioner, the blocks of the Cellular Jail had been destroyed by the Japanese.

In this scenario, the first memorandum dated 8th April 1968, signed by fifty-six ex-Andaman freedom fighters, was submitted to the Prime Minister proposing Cellular Jail to be declared as a National Memorial. They also made demands, referring to a Parliament debate, to declare it a national museum, keep the memory of Netaji alive, and organise an official inauguration to which all the surviving freedom fighters or political prisoners should be invited. Shri Bhupesh Gupta, Member of Parliament from West Bengal, while mentioning the first memorandum of the Fraternity Circle, raised the matter in the Rajya Sabha on 1st May 1968 and asked the Government to preserve it as a national memorial.

The members of the Fraternity Circle, in their letter dated 8th April 1969, signed by five freedom fighters, addressed to the Prime Minister of India, reiterated their demand and in response, the Ministry of Home Affairs informed via a letter dated 29th April 1969 that "It has since been decided that these three existing wings, including the Central Tower, should be preserved as a national monument."[7]

The members of the Fraternity Circle were also invited to the Republic Day function on 26th January 1974, held at Gymkhana Ground, now Netaji Stadium.

Shri Ram Niwas Mirdha, Minister of State in the Ministry of Home Affairs, Government of India, while answering the Parliament (Rajya Sabha) Starred Question no. 21 dated 2nd May 1973, said, "As regards the question about the various wings, Sir, in the original building there were seven wings, which were in a star-shaped fashion. When the Japanese bombarded the place in 1942, some wings were damaged, and the others were rendered unsafe. So, when the Andamans were reoccupied in 1945, some of the unsafe wings were demolished, and all that remains now are the three wings of the original seven wings..."[8]

The long struggle undertaken by the Fraternity Circle ultimately culminated on a positive note. When the matter came to the notice of the then Prime Minister Shri Morarji Desai, he said, "It has been delayed. I agree. It is unfortunate. But now, we will not delay it much further."[9] The Government of India finally accepted their proposal to preserve it as a National Memorial without making any substantial changes. The Memorial was dedicated to the nation by the then Prime Minister of India on 11th February 1979 in a function held in the Cellular Jail. However, no notification to this effect has been issued so far.

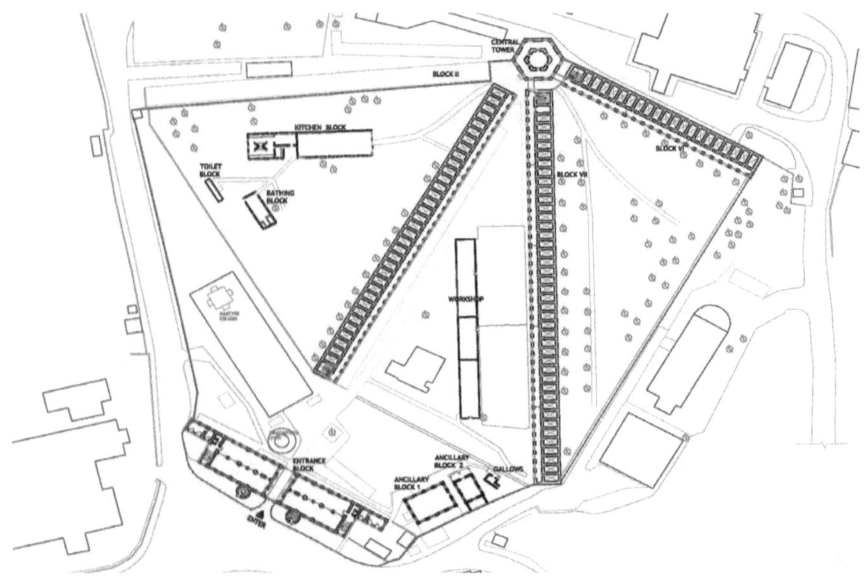

Plan of the remaining three blocks, including the Administrative block and Central Tower of the Cellular Jail

Cellular Jail – A Memorial

Presently, there are only 283 cells remaining. This monument has suffered along with its inmates in its journey from prison to pilgrimage.

Today, Cellular Jail, the National Memorial, is one of the greatest monuments of the freedom struggle. The Andaman and Nicobar

Administration and the Government of India have taken all steps for its preservation and development.

After the massive earthquake and tsunami that shook the Islands in December 2004, the Archaeological Survey of India (A.S.I.) was tasked with studying and highlighting conservation issues of the Cellular Jail. Their preliminary report indicated that the structure is generally in good condition with no major foundation issues, although water seepage from the terrace is a concern due to ineffective repairs. A.S.I. suggested additional conservation measures, including documentation and a geo-technical study, which were completed by the concerned department of the Administration. These efforts laid the groundwork for the conservation and restoration of the jail. The first phase of the conservation plan, which began in 2019, focused on minimal intervention to preserve the architectural integrity and historical significance of the structure while enhancing their longevity. The project was expected to be completed by the end of 2021; however, due to COVID protocols, the work was delayed and completed by March 2022.Now, it is high time to take up the matter with ASI for conservation of the remaining part of the structure and notify the monument under the provisions of *The Ancient Monuments and Archaeological Sites and Remains Act 1958* .

Even today, it takes us through a time zone which reminds us of oppressive rulers and sacrifices of our freedom fighters. The workshop and museum galleries display the extracts from autobiographies of freedom fighters and archival documents that narrate the advent of Cellular Jail, its history, atrocities committed, and the great struggle for freedom that took place within its four walls. The eternal flames, the martyr's memorial, and the sound and light show are all part of the dedicated effort to highlight the heroes of India's freedom struggle who were incarcerated in these Islands during their ceaseless struggle for freedom.

The administrative block of the Cellular Jail has been converted into museum galleries, which depict case histories and photographs of freedom fighters. The relevant extracts from autobiographies and archival documents have been used in the permanent exhibition gallery to outline the torture inflicted on the revolutionaries. There is an Art Gallery on the first floor that features paintings of national-level artists depicting inhuman treatment meted out to our freedom fighters. The gallery on Netaji houses photographs with special reference to his historic visit to the Cellular Jail. There is a reference library and a small archive attached to it, which houses books on the freedom movement. The autobiographies and biographies of political prisoners are the most valuable collections, which are referred to by researchers from India and abroad.

On the ground, visitors can pay their floral tribute at the Martyr's Column and fold their hands in remembrance of great souls while looking at the eternal flames on both sides and reading out the inspiring quote of Veer Savarkar, Netaji and others inscribed on the bronze plaques of the flames. On the way to the cells, visitors can see the workshed where prisoners were engaged in different types of work such as oil grinding, coir pounding, and rope making. Political prisoners were required to produce a daily quota of coconut and mustard oil—targets that were beyond the physical capacity of all. Dire punishments followed for those who failed to meet the quotas. Here, mannequins are used to display the three different kinds of chains used to punish prisoners for breaking the jail rules. On the other side of the workshed, one can see the raised slab where the last rituals were performed before execution. However, it is a fact that no revolutionary with a death sentence was deported to the Cellular Jail. It was inflicted only in the case of those prisoners who, being already under severe sentence, attempted the lives of jail officials, fellow inmates, and others in the penal settlement.

Every evening, Cellular Jail hosts a sound and light show that narrates its history and the great struggle that took place within its four walls. The visitors to the museum and light and sound show are moved emotionally with patriotic fervour. Their expectations are high from the management, and it is the responsibility of the authorities to ensure that they are not disappointed in any way.

I am fortunate enough to have served in the National Memorial Cellular Jail for over two decades, and I can proudly say that it has now become one of the most favoured pilgrimage destinations for all those Indians who prefer to pay their obeisance to the freedom fighters by visiting the Islands and the Cellular Jail once in a lifetime.

Block No 1 of the Cellular Jail was used as District Jail untill the construction of a new Jail at Protheropur

NOTES AND REFERENCES

1. Gauri Shankar Pandey, The Cellular Jail - The National Memorial, Sangeeta Publishing House, Port Blair, 1987, p. 27

2. *Ibid*, pp. 31-33

3. Ex-Andaman Political Prisoners' Fraternity Circle, Uphold Cellular Jail National Memorial, Kolkata, 1978, p. 40

4. *Ibid*, p. 4

5. *Ibid*, p. 3

6. *Ibid*, p. 12

7. *Ibid*, p. 14

8. *Ibid*, p. 46

9. Brief report by Chief Commissioner on the historic occasion of inauguration of Cellular Jail National Memorial, Port Blair, p. 3

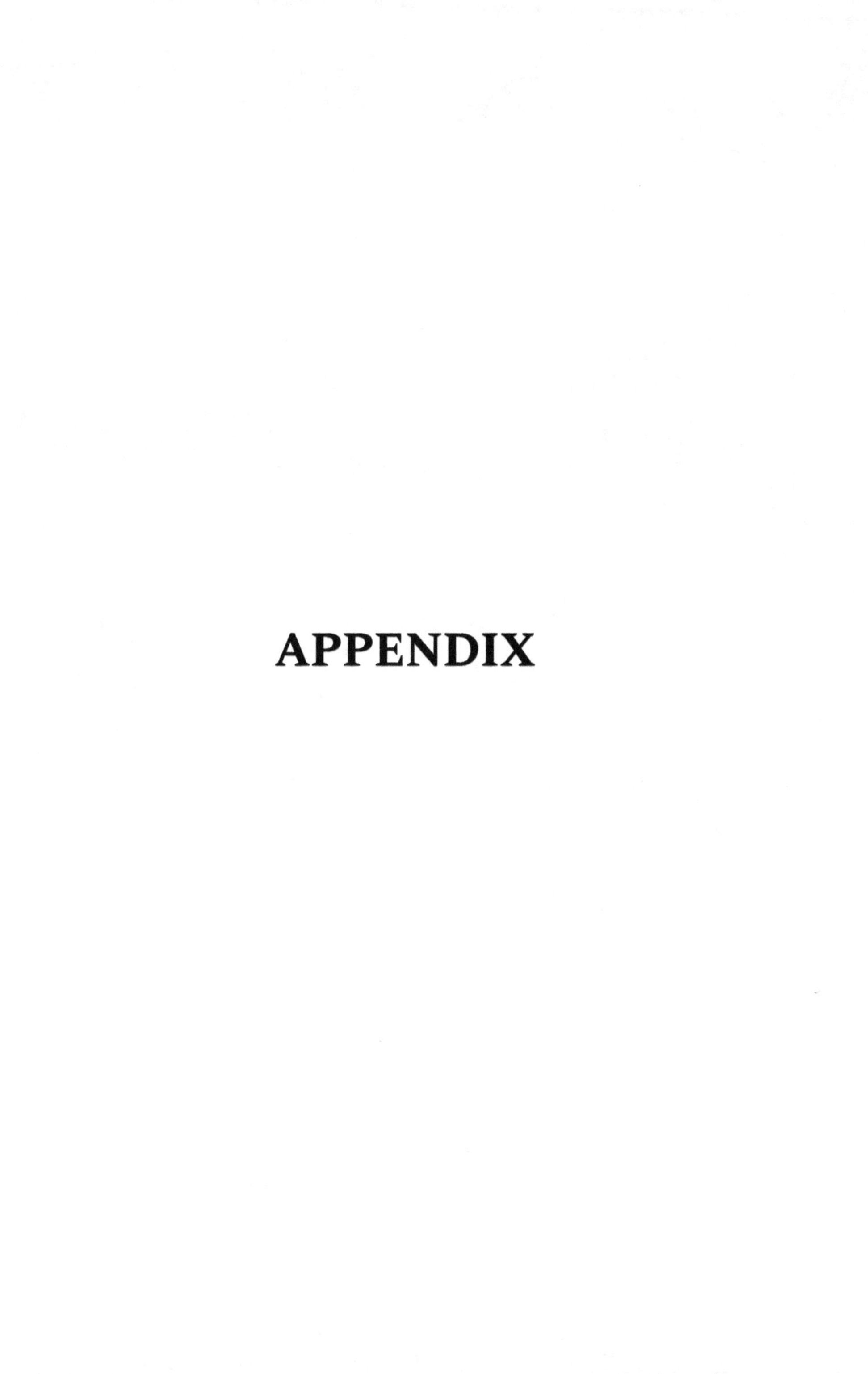

APPENDIX

Appendix I
List of Freedom Fighters

Sl. No.	Names	Residence	Case
1.	Ladha Ram Kapoor	Varaychawala, Gujarat	Revolutionary Writing Case 1908-09
2.	Nand Gopal Chopra	Gujranwala, Punjab	
3.	Hoti Lal Verma	Meerut, Uttar Pradesh	
4.	Govindram	Lahore, Punjab	
5.	Babu Ram Hari	Gurdaspur, Punjab	
6.	Roshan Lal	Uttar Pradesh	
7.	Pandit Ram Charan Lal Sharma	Etah, Uttar Pradesh	
8.	Mokshada Babu	-	
9.	Barindra Kumar Ghosh	Hooghly, Bengal	Alipore Conspiracy Case 1908-09
10.	Ullaskar Dutta	Shibpur, Bengal	
11.	Upendra Nath Banerjee	French Chandannagar, Bengal	
12.	Bhibhuti Bhushan Sarkar	Nadia, Bengal	
13.	Hrishikesh Kanjilal	Shrirampore, Bengal	

Sl. No.	Names	Residence	Case
14.	Birendra Chandra Sen, alias Durga Das	Sylhet, Assam	
15.	Sudhir Kumar Sarkar	Bengal	
16.	Abinash Chandra Bhattacharjee	Sinthee, Calcutta	
17.	Hem Chandra Das Kanungo	Midnapore, Bengal	
18.	Indu Bhusan Roy	Khulna, Bengal	
19.	Nirpada Roy	Nadia, Bengal	
20.	Abani Bhushan Chakraborty	Jessore, Bengal	Khulna (Nangla) Conspiracy Case 1909-10
21.	Bidhu Bhushan Dey	Abhoynagar, Bengal	
22.	Kalidas Ghosh, alias Kali Charan Ghosh	Narail, Bengal	
23.	Sudhir Chandra Dey	Bengal	
24.	Ashwini Kumar Basu	Jessore, Bengal	
25.	Kinu Ram Pal, also known as Priya Nath	Khulna, Bengal	Jessore-Khulna Conspiracy Case 1909-10
26.	Brojendra Nath Dutt	Dacca, Bengal	
27.	Satish Chandra Chatterjee/ Bhattacharjee	Abhoynagar, Bengal	
28.	Nagendra Nath Sarkar	Narail, Bengal	
29.	Nagendra Nath Chandra, alias Nagendra Chandra Chandra	Bengal	

Sl. No.	Names	Residence	Case
30.	Sachindra Lal Mitra	Khulna, Bengal	
31.	Vinayak Damodar Savarkar	Nasik, Bombay	Nasik Conspiracy Case 1909-10
32.	Ganesh Damodar Savarkar	Nasik, Bombay	
33.	Daji Waman Narayan Joshi	Nasik, Bombay	
34.	Jyotirmoy Behari Roy	Dacca, Bengal	Dacca Arms Conspiracy Case 1910
35.	Pulin Behari Das	Faridpur, Bengal	
36.	Suresh Chandra Sengupta	Dacca, Bengal	Rajendrapur Supplementary Train Action Case 1910-11
37.	Nani Gopal Mukherjee, also known as Jogendra Nath Mukherjee	Chinsurah, Bengal	Dalhousie Square Bomb Case - 1911
38.	Jyotindra Chandra Ghosh	Dacca, Bengal	First Barisal Conspiracy Case - 12
39.	Khagendra Nath Chaudhary, alias Suresh Chandra	Dacca, Bengal	Second Barisal Conspiracy Case - 1913
40.	Trailokya Nath Chakraborty	Mymensingh, Bengal	
41.	Madan Mohan Bhowmick	Keraniganj, Bengal	Nangalband Action Case 1913
42.	Amrit Lal Hazra	Dacca, Bengal	Raja Bazaar Bomb Case - 1913
43.	Bhan Singh	Ludhiana, Punjab	Lahore Conspiracy Case 1915
44.	Balwant Singh	Amritsar, Punjab	
45.	Kirpal Singh	Ludhiana, Punjab	
46.	Sohan Singh Bhakna	Amritsar, Punjab	

Sl. No.	Names	Residence	Case
47.	Sawan Singh		
48.	Lal Singh		
49.	Bishen Singh		
50.	Bishen Singh		
51.	Bishen Singh		
52.	Kushal Singh		
53.	Hazara Singh		
54.	Kehar Singh		
55.	Mangal Singh		
56.	Wasakha Singh		
57.	Wasawa Singh		
58.	Sher Singh		
59.	Indar Singh	Ludhiana, Punjab	
60.	Indar Singh	Lahore, Punjab	
61.	Inder Singh		
62.	Jawand Singh	Amritsar, Punjab	
63.	Kala Singh		
64.	Kala Singh		
65.	Gurdit Singh		
66.	Jwala Singh		
67.	Harnam Singh	Hoshiarpur, Punjab	
68.	Jagat Ram		
69.	Piara Singh		
70.	Shiv Singh		
71.	Hirde Ram	Mandi	
72.	Nidhan Singh	Ferozepur, Punjab	
73.	Pandit Parmanand (Jhansi)	Hamirpur, Uttar Pradesh	
74.	Bhai Parmanand	Rawalpindi, Punjab	
75.	Prithvi Singh Azad	Patiala, Punjab	
76.	Ram Saran Das	Kapurthala, Punjab	
77.	Roda Singh	Ferozepur, Punjab	
78.	Rur Singh		
79.	Chuher Singh	Raikot, Punjab	

Sl. No.	Names	Residence	Case
80.	Gurumukh Singh (1916 & 1937)	Ludhiana, Punjab	
81.	Kesar Singh	Amritsar, Punjab	
82.	Madan Singh	Lahore, Punjab	
83.	Nand Singh	Ludhiana, Punjab	
84.	Rulla Singh		
85.	Udham Singh	Amritsar, Punjab	
86.	Ashutosh Lahiri	Pabna, Bengal	Pragpur (Gopalpura) Action Case 1915
87.	Gopendra Lal Roy	Sylhet, Bengal	
88.	Kshitish Chandra Sanyal	Bengal	
89.	Phanindra Bhushan Roy	Bengal	
90.	Jyotish Chandra Pal	Nadia, Bengal	Balasore Action Case (Buribalam War) - 1915
91.	Narendra Mohan Ghosh Chowdhury, alias Naren Ghosh Chowdhury	Serpentine Lane, Bengal	Shibpur Political Dacoity Case 1916
92.	Nikhil Ranjan Guha Roy (1916 & 1932)	Krishnanagar, Bengal	
93.	Surendra Nath Biswas	Bengal	
94.	Sanukal Chatterjee		
95.	Jatindra Mohan Nandi, alias Jatindra Nath Nandi		

Sl. No.	Names	Residence	Case
96.	Bhupendra Nath Ghosh		
97.	Harendra Nath Bhattacharjee		
98.	Sachindra Nath Dutta		
99.	Satya Ranjan Bose		
100.	Hardit Singh	Ludhiana, Punjab	First & Second (Burma) Mandalay Conspiracy Case 1916-17
101.	Kirpa Ram	Gujarat, Punjab	
102.	Chet Ram	Sialkot, Punjab	
103.	Jeevan Singh	Gujranwala, Punjab	
104.	Kapur Singh	Ludhiana, Punjab	
105.	Budha Singh	Gujranwala, Punjab	
106.	Mujtaba Hussain, alias Mulchand	Jaunpur, Uttar Pradesh	
107.	Amar Singh Nandbol	Ludhiana, Punjab	
108.	Ali Ahmed Siddiqui	Faizabad, Uttar Pradesh	
109.	Ram Rakha	Hoshiarpur, Punjab	
110.	Sachindra Nath Sanyal (1916 &1925)	Varanasi, Uttar Pradesh	Benaras Conspiracy Case 1916 & Kakori Conspiracy Case - 1925
111.	Gobinda Chandra Kar	Mymensingh, Bengal	Bengal Arms Act Case 1918
112.	Nikunja Behari Pal	Tippara, Bengal	
113.	Bishen Singh	Amritsar, Punjab	Dugsai Court-Martial Law 1919
114.	Bishen Singh		
115.	Kehar Singh		
116.	Channan Singh		
117.	Natha Singh, alias Nathuwa Singh		
118.	Nand Singh		

Sl. No.	Names	Residence	Case
119.	Chattar Singh	Punjab	
120.	Girdhari Lal	Gujranwala, Punjab	
121.	Mohammed Akram Khan	North-West Province	
122.	Wilyati Singh - Amritsar Riot	Punjab	
123.	Ratan Chand - Amritsar National Bank Murder Case	Amritsar, Punjab	
124.	Sunder Singh	Ramgadi	
125.	Bugdah - Amritsar National Bank Murder Case	Punjab	
126.	Harnam Singh - Amritsar Riot, National Bank Murder Case		
127.	Deena		Amritsar Alliance Bank Action Case & National Bank Action Case-1919
128.	Jalaldeen		
129.	Karamchand		
130.	Mehardeen		
131.	Mohammadi		
132.	Sadiq		
133.	Sandhi		
134.	Jayram		
135.	Manohar Singh		
136.	Harnam Singh		
137.	Raja Ram		Malakwal Riot Case 1919
138.	Ala-ud-din		Kasur Supplementary Riot Case 1919
139.	Nadir Ali Shah		
140.	Artia Majhi	Daspalla, Odisha	Daspalla Riyasat Case/ Orissa Conspiracy Case

Sl. No.	Names	Residence	Case
141.	Bhagbatiya Behra		
142.	Mahadev Pradhan		
143.	Kendu Paan		
144.	Charitra Nayak		
145.	Chota alias Chote Singh		
146.	Jogiya Jaani		
147.	Bidhu Bhushan Sarkar	Bengal	Various Revolutionary Activities Cases 1909-1921
149.	Shantabhanu Lahiri	Bihar	
150.	Sucharan Lal Sharma	-	
152.	Gulam Sarwar Khan	North West Province	

Moplah Rebellion 1921-22

1.	Poovakundil Maayin Haji	Malabar,Kerala
2.	Aripra Poker Haji	
3.	Nelliparamban Alavi Haji	
4.	Mathungal Marakkar	
5.	Kolamban Moideen Kutty	
6.	Machingal Rayin	
7.	Mattungal Ahmed Kutty	
8.	Chelekodan Ahmed	
9.	Nalakath Unneen Choudhary	
10.	Kutha Kallan Kunjara	
11.	Kolaparanban Kunjalvi	
12.	K.T Ahammed Kutty Haji	
13.	Kozhisseri Koya Kutty	
14.	Poovakundil Alavi	
15.	Puthampeedi Kayet Kunji Kader Molla	
16.	Neehiyil Kunjeedu	

17.	Chakkupurakkal Kutty Hasan
18.	Pooyikuman Marakkar
19.	Poolakuyyil Kunhi Moideen Kutty
20.	Ambattuparamban Saidalippa
21.	Variyath Valappil Ahmed Kutty
22.	Machincheri Alavi
23.	Chungatto Athan
24.	Pokat Kayarni
25.	Kayakhatiparambil Kunjeni
26.	Mmukri Kunjayammun

Rampa Rebellion 1922-24

1.	Bonangi Pandu Padal	Visakhapatnam, Andhra Pradesh
2.	Korrabu Kotayya	
3.	Golivil Sanayasayya	
4.	Kunchatti Sanyasi	
5.	Vegiraji Satyanarayana Raju	
6.	Gam Mallu Dora	
7.	Taggi Veerayya Dora	

1922-30

1.	Sunder Singh Maksudpur	Punjab	First & Supplementary Babbar Akali Conspiracy Case 1923
2.	Pratap Singh Chabelpur		
3.	Bhola Singh Katha		
4.	Surain Singh Kang		
5.	Munsha Singh Samravan		
6.	Udham Singh Suranusi		
7.	Gian Singh Alowal		
8.	Banta Singh Alowal		
9.	Karam Singh Jhinger		
10.	Man Singh Gobindpur		
11.	Piara Singh Dhamian		
12.	Thakar Singh Bharata		
13.	Bachint Singh Damunda		
14.	Isher Singh Dichkotia		
15.	Vishnu Sharan Dublis	Meerut, Uttar Pradesh	Kakori Conspiracy Case - 1925

Cellular Jail 1932-38

Sl. No.	Name	Residence	case
1.	Dhrubesh Chandra Chattopadhyay	Hooghly, Bengal	Dakshineswar Bomb Case & Alipore Murder Case - 1926
2.	Ananta Kumar Chakraborty, also known as Bhola	Barisal, Bengal	
3.	Rakhal Chandra Dey	Chittagong, Bengal	
4.	Kalipada Chakraborty		Killing of Sub-Inspector Tarini Mukhopadhyay in Chittagong Case 1929
5.	Ramesh Chandra Chatterjee	Barisal, Bengal	
6.	Batukeshwar Dutt	Burdwan, Bengal	Central Assembly Bomb Case 1929
7.	Dr. Gaya Prasad, also known as B.S. Nigam	Kanpur, U.P	Second Lahore Conspiracy Case 1930
8.	Jaidev Kapoor, also known as Harish Chandra	Hardoi, U.P	
9.	Kundan Lal Gupta, also known as Pratap Gupta	Faizabad, U.P	
10.	Mahavir Singh	Etah, U.P	
11.	Bejoy Kumar Sinha	Kanpur, U.P	
12.	Kamal Nath Tiwari, also known as Kanwal Nath Trivedi	Champaran, Bihar	
13.	Gurumukh Singh, also known as Anup Singh (deported twice in 1916 and 1937)	Ludhiana, Punjab	
14.	Randhir Singh	Punjab	
15.	Shiv Verma, also known as Hari Narayan	Hardoi, U.P	
16.	Suresh Chandra Das	Faridpur, Bengal	Armenian Street Action Case 1930

Sl. No.	Name	Residence	case
17.	Anant Lal Singh	Chittagong,	Chittagong
18.	Loknath Bal	Bengal	Armoury Raid Case/
19.	Himangshu Bhowmick, also known as Raja		Chittagong Youth Revolution-1930
20.	Subodh Kumar Chowdhury	Bardhaman, Bengal	
21.	Hirday Ranjan Das	Chittagong, Bengal	
22.	Sahay Ram Das	Nadia, Bengal	
23.	Randhir Dasgupta	Chittagong, Bengal	
24.	Sukhendu Bikash Dastidar		
25.	Ganesh Ghosh, also known as Ganesh Chand Ghosh		
26.	Saroj Kanti Guha		
27.	Ananda Prasad Gupta		
28.	Phanindra Lal Nandi		
29.	Fakir Chand Sen, also known as Fakir Chand Sengupta		
30.	Lal Mohan Sen	Noakhali, Bengal	
31.	Subodh Chandra Roy	Chittagong, Bengal	
32.	Dinesh Chandra Dasgupta		
33.	Sushil Kumar Dey		
34.	Kali Kinker Dey		
35.	Harihar Dutta		
36.	Dr. Bhupal Chandra Bose	Dacca, Bengal	Dalhousie Square Bomb Case 1930
37.	Surendra Nath Dutta	Barisal, Bengal	
38.	Narayan Chandra Roy	Calcutta, Bengal	
39.	Nisha Kanti Roy Chowdhury	Jessore, Bengal	Mechua Bazar Bombing Case 1930
40.	Satish Chandra Prakashi	Bengal	
41.	Sachindra Lal Kar Gupta	Barisal, Bengal	
42.	Sudhangshu Lal Dasgupta		
43.	Laxmi Kant Shukla	Unnao, Uttar Pradesh	British Commissioner of Jhansi's Murder Case - 1930

Sl. No.	Name	Residence	case
44.	Dhirendra Nath Chowdhury	Calcutta, Bengal	Alipore Arms Conspiracy Case 1930-36
45.	Chinta Haran Das	Faridpur, Bengal	
46.	Usha Ranjan Dey		
47.	Abani Ranjan Ghosh	Mymensingh, Bengal	
48.	Kalipada Roy	Tippara, Calcutta	
49.	Sudhir Chandra Roy	Faridpur, Bengal	
50.	Suneermal Sen	Dacca, Bengal	
51.	Sudhendu Chandra Dam	Mymensingh, Bengal	Sealdah Action Case 1931
52.	Nagendra Chandra Modak		
53.	Rabindra Chandra Niyogi		
54.	Prabodh Kumar Roy		
55.	Koumudi Kanta Bhattacharjee	Barisal, Bengal	Barisal Political Dacoity Cases 1931-34
56.	Bimalendu Chakraborty	Dacca, Bengal	
57.	Hira Mohan Chatterjee	Faridpur, Bengal	
58.	Keshab Lal Chatterjee	Barisal, Bengal	
59.	Nand Lal Dasgupta		
60.	Nanigopal Dasgupta		
61.	Bhupesh Chandra Guha		
62.	Sudhangshu Narayan Das Majumdar		
63.	Nibaran Chandra Chakraborty	Mymensingh, Bengal	Kishoreganj, Mymensingh Political Dacoity Case - 1931
64.	Jyotindra Chandra Dey, also known as Jatindra Dey		
65.	Dinesh Chandra Dhar, also known as Dinesh Dhar		
66.	Dwijendra Nath Naha, alias Dwijendra Chandra Naha	Dacca, Bengal	
67.	Purna Chandra Roy, also known as Kshitij Roy	Mymensingh, Bengal	
68.	Purna Chandra Goswami		

Sl. No.	Name	Residence	case
69.	Mahendra Bhowmick, also known as Mahendra Chandra Bhowmick.	Dacca, Bengal	
70.	Shashindra Chakraborty	Mymensingh, Bengal	
71.	Chandrika Singh	Saran, Bihar	Hajipur Station Action Case, 1931
72.	Jogendra Shukla, also known as Sohan Singh	Muzaffarpur, Bihar	Motihari Conspiracy Case 1930-31
73.	Nanku Singh	Saran, Bihar	
74.	Gulab Chand Gupta, also known as Gulali Sunar.	Champaran, Bihar	
75.	Kedarmani Shukla		
76.	Gopal Chandra Acharya	Mymensingh, Bengal	Atharabari Conspiracy Case, 1931
77.	Hemendra Nath Chakraborty	Pabna, Bengal	
78.	Sachindra Chandra Home	Mymensingh, Bengal	
79.	Bimal Kumar Dasgupta alias Makhan	Midnapore, Bengal	Attempt to Murder Villiers-President Europeans Association Case 1931
80.	Dharni Kanta Biswas	Mymensingh, Bengal	Puthia Mail Action Case 1932
81.	Bijan Kumar Sengupta	Rajshahi, Bengal	
82.	Mukul Ranjan Sengupta	Barisal, Bengal	
83.	Sushil Kumar Dasgupta	Rangpur, Bengal	
84.	Amlendu Bagchi	Rajshahi, Bengal	
85.	Promod Ranjan Bose	Faridpur, Bengal	Attempt to Kill Alfred Watson Case - 1932
86.	Sunil Kumar Chatterjee	24 Pargana, Bengal	
87.	Haripad Chowdhury	Faridpur, Bengal	
88.	Bankim Chandra Chakraborty, also known as Prabodh Chandra Chakraborty	Agartala, Tripura	Brahmanbaria Arms Case 1932
89.	Kamini Kumar Dey	Tippara, Bengal	
90.	Radhika Mohan Das		

Sl. No.	Name	Residence	case
91.	Subal Chandra Roy Karmakar	Dacca, Bengal	Charmugarh Political Dacoity Case - 1932
92.	Surendra Mohan Kar Roy	Faridpur, Bengal	
93.	Ram Chandra Saha, also known as Ram Chandra Das Shah	Dacca, Bengal	
94.	Santosh Kumar Dutta	Calcutta	
95.	Chandra Nath Bhattacharya, alias Chandra Kant Bhattacharya	Tippara, Bengal	Comilla Political Dacoity Case 1932
96.	Chunni Lall Deb	Tippara, Bengal	
97.	Anant Lal Dey	Dacca	
98.	Chitranjan Dutta	Dacca	
99.	Nirpendra Dutta Roy	Bengal	
100.	Rabindranath Guha Roy	Faridpur, Bengal	
101.	Gopi Mohan Shah	Tippara, Bengal	
102.	Revati Mohan Shah	Tippara	
103.	Bharat Chandra Sharma Shastri, also known as Bharat Sharma Roy	Brahmanbaria, Bengal	
104.	Lalit Chandra Chakraborty	Mymensingh	Netrakona Arms Conspiracy Case
105.	Mohan Kishore Nama Das, alias Man Krishna Nama Das	Mymensingh, Bengal	
106.	Upendra Nath Saha		Attempt to Kill Graham, Magistrate of Mymensingh District Case 1932
107.	Bhupesh Chandra Bhattacharjee		
108.	Joyesh Chandra Bhattacharjee		
109.	Sitangshu Bhushan Dutta Roy		
110.	Mohit Chandra Adhikari	Bhagalpur, Bihar	Gaya/Patna Conspiracy Case - 1932-33

Sl. No.	Name	Residence	case
111.	Shyam Krishna Agarwal	Patna, Bihar	Gaya/Patna Conspiracy Case – 1932-33
112.	Vishwanath Mathur	Darbhanga, Bihar	
113.	Kanai Lal Michir	Patna, Bihar	
114.	Mahavir Michir		
115.	Shamdev Narayan	Siwan, Bihar	
116.	Ram Pratap Singh	Patna, Bihar	
117.	Suraj Nath Chaubey	Shahabad, Bihar	
118.	Dr. Keshav Prasad	Gaya, Bihar	
119.	Shyam Charan Bharatwar		
120.	Sashimohan Bhattacharya, also known as Vali	Tippara, Bengal	Tangail Action Case 1932
121.	Prafulla Chandra Bhowmick	Mymensingh, Bengal	
122.	Satya Ranjan Ghosh		
123.	Bhupesh Chandra Saha	Faridpur, Gopalgunj	Dhamrai Mail Robbery Case 1932
124.	Makhanlal Dey, also known as Tona	Dhamrai, Dacca	
125.	Sharat Dhupi Das / Sharat Chandra Das Dhupi	Mymensingh, Bengal	Kuniati Action Case-1932
126.	Surendra Nath Sarkhel	Barisal, Bengal	Barisal (Singa-Gournadi) Robbery Case 1932
127.	Nepal Chandra Sarkar, also known as Upendra Narayan Sarkar	Barisal, Bengal	
128.	Phani Bhushan Dasgupta	Barisal, Bengal	
129.	Chitranjan Biswas, also known as Chitta Biswas	Mymensingh, Bengal	Attempt to Kill Luke, Jail Superintendent's Case 1932
130.	Bhola Nath Roy Karmakar	Rajshahi, Bengal	
131.	Gaurgopal Dutta		
132.	Haripada Bhattacharjee	Chittagong, Bengal	Ahsanullah Murder Case – 1932
133.	Benoy Bhushan Roy	Dacca, Bengal	Attempt to Assassinate Additional Superintendent of Police, C.G. Grasby Case 1932

Sl. No.	Name	Residence	case
134.	Suresh Chandra Acharya	Mymensingh, Bengal	Mymensingh Political Dacoity Case 1932-33
135.	Adhir Chandra Singh, also known as Madhu Singh		
136.	Dhirendra Chandra Chakraborty		
137.	Dinesh Chandra Das		
138.	Jamini Kumar Dey		
139.	Manmat Nath Dutta		
140.	Mathura Nath Dutta		
141.	Govinda Chandra Kar		
142.	Lalit Chandra Raha		
143.	Amar Chandra Sutradar		
144.	Bhabesh Chandra Talukdar		
145.	Debendra Chandra Talukdar		
146.	Shailesh Chandra Dutta		
147.	Jagneshwar Das, also known as Jageshwar Das	-	Angaria Robbery Case - 1932
148.	Jogesh Chandra Chakraborty	Faridpur, Bengal	
149.	Anukul Chandra Chatterjee	-	
150.	Dharni Kanta Chakraborty, also known as Dharni Chakraborty	Mymensingh, Bengal	Arniyapasha Conspiracy Case 1932
151.	Prafulla Kumar Majumdar	Dacca, Bengal	
152.	Sudhir Chandra Bhattacharjee	Mymensingh, Bengal	
153.	Bhupesh Chandra Banerjee	Dacca, Bengal	Dacca Arms Conspiracy Case 1932
154.	Surendra Chandra Dhanik	Dacca, Bengal	
155.	Parimal Ghosh, also known as Parimal Chandra Ghosh.		
156.	Adhir Ranjan Nag		
157.	Prasanta Kumar Sengupta		
158.	Sailesh Chandra Roy	Noakhali, Bengal	

Sl. No.	Name	Residence	case
159.	Madhusudan Dutt	Mymensingh, Bengal	Jamalpur Dacoity and Arms Conspiracy Case, 1932
160.	Bidhu Bhushan Sen		
161.	Ajay Singh, also known as Jogi Ajay Chandra Singh	Chittagong, Bengal	Calcutta Arms Act Case 1932–33
162.	Satyendra Kumar Bose	Faridpur, Bengal	
163.	Jogendra Nath Guha	Barisal, Bengal	
164.	Surendra Nath Dutta Gupta	Calcutta, Bengal	
165.	Rakhal Das Mallick	Calcutta, Bengal	
166.	Ajith Kumar Mitra		
167.	Mohit Mohan Moitra	Pabna, Bengal	
168.	Saroj Bhushan Roy	Tezpur, Assam	
169.	Sudhindra Mohan Roy	Calcutta, Bengal	
170.	Kamal Kanta Shrimani		
171.	Manoranjan Guha Thakurta		
172.	Siraj-Ul-Haq, alias Saroj Kumar Bose		
173.	Kshitij Chandra Chowdhury	Mymensingh, Bengal	
174.	Barindra Kumar Ghosh	Calcutta, Bengal	
175.	Radha Ballab Gope	Faridpur, Bengal	
176.	Kartick Chandra De Das	Barisal, Bengal	
177.	Jogendra Nath Banerjee	Calcutta, Bengal	
178.	Mukul Chandra Roy	Dacca, Bengal	
179.	Mani Ganguly	–	
180.	Jagat Bandhu Bose	Jessore, Bengal	Arms and Explosives Case 1932
181.	Jeeban Molla, alias Abdul Jabbar	Faridpur, Bengal	
182.	Achyut Nath Ghatak	Dacca, Bengal	
183.	Abhayapada Mukherjee	Rajshahi, Bengal	
184.	Amrendra Nath Mukherjee	Khulna, Bengal	
185.	Mohan Lal Nag	Howrah, Bengal	

Sl. No.	Name	Residence	case
186.	Khokha, also known as Sudhindra Kumar Roy	Mymensingh, Bengal	
187.	Sudhanshu Kumar Sengupta	Barisal, Bengal	
188.	Anand Charan Pal	Dacca, Bengal	
189.	Malay Krishna Brahmachar	Faridpur, Bengal	
190.	Keshab Chandra Samajdar	Calcutta, Bengal	
191.	Sudangshu Lal Dasgupta	-	
192.	Sarada Prasanna Bose	Dacca, Bengal	Murad Nagar Mill Robbery Case 1932
193.	Gopal Chandra Dey	Tippara, Bengal	
194.	Krishnapada Chakraborty	Dacca, Bengal	Tippera Arms Act Case, 1932
195.	Dhanvantri	Durga Dutt Kashmiri	Delhi Conspiracy Case (Hazrat Nizamuddin Railway Track Case) - 1932
196.	Jagat Bandhu Roy	Ram Kishan Ram	Chinsurah Conspiracy Case - 1932
197.	Bhaba Ranjan Patitunta	Rasik Chandra Patitunta	Bakarganj Action Case 1932
198.	Abani Kumar Mukherjee	Shibpur, Bengal	Shibpur -Nadia Political dacoity Case -1932-33
199.	Nikhil Ranjan Guha Roy (1916 & 1932)	Faridpur, Bengal	Shibpur -Nadia Political dacoity Case-1915-16 and Kandi Bomb Case - 1932
200.	Gauri Shankar Dubey	Champaran, Bihar	Muzaffarpur Political Dacoity Case 1932
201.	Kamakya Charan Ghosh	Bengal	B.E.J. Burge Murder Case - 1933
202.	Nand Dulal Sinha	Bengal	
203.	Sanatan Roy	Midnapore, Bengal	
204.	Sukumar Sengupta		

Sl. No.	Name	Residence	case
205.	Dharni Mohan Banik	Mymensingh, Bengal	Kamalpur Dacoity Case 1933
206.	Dinesh Chandra Banik		
207.	Haribol Chakraborty, also known as Kali Kumar Chakraborty		
208.	Jogendra Chandra Chakraborty		
209.	Bhushan Mohan Chandra	Dacca	
210.	Indu Bhushan Das	Mymensingh, Bengal	
211.	Janaki Mohan Das	Dacca	
212.	Hem Chandra Dutta, alias Hemendra Chandra Dutta	Mymensingh, Bengal	
213.	Shridhar Goswami		
214.	Dr. Birendra Chandra Lahiri		
215.	Sudhangshu Kiran Lahiri, also known as Jamini Lahiri		
216.	Manindra Chandra Sen	Dacca	
217.	Dinesh Chandra Saha	Mymensingh Bengal	
218.	Prakash Chandra Sheel		
219.	Prativadi Bhayankara Venkateshwara Rao	East Godavari, Andhra Pradesh	Kakinada Bomb Conspiracy Case 1933
220.	Haripada Bose	Faridpur, Bengal	Hilli Station Political Dacoity Case - 1933
221.	Bijoy Krishna Chakraborty, also known as Bijoy Banerjee	Dacca	
222.	Pran Krishna Chakraborty, also known as Paran	Faridpur, Bengal	

Sl. No.	Name	Residence	case
223.	Abdul Qadir Chowdhury	Bogra, Bengal	
224.	Kiran Chandra Dey	Dinajpur, Bengal	
225.	Prafulla Narayan Sanyal	Faridpur, Bengal	
226.	Ramakrishna Sarkar, also known as Mondal	Bogra,, Bengal	
227.	Hrishikesh Bhattacharjee	Dinajpur, Bengal	
228.	Saroj Kumar Bose, alias Ketu		
229.	Satyabrata Chakraborty, also known as Moni		
230.	Pramtha Nath Ghosh	Bankura, Bengal	Jharia Conspiracy Case 1933
231.	Jyotirmoy Roy	Birbhum, Bengal	
232.	Jagadananda Mukherjee	Pargana, Bengal	Cornwallis Street Shooting Case, 1933
233.	Raj Mohan Karanji	Rangpur, Bengal	Kurigram (Rangpur) Conspiracy Case 1933-34
234.	Kumud Bihari Mukherjee		
235.	Sachindra Kumar Nandi		
236.	Satish Chandra Bose Roy		
237.	Haridas Shah		
238.	Bachu Lal, also known as Bachu Ram	Amritsar, Punjab	Ooty Bank Robbery and Bombing Case - 1933
239.	Hazara Singh, also known as Banta Singh.	Hoshiarpur, Punjab	
240.	Kushiram Mehta		
241.	Prem Prakash, also known as Devanab	Garhwal	
242.	Puran Chand	-	
243.	Shambu Nath Azad	Uttar Pradesh	
244.	Bangeshwar Roy	Dacca, Bengal	Dacca Post Office Robbery Case - 1933
245.	Binoy Kumar Bose		
246.	Nagendra Nath Gupta	Barisal, Bengal	Kushtia Arms Conspiracy Case 1933

Sl. No.	Name	Residence	case
247.	Prabhakar Biruni	Bankura, Bengal	Illegal Arms Act Case 1933-34
248.	Hem Chandra Bakshi	Rangpur, Bengal	
249.	Bibhuti Bhushan Banerjee	Dacca, Bengal	
250.	Susheel Kumar Banerjee	Calcutta, Bengal	
251.	Hrishikesh Bose		
252.	Kalipada Chakraborty, also known as Kali Bhattacharya	Faridpur, Bengal	
253.	Shanti Pada Chakraborty	Chittagong, Bengal	
254.	Deb Kumar Das	Barisal, Bengal	
255.	Dhirendra Chandra Dutta, also known as Dhiren Dutta	Dacca, Bengal	
256.	Dhirendra Chandra Das, also known as Nani Gopal Das	Mymensingh, Bengal	
257.	Durga Shanker Das	Barisal, Bengal	
258.	Sudhanshu Bhushan Dasgupta	Bankura, Bengal	
259.	Manindra Lal Dutta	Chittagong, Bengal	
260.	Pravir Kumar Goswami	Mymensingh, Bengal	
261.	Lalit Mohan Sinha	24 Pargana, Bengal	
262.	Amritendu Mukherjee	Krishna Nagar, Bengal	
263.	Anant Kumar Mukherjee, also known as Haldar	Midnapore, Bengal	
264.	Nalini Ranjan Sengupta	Dacca, Bengal	
265.	Kripa Nath Dey, alias Haren	Faridpur, Bengal	
266.	Nagendra Chandra Deb	Mymensingh, Bengal	
267.	Harbandu Samajdar	Faridpur, Bengal	
268.	Hrishikesh Dutta	Howrah, Bengal	
269.	Bhabatosh Karmakar	Bankura, Bengal	
270.	Govind Bera, also known as Govind Prashad Bera	Midnapore, Bengal	Mayana Political Dacoity Case 1933

Sl. No.	Name	Residence	case
271.	Samarendra Nath Ghosh	Dacca, Bengal	Manickgunj Post Office Action Case 1933
272.	T. Sachidanand Sivam	Madras	2nd Madras Conspiracy Case - 1933
273.	Hari Krishna Khar	Bengal	Burdwan Political Dacoity Case, 1933
274.	Jitendra Chandra Dey Majumdar, alias Jitendra Majumdar	Faridpur, Bengal	Gauripur Post Office Action Case 1933
275.	Kartik Chandra Sarkar	Pabna, Bengal	Threatening Letter Case 1934
276.	Sudhir Kumar Samajdar	Calcutta, Bengal	
277.	Jogesh Chandra Das	Rangpur, Bengal	Rangpur Conspiracy Case 1933-34
278.	Nagendra Nath Dasgupta	Barisal, Bengal	
279.	Narendra Nath Das	Rangpur, Bengal	
280.	Nagendra Mohan Mustafi	Jalpaigudi, Bengal	
281.	Paresh Chandra Chowdhury	Rangpur, Bengal	
282.	Purnendu Sekhar Guha	Faridpur, Bengal	
283.	Benoy Kumar Tarafdar	Bogra, Bengal	
284.	Bimal Ranjan Dey Bhowmick	Dacca, Bengal	
285.	Shashi Mohan Maitra	Rangpur, Bengal	
286.	Biru Bhushan Chakraborty	Faridpur, Bengal	
287.	Dhirendra Kumar Biswas	Nadia, Bengal	
288.	Gyanan Govind Gupta	Pabna, Bengal	
289.	Gauranga Das, also known as Gauranga Mohan Das	Sylhet, Bengal	Itahkhol Sylhet Robbery Case 1933-34
290.	Dhirendra Chakraborty	Tippara, Bengal	
291.	Bidyadhar Shah		
292.	Biraj Mohan Deb, alias Bagha		

Sl. No.	Name	Residence	case
293.	Kala Chand alias Makhan Lal Chakraborty	Bakerganj, Bengal	Faridpur Bomb Case 1933
294.	Madan Mohan Roy Chowdhury	Faridpur, Bengal	
295.	Hriday Kanta Das		
296.	Ramani Ranjan Ganguly		
297.	Nirmalendu Guha		
298.	Amulya Charan Mitra		
299.	Birendra Nath Roy	Dacca, Bengal	
300.	Atul Chandra Dutta	Faridpur, Bengal	
301.	Sachindra Nath Mitra		
302.	Santigopal Sen	Dacca, Bengal	Midnapore Conspiracy Case 1933
303.	Bhupal Chandra Panda	Midnapore, Bengal	
304.	Madhusudhan Banerjee, alias Amiya Banerjee	Dacca, Bengal	Lebong Governor Outrage Shooting Case - 1934
305.	Manoranjan Banerjee, alias Naresh Chowdhury		
306.	Sukumar Ghosh		
307.	Sushil Kumar Chakraborty alias Ajith Kumar Dhar		
308.	Mahesh Chandra Barua	Chittagong, Bengal	Bathua Dacoity Case - 1934
309.	Nirendra Lal Barua		
310.	Saradindu Bhattacharjee		
311.	Mokshada Ranjan Chakraborty		
312.	Priyada Nandan Chakraborty		
313.	Jibendra Kumar Das alias Durga Das		
314.	Arvind Dey		
315.	Gagan Chandra Dey		
316.	Nagendra Lall Dey		
317.	Kirti Majumdar, also known alias Bhushan Majumdar		
318.	Manmohan Shah		
319.	Manindra Chandra Dey		

Sl. No.	Name	Residence	case
320.	Manoranjan Chowdhury alias Manoranjan Banerjee Chowdhury		
321.	Sudhir Ranjan Chowdhury		
322.	Bimal Chandra Bhattacharjee	Mymensingh, Bengal	Interprovincial Conspiracy Case 1934-35
323.	Dhirendra Kumar Bhattacharjee alias Dhirendra Nath Bhattacharjee	Tippara, Bengal	
324.	Provost Chandra Chakraborty		
325.	Manindra Lall Chowdhury	Chittagong, Bengal	
326.	Surendra Dhar Chowdhury	Tippara, Bengal	
327.	Haripada Dey	Dacca, Bengal	
328.	Narendra Prasad Ghosh	Mymensingh, Bengal	
329.	Paresh Chandra Guha	Srinagar, Dacca	
330.	Jitendra Nath Gupta	Faridpur, Bengal	
331.	Jyotish Majumdar	Tippara, Bengal	
332.	Satyendra Narayan Majumdar	Jessore, Bengal	
333.	Pravat Kumar Mitra	Serampore, Kolkata	
334.	Dwijendranath Talapatra	Rajshahi, Bengal	
335.	Amulya Charan Sen Gupta	Dacca, Bengal	
336.	Jitendra Nath Chakraborty alias Abani Mukherjee	Tippara, Bengal	
337.	Bimal Kumar Sarkar	Bankura, Bengal	Bankura Political
338.	Mritunjay Banerjee		Robbery Case 1934
339.	Gopendra Lal Roy alias Gopen Roy	Sylhet, Bengal	Umed Nagar Mail Robbery Case - 1934
340.	Satyendra Chandra Roy		

Sl. No.	Name	Residence	case
341.	Amulya Kumar Roy	Dacca, Bengal	Arms Rules Conspiracy Case
342.	Akshay Kumar Chowdhury	Dinajpur, Bengal	Dinajpur Political Dacoity Case 1934
343.	Nitya Ranjan Chowdhury		
344.	Dinesh Chandra Das, alias Tagore		
345.	Nani Gopal Das		
346.	Kumudini Nath Ghosh		
347.	Narendra Chandra Ghosh alias Nani		
348.	Upendra Mondal		
349.	Ramendra Nath Samajdar		
350.	Gamir Sheikh alias Gamiruddin Sarkar		
351.	Rajani Kanta Sarkar		
352.	Anaath Bandhu Saha		
353.	Harendra Das		
354.	Pran Krishna Chowdhury alias Pran Kristo Chowdhury.		
355.	Rajendra Nath Chakraborty	Bakargunj, Bengal	Agalpasha Robbery Case - 1934
356.	Uma Shankar Keor	Birbhum, Bengal	Birbhum Conspiracy Case, 1934
357.	Kali Prasanna Roy Chowdhury alias Kali Prasanna Bhattacharya		
358.	Dharni Dhar Roy alias Shialmara		
359.	Pradyut Kumar Chowdhury alias Pradyut Roy Chowdhury	Murshidabad, Bengal	
360.	Pravas Chand Roy	Birbhum, Bengal	
361.	Pran Gopal Mukherjee	Murshidabad, Bengal	

Sl. No.	Name	Residence	case
362.	Pravat Kumar Ghosh alias Prasant Kusum Ghosh	Birbhum, Bengal	
363.	Bijoy Kumar Ghosh		
364.	Rajat Bushan Dutta		
365.	Samadish Chandra Ray		
366.	Haripad Banerjee	Hooghly, Bengal	
367.	Haran Chandra Khangar	Birbhum, Bengal	
368.	Rabindranath Banerjee, alias Samarjeet Banerjee	Dacca, Bengal	Bengal Criminal Law Act 1934
369.	Bhagwan Chandra Biswas	Noakhali, Bengal	
370.	Jiben Kristo Guha Thakurta	Barisal, Bengal	
371.	Shirod Banerjee	Bakerganj, Bengal	
372.	Niranjan Sengupta	Bengal	
373.	Sudhir Chandra alias Sudhir Kumar Ghosh	Calcutta	
374.	Nalini Mohan Das	Barisal, Bengal	
375.	Moti Lal Roy	Sylhet, Bengal	Lord Hardinge Bomb Case - 1934
376.	Anant Kumar Bhattacharya	Murshidabad, Bengal	Disobeying Government Orders Case 1934-36
377.	Anil Chandra Mukherjee	Dacca, Bengal	
378.	Anant Kumar Chakraborty	Dacca, Bengal	
379.	Birendra Vinod Chowdhury	Chittagong, Bengal	
380.	Kali Mohan Banerjee	Calcutta, Bengal	
381.	Sudhindra Bhattacharya	Rajshahi, Bengal	
382.	Binay Bhushan Laskar	Sylhet, Bengal	Sylhet Assam Dacoity Case 1934
383.	Tarapad Das alias Mohammed Ibrahim	Calcutta, Bengal	Calcutta Letter Conspiracy Case 1935
384.	Ramesh Chandra Das	Barisal, Bengal	
385.	Khudiram Bhattacharya alias Umesh Chandra Bhattacharya	Nadia, Bengal	Nawadwip-Nadia Arms Conspiracy Case 1935
386.	Murarimohan Goswami		

Sl. No.	Name	Residence	case
387.	Prafull Kumar Biswas	Faridpur, Bengal	Manicktala Arms Conspiracy Case 1936
388.	Ram Singh alias Ram Kishore	Mathura, Uttar Pradesh	P. A. Dogra, D.S.P., C.I.D. Murder Case 1936
389.	Dwaraka Prasad Pandey	Bengal	Various Revolutionary Activities Cases 1922-1936
390.	Dhirendra Chandra Das		
391.	Hem Chandra Bhattacharya	Chittagong, Bengal	
392.	Krishna Chandra Roy	Bengal	
393.	Krishna Biswas		
394.	Madanlal Dasgupta		
395.	Manan Chandra Dey		
396.	Md. Ilahi Baksh	Mymensingh, Bengal	
397.	S.N. Chakraborty	Bengal	

Appendix II

Pages from the diary of Veer Savarkar, used in the Cellular Jail.

Credit: Shri Ranjit Savarkar, Swatantrya Veer Savarkar Smarak, Mumbai

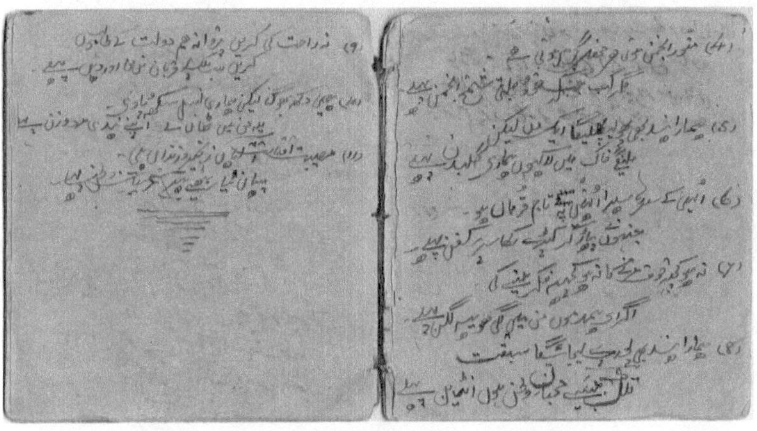

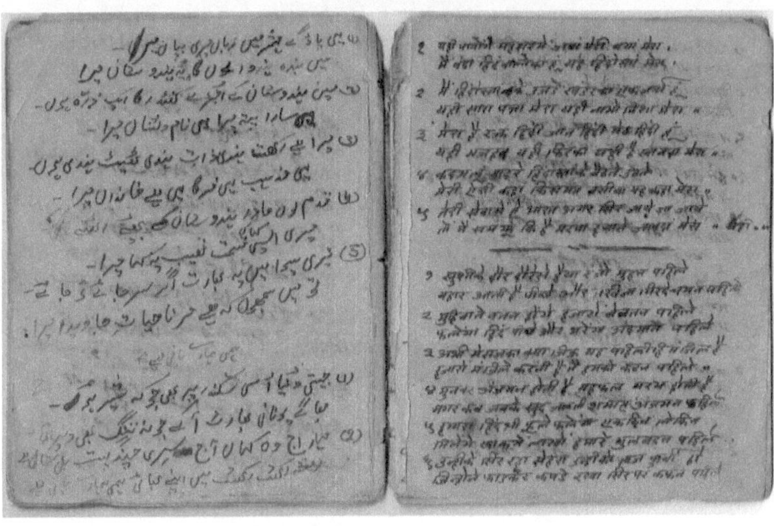

30ᵗʰ December 1997: Spouses of deceased freedom fighters of Cellular Jail during a felicitation function

11ᵗʰ March 2006: Veteran freedom fighter Viswanath Mathur's ashes brought to the Cellular Jail, accompanied by other veterans and his son, Prakash. His ashes were immersed in the Andaman Sea

An old photograph of block no 2 of the Cellular Jail

An old picture of Cellular Jail with blocks no 1 & 2. The Jail hospital
can also be seen.

Author speaking at a function organised in Cellular Jail in the presence of historians and others (From right to left) Shri Madan Mohan Singh, Sq. Leader (Retd.) Bali, relative of Shaheed Ram Rakha Bali, Shri G.S. Pandey and Shri Ashok Srivastav

Shri Mukeshwar Lall, Historian and Founder of KalaPani Museum, educating the students on the unsung heroes as part of the Azadi Ka Amrit Mahotsav programme

5th May 2005 - Dr. A.P.J. Abdul Kalam, Former President of India being briefed during his visit to the National Memorial Cellular Jail

Author with the family of Freedom fighter Prativadi Bhankara Venkatacharya

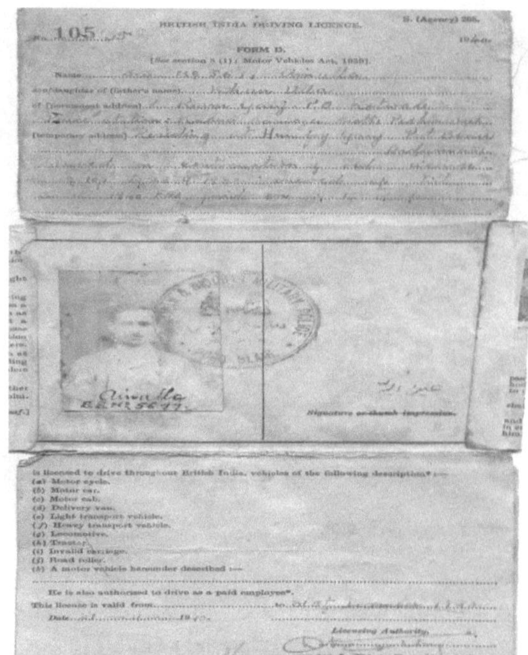

The driving licences of the author's father, Shri Ainulla Khan, convict, later Self-Supporter, No. 5677. The licences were issued from Peshawar and Andaman.

नृपेन्द्र मिश्र
Nripendra Misra
Principal Secretary to Prime Minister

December 26, 2018

Dear Dr. Rasheeda Iqbal,

This is to thank you for making our visit to Andaman & Nicobar Island memorable. Your enthusiasm and personal attention to our needs and comforts deserves special mention.

We were particularly impressed by your intellectual capacity and in-depth knowledge of the history of Island. I wish you great success in your future career.

With regards,

Yours sincerely,

(Nripendra Misra)

Dr. (Ms.) Rasheeda Iqbal
Assistant Director (Art & Culture)
Cellular Jail
Andaman & Nicobar Islands
Port Blair.

प्रधान मंत्री कार्यालय, साउथ ब्लॉक, नई दिल्ली-110 011
PRIME MINISTER'S OFFICE, SOUTH BLOCK, NEW DELHI-110 011
TEL. 23013040 FAX-23017475

Humbled & Honoured

Late Shri Anup Dasgupta, working President, Ex-Andaman Political Prisoner's Fraternity Circle and Freedom Fighters family members paying floral tribute at the Martyr's column

Author with (right to left) Shri G.S.Pandey, Late M.A.Mujtaba, eminent historian and Shri Hasan Ali (Retd.) Archivist

Members of Local Born Association with Late John Lobo, member of the Indian National Army, Andaman branch (centre) during a function held at Chatham Memorial to pay tribute to the first batch of Freedom Fighters of 1857

Bibliography

PRIMARY SOURCES

A. Archival Material

F. No. 158, Central Records Section, Secretariat, Port Blair

F. No. 21/4/47, Central Records Section, Secretariat, Port Blair

F. No. 41-1/68 - Home, Central Records Section, Secretariat, Port Blair

F. No. 41-1/69-Home, Central Records Section, Secretariat, Port Blair

F. No. 41-23/69-Home, Central Records Section, Secretariat, Port Blair

F. No. 15-92/77 Home, Central Records Section, Secretariat, Port Blair

F.NO. 41-1/7, Home, Central Records Section, Secretariat, Port Blair

Files related to the attack on Hyderabad Residency in the State Archives, Hyderabad.

Files relating to the Moplah Rebellion of 1921, Regional Archives, Kozhikode, Kerala.

Home Department Proceedings from 1873-1920, Cellular Jail Library

Punjab Government, Civil Secretariat, 1858, Department, Judicial Proceedings, Nos. 34-7 & Nos. 42-3

B. Rules/ Regulations/ Manuals/ Reports

Andaman and Nicobar Islands, At a Glance, Directorate of Economics and Statistics, Andaman and Nicobar Administration, 2002.

Andaman and Nicobar Circulars, 1933, Central Records Section, Secretariat.

The Andaman and Nicobar Islands Regulations of 1876.

The Andaman & Nicobar Manual, Calcutta, Government Printing, India, 1908.

Report on the Administration of the A&N Islands (1945-1946), Central Records Section, Secretariat

C. Autobiographies/Biographies

Azad, Prithvi Singh Azad, *Kranti Path ka Pathik-Meri Atmakatha*, Haryana Sahitya Academy, Chandigarh, 1990 (Hindi).

Bandopadhyay, Upendra, *Nirvasiter Atmakatha (Autobiography of an Exile)* (Bengali), 7th Edition, National Publishers, Calcutta.

Chakraborty, Trailokya Nath, *Jaile Tris Bachhar (Thirty Years in Prison)* (Bengali), Calcutta, 1948.

Dhillon, Mohinder Singh, *A Titan in the Andamans - Diwan Singh Kalepani*, Angad Publishers, Chandigarh, 1994.

Ghosh, Barindra Kumar, *The Tale of My Exile*, Pondicherry, 1922.

Parmanand, *The Story of My Life*, New Delhi, 1982.

Parmanand, Bhai, *Aap Beeti*, Prabhat Prakashan, New Delhi, 2002.

Sanyal, Sachindranath, *Bandi Jiwan* (Hindi), Atmaram and Sons, Delhi, 1986.

Savarkar, V.D. Mera *Aajeevan Karavaas* (Hindi). Nagpur: Savarkar Tatvagyan Prasar Kendra, 1966.

Savarkar, V. D., *The Story of My Transportation*, Bombay, 1950.

Sinha, Bejoy Kumar, *In Andaman, the Indian Bastille*, People's Publishing House, New Delhi, 1939.

Shukla, Lakshmi Kant, *Kya Choroo Kya Bandh Chaloon*, (Hindi) Nidhi Prakashan, Delhi, 1990.

Barindra Kumar Ghosh, *The Tale of My Exile*, Arya Office, Pondicherry, 1922

Prativadi Bhayankara Venkatacharya, *Craik's Paradise (Life in Andamans)*, 1938

D. Census Reports/Gazetteers

Census Report of the Andaman and Nicobar Islands, 1901 by Sir Richard Temple.

Census Report of the Andaman and Nicobar Islands, 1911 Vol. II by R.F. Lowis.

Census Report of the Andaman and Nicobar Islands, 1921 Vol. II by R.F. Lowis.

Census Report of the Andaman and Nicobar Islands, 1931 Vol. II by C.J. Bonington.

Imperial Gazetteer of India, Provincial Series, A & N Islands, 1st Edition - 1909, Reprint 1985.

Kerala District Gazetteers - Kozhikode by A. Sreedharan Menon, 1962.

Kiran Dhingra, *Gazetteer - The Andaman and Nicobar Islands in the 20th Century*, Oxford University Press, 2005.

Punjab District Gazetteers - Sangrur by B. R. Sharma, 1984.

Punjab District Gazetteers - Ferozepur by B.R. Sharma, 1983.

SECONDARY SOURCES

A. Books

Adam, H.L., *Crime & Criminology*, Printwell, Jaipur, Reprinted 1997.

Agarwal, S.N., *The Heroes of Cellular Jail*, Rupa & Co, New Delhi, 2006.

Bali, Yogendra & Kalika, *The Warriors in White, Glimpses of Kooka History*, Har-Anand Publications, New Delhi, 1995.

Balkhi, Fasihuddin, *Wahhabi Movement*, Classical Publishing Company, New Delhi, 1983.

Choudhary, Sukhbir, *Moplah Uprising (1921-23)*, Agam Prakashan, Delhi, 1977.

Chak, B.L., *Green Islands in the Sea*, Delhi, Publications Division, 1957.

Chandra, Bipan, *India's Struggle for Independence*, Penguin Books, New Delhi, 1989.

Chopra, Prabha, *Forgotten Heroes of India's Freedom Struggle*, A Who's Who, Delhi, 1992.

Chowdhury, Rabin Roy, *Black Days in Andaman and Nicobar Islands*, Manas Publications, New Delhi, 2004.

Chopra, P. N., *Who's Who of Indian Martyrs*, Vol. III, Department of Culture, Ministry of Education & Social Welfare, Government of India, New Delhi, 1973.

Cooper, Zarine, *Archaeology and History*, Early settlements in the Andaman Islands, Oxford University Press, New Delhi, 2002.

Dasgupta, Jayant, *Japanese in Andaman and Nicobar Islands*, Manas Publications, New Delhi, 2002.

Dass, F.A.M., *The Andaman Islands*, first published in 1937, reprint 1988, Asian Educational Services, New Delhi, Madras, 1988.

Dharamvir, *Bhai Parmanand Aur Unka Yug* (Hindi), Bhai Parmanand Smarak Samiti, Second Edition, Delhi, 1990.

Divekar, V. D., *South India in 1857: War of Independence*, Lokmanya Tilak Smarak Trust, Pune, 1993.

Ghadar Party's Lahore Conspiracy Case, 1915 Judgement, Archana Publications, Meerut, 2006.

Hennessy, H. E., *Administrative History of British India*, Neeraj Publishing House, Delhi, First published in 1925, First Indian Reprint - 1983

Hussain, Yusuf, *Pen Picture of the Andaman and Nicobar Islands*, Port Blair, Lucknow, 1954.

Iqbal, Rashida (ed), *Unsung Heroes of Freedom Struggle in Andamans*, Who's Who, Directorate of Youth Affairs, Sports & Culture, A & N Administration, 1998.

Jain, Phoolchand, *Swatantratha Senani Granthmala-2 Bandi Nama*, Andaman Jail, Institute of Social Sciences, New Delhi, 1998.

Jain, *Swatantratha Senani Granthmala-6 Karantikari Aandolan*, Institute of Social Sciences, New Delhi, 1999.

Keer, Dhananjya, *Veer Savarkar*, Popular Prakashan, Mumbai, Third Edition 2012.

Kloss, Boden C., *In the Andamans and Nicobars*, Vivek Publishing House, Delhi-7, 1902, Reprinted 1971.

Lall, B.B., *A Regime of Fears and Tears*, Farsight Publishers & Distributors, Revised Edition, Delhi, 2000.

Majumdar, R.C., *Penal Settlement in Andamans*, Gazetteers Unit, Department of Culture, Ministry of Education and Social Welfare, Government of India, New Delhi, 1975.

Man, Edward Horace, *The aboriginal inhabitants of the Andaman Islands*, Mittal Publication, New Delhi, first published in 1883. Photographically reproduced in 2001.

Manipur, Who's Who 1891, Manipur State Archives, 1990.

Mathur, L.P., *Kala Pani History of Andaman and Nicobar Islands with a Study of India's Freedom Struggle*, Eastern Book Corporation, Delhi, 1985.

Mouat, F.J., *The Andaman Islanders*, Mittal Publications, New Delhi, (1863), 1995.

Mujtaba, M. Ahmed, *Few Freedom Fighters of 1857*, Port Blair.

Mukherjee, Madhushree, *The Land of the Naked People: Encounters with Stone Age Islanders*, Penguin Books, New Delhi, 2003.

Moorthy, Pala Krishna, *The Grand Rebel*, Kavitha Publishers, Hyderabad, 2006.

Nagar, Amrit Lal, *Gadar ke Phool* (Hindi), Rajpal & Sons, Delhi, 1991.

Naidu, S.P.P.K., *The British Prison System in Andaman*, Phenomena Publications, Port Blair, 2007

Naidu, S.P.P.K., *The Chronicles of Andaman and Nicobar Islands*, Phenomena Publications, Port Blair, 2003.

Negi, D.S., *Andaman and Nicobar Islands*, Tushar Publications, New Delhi, 1992.

Narang, S.K., Under the Shadow of Death, Prime Publishers, Delhi, 1988

Pandey, Gauri Shanker, The Cellular Jail - The National Memorial, Sangeeta Publishing House, Port Blair, 1987.

Parratt, John & Saroj N. Arambam, *Queen Empress Vs Tikendrjit*, Prince of Manipur - The Anglo-Manipur Conflict of 1891, Har-Anand Publications, New Delhi.

Portman, M. V., *A History of Our Relations with the Andamanese'*, Vol. I & II, Calcutta (1899), 1990.

Promod Kumar, *Hunger Strike in Andamans*, Martyrs' Memorial and Freedom Struggle Research Centre, Lucknow, 2004.

Ram, S., *Andaman and Nicobar Islands: Past and Present*, Akansha Publishing House, New Delhi, 2001.

Ray, Santimoy, *Freedom Movement and Indian Muslims*, 1983.

Sahabi, Mufti Intezam-ullah, *Gadar Ke Chand Ulema*, Urdu, Deeni Book Depot, Bazar Jama Masjid, New Delhi.

Sherwani, Maulana Shahi Ahmed Khan, *Baghi Hindustan*, Al-Majma-Al-Islami, Mubarakpur, District Azamgarh (U.P.), 5th Edition.

Sen, Shatadru, *Disciplining Punishment*, colonialism and convict society in the Andaman Islands, Oxford University Press, 2000.

Sharma, Shukhdeba Janjabam & Aheibam Koireng Singh, "Unsung Anglo-Manipur War Heroes at Kalapani" - India @75 series, 2022.

Shukla, Prof. Chintamani, *Yatnabhoomi Andaman ka Romanchak Itihaas* (Hindi), 1985

Shukhdeba Sharma Hanjabam & Aheibam Koireng Singh, Unsung Anglo-Manipur War Heroes at Kalapani, National Book Trust, New Delhi 20

Sircar, Pronob Kumar, History of the Andaman Islands, NotionPress.com, 2021

Singh, Bhai Nahar & Kirpal, *Struggle for Free Hindustan*, Vol. 2 Part I, Atlantic Publishers and Distributors, New Delhi, 1988.

Singh, Bhai Nahar & Kirpal, *Struggle for Free Hindustan*, Vol. 3 Part I, Nirmal Publishers and Distributors, New Delhi, 1987.

Singh, Bhai Nahar & Kirpal, *Struggle for Free Hindustan*, Vol. 1, Atlantic Publishers and Distributors, New Delhi, 1986.

Singh, Iqbal N., *The Andaman Story*, Vikas Publishing House Pvt. Ltd, Delhi, 1978

Singh, K. S., *Andaman and Nicobar Islands*, A.S.I. People of India Series, Vol. XII, Madras, 1994.

Singh, Nagendra Kumar, *Encyclopedia of Indian Biographies*, Vol. 6, APH Publishing Corporation, New Delhi, 2000

Singh, Ujjawal Kumar, *Political Prisoners in India*, Delhi: Oxford University Press, 1998.

Sinha, Bejoy Kumar, *Indian Revolutionary Movement*, Lokmanya Tilak Smarak Trust, Pune, 1994.

Tamta, B.R., *Andaman and Nicobar Islands*, National Book Trust, Delhi, 1992.

Thanesar, Maulana Mohammad Jafar Ali, *Kala Pani–ya-Tawareek-e-Ajeeb*, Reprinted, 1969, Maulana Waheedudin Qasmi, Delhi.

The Freedom Struggle in Hyderabad, A Connected Account, Vol. II 1857-1885, published by the Hyderabad State Committee appointed for the compilation of a History of the Freedom Movement in Hyderabad, 1956.

Tripathi, Vachnesh, *Mahan Krantikari Vasudev Balwant Phadke*, (Hindi), Praveen Prakashan, New Delhi, 1992.

Turner, C.H. *Notes on the Andaman Islands from the existing information*, Rangoon, 1887.

Waraich, Prof. Malwinderjit Singh & Dr. Gurdev Singh Sidhu, *Komagata Maru: A Challenge to Colonialism*, Unistar Books Pvt. Ltd., 2005.

Waraich, Malwinder Jit Singh & Harinder Singh, *War against King Emperor*, Ghadr of 1914-15, Bhai Sahib Randhir Singh Trust, Punjab, 2001.

Wood, Conrad, *Moplah Rebellion and its Genesis*, People's Publishing House, revised print, New Delhi, 1987.

B. Articles/Souvenirs/Journals/Booklets

Andaman and 1857 by Dr. Narayan H. Kulkarni published in *Mukti-Thirtha*, Andaman, Ex-Andaman Political Prisoners' Fraternity Circle, Calcutta, 1976.

Another Ghadr, 1914 by Prof. Malwinderjit Singh Waraich

Bastion of India, The Directorate of Information, Publicity & Tourism, Andaman and Nicobar Administration, 1998.

Dr. Diwan Singh Kalepani - a profile, Punjab Govt. Press, SAS Nagar

1857 Uprising and the Nationalist Discourse by P.K. Shukla.

Maharaja Dibyasingha Deva III and the British Crown in Odisha" by Dr. Janmejay Choudhury, published in June 2017

Moplahs - part of Andamanians by C.M. Mohd published in the Annual Number of Hamari Awaz, Port Blair.

Mukti-Thirtha-Andaman, Ex-Andaman Political Prisoners' Fraternity Circle, Calcutta, 1976.

My I.N.A. Days in the Andamans, R.L. Avasthi, 1987

Swarajya, the paper that inspired Freedom Movements in U.P. by Bishambhar Nath Pande.

Two Rebel Leaders of 1857 in the Andamans by Prof. Iqbal Hussain, *Souvenir on the Centenary Year of Cellular Jail,* Andaman and Nicobar Administration, 2006

C. Oral Transcript/Interviews

Interviews of Ex-Andaman Political Prisoners by Promod Kumar, Martyrs' Memorial and Freedom Struggle Research Centre, Lucknow.

Oral transcripts of interviews with Ex-Andaman Political Prisoners and old residents of Andaman and Nicobar published in various newspapers and magazines from time to time by Shri Madan Mohan Singh.